HORACE: A PORTRAIT

HORACE:
A PORTRAIT

By
ALFRED NOYES

NEW YORK
SHEED & WARD · 1947

TO E.V.M.

in whose house, between the Santa Ynez Mountains and the Pacific, and far beyond the sunset islands of the sixteenth epode, the Roman poet is neither dust nor a shadow, but a living voice.

CONTENTS

PREFACE

IT IS SAID THAT WHEN ROBERT LOUIS STEVENSON LAY SERIOUSLY ill at Davos he asked that a Scottish minister who lived in the neighborhood should be summoned to his bedside. It was very early in the morning; but the good divine, fearing the worst, immediately dressed and hastened to the chalet where his fellow-countryman lodged. He found Stevenson apparently in the article of death; but, as the kindly visitor leaned over the bed to whisper some word of ghostly consolation, the sick man opened his eyes and gasped, faintly, "For God's sake, have you a Horace?"

It is with this Horace, the lover of life, the friend of poets, the wise adviser of so many different kinds of men, that my book is engaged. What was the secret of that perennial charm which, as Sainte-Beuve said, has made his book a secular breviary of good taste, poetry, and wisdom for two thousand years? The Horace of the poets is necessarily, perhaps, a somewhat different person from the Horace of the scholars and linguistic experts. The short essay of Sainte-Beuve, usually printed with his longer study of Virgil, suggests that the appreciation of Horace is not primarily for the specialist in classical studies. Every civilized man, he says, must have one book at least to which he turns as to a familiar friend, who will comment on all his daily affairs, as well as on all his exceptional adventures. There was a time when Homer was a kind of secular bible for scholars. St. Augustine, Montaigne, and Virgil have served in the same way. But among ancient authors there is none that comes more nearly home to us than Horace. To enjoy him, we do not have to discard our own habits of thought; and yet he brings us by so many ways into the very life of a vanished world:

ix

Je ne connais rien de plus doux, quand on vieillit . . . que de penser ainsi a l'aide d'un livre familier et mainte fois relu; c'est une manière de marcher en s'appuyant, en prenant un bras pour faire un tour de promenade en soleil.

I have found Horace a very good friend by my own fireside in English winters, and an equally good friend within sight of Soracte, or among the olive trees of California which so often seem to remember Italy.

Textual criticism is for the expert Latinist; and into that den of lions there is at least one Daniel who will never venture. But Horace, after all, was primarily a poet; and, in the interpretation of his poetry, the textual experts have occasionally shown a certain lack of familiarity with the ways of poets and the impulses under which poets write. I feel quite sure, for instance, despite the German argument based on the word *nauseam* and so strongly supported by writers like Professor Campbell and Professor Tenney Frank, that Horace did not write the ninth epode during a bout of seasickness, on the salt and heaving scene, and during the actual progress of the battle of Actium. "It is now generally agreed that he did," says Professor Frank; but I am relieved to find that Mr. L. P. Wilkinson, in his recent book on the lyric poetry of Horace (a most valuable contribution to the study of his metrical technique), is apparently unaware of any such agreement, and quite rightly assumes that Horace was not there.

Mr. H. J. Haskell, in his delightful and extremely illuminating book *This Was Cicero*, points out that scholars of the greatest eminence have sometimes fallen into real mistakes about the public men of ancient Rome through a lack of familiarity with the ways of politicians in all ages. "I have constantly been horrified," he says, "to find historians accepting political speeches as statements of fact." There are similar causes of confusion in some of the most erudite books written on the poets, though the error is of a different kind. I have constantly been horrified to find scholars of the widest knowledge misunderstanding the nature of poetry, and describing a perfectly sincere and deeply felt passage as a "conventional insincerity." The poem *Diffugere nives*, which Housman, and all those who put the poetry first, regard as one of the supreme masterpieces of pure literature, was held to be "commonplace" and described as "insignificant" by that learned, but ideological pundit, Wilamowitz. Cicero, who was one of the chief influences on the mind of St. Augustine, and among the most effective humanizing influences in what was once European civilization, was described by Mommsen as the "worst type of journalist." In many cases there seems to be a real conflict between erudition and the appreciation of literature. The commentators on Horace often flatly contradict one another when they stray into the field of poetry. Professor Campbell, for instance, in his immensely valuable book on Horace, goes so far as to call the equally eminent Professor Tyrrel "pig-headed"—surely a deplorable expression in a contest of celestial minds, even though Horace did call himself *"Epicuri de grege porcum."*

"Poetry," said one of its most exquisite craftsmen, "is like shot silk, glancing with many colors." [1] In Horace, one of these colors is a subtle and unexpected irony. It is sometimes not realized by the textual critics, who necessarily examine the work piecemeal, that poets use irony, not only as a weapon, but as a shield. When Horace compares himself with a "hog from the herd of Epicurus," his irony glances in many different directions. In the first place, he is laughing at himself, an obviously self-protective device. In the second place, he is a little ironical about a very common misinterpretation of the creed of Epicurus. Horace knew far too much about Epicurus and his philosophy as expounded by Lucretius to associate them with

[1] Tennyson.

the hedonism of the swine-trough, or with merely materialistic indulgence. In the third place, his irony glances at those who insist that he is himself, primarily, a disciple of Epicurus, whereas—like almost all poets—he is an eclectic, binding himself to no school of philosophy. He took from Epicurus what fitted into his own way of looking at things. But he also took what he wanted from the Stoics, at whose expense he was also ironical. He took a good deal from Plato, especially some of the Socratic irony in the lighter dialogues. This is apparent in the *Satires* and *Epistles.* Horace definitely stated that he could follow no one master in these things. Philosophical critics, looking for a system, and unaccustomed to this wayward behavior on the part of the poets, are thereupon plunged into an argument which can never end, since they are looking for the wrong answer.

It is clear enough that there is something to be said from the side of poetry when one considers the fact that the *Art of Poetry,* as it is called, cannot be mentioned in the same breath with many systematized essays, on the point of philosophical treatment. But the systematized essays fade away, and the epistle to the Pisos has delighted readers and influenced the course of literature for two thousand years. Furthermore, in the matter of translation, there is something to be said from the side of poetry. By far the best Horatian alcaics in the English language are those of a single stanza by Stevenson:

> Brave lads in olden musical centuries
> Sang, night by night, adorable choruses;
> Sat late by ale-house doors in April
> Chanting for joy as the moon was rising.

He did not keep it up, for the second stanza was not so good. But those four lines, in which not a syllable goes astray from the strict law of the metre, are perfect, and all the more vital and joyous for the discipline. Tennyson's alcaics on Milton are also perfect, but they follow the Greek rather than the Horatian model. One has only to compare these lines with Lytton's unrhymed translations of Horace to discover how much is sometimes missed by disregarding the metrical pulse of the original. Mr. L. P. Wilkinson is quite right in saying that Lytton's unrhymed translations stand out in comparison with many others, but when the first line of a poem in alcaics is rendered thus:

> Coeval with me, born when Manlius was consul

one turns back to:

> Brave lads in olden musical centuries

and discovers that one is nearer to Horace, after all, in the lines of Stevenson.

I am encouraged to think that there is room for a book on Horace, written primarily from the point of view of poetry. But all lovers of Horace necessarily owe an immense debt to the work of that great company of scholars who have done so much in recent years to bring the legacy of Rome to the English-speaking world. In their field I am no more than a student; but I hope a faithful one. I have consulted the works of Sellar, Macleane, Wickham, Greenough, Warde Fowler, Mackail, Bailey, and many others to whom acknowledgment is made in the text. The writings of E. K. Rand, too, of Harvard, were among those in which scholarship and the love of letters went hand in hand. So also, were those of Shorey and Merrill, whose edition of Catullus contains the best comparison between that poet and Horace which I have seen anywhere.

HORACE: A PORTRAIT

THE EMPEROR'S LETTER

ABOUT TWO THOUSAND YEARS AGO, IN THE PORTICO OF A country-house among the Sabine hills, not far from the place which is now called Tivoli, a small dark-eyed man sat at a white stone table reading a letter. It had come by imperial post, express delivery (*cursus velox*), and it appeared to trouble him.

Davus, the slave who waited on him, was a little troubled, too; for his master, Quintus Horatius Flaccus, had hardly touched the frugal meal before him. This was very unusual. He always liked things to be served in the right way. He objected strongly to finger-prints on the silver. But he was not difficult to please. On this occasion the expression of his face might suggest that he had been eating "olives fresh from the bough," as one of his modern translators has it. But the olives on his table had been well pickled. The salad was delicious. The young roasted pigeon was done to a turn. The big dark figs were ripe and unpecked by the thrushes. The wine, though it was home-made, tasted of the grape, and had been approved by Maecenas himself when that eminent statesman had been a guest. There was no fault to be found with the table which, incidentally, was an old friend. It was as bright and spotless as it had ever been in his old quarters at Rome, where it played a part in one of his poems, at a time when it was almost his only piece of furniture. It had been brought twenty-eight miles by wagon to these more pleasant surroundings at the Sabine Farm, partly because it could stand in the open portico without being damaged by weather, and partly because Horace was fond of his old friends. Occasionally, when nobody was about, a pigeon would flutter down from the turret-shaped *columbarium*, or the roof, to admire itself in the polished surface; "and that," as Davus would say, "made more work."

But all had been well today. There was not even the smallest blue feather drifting between the dishes on his *lapis albus*. It was laid exactly as the poet liked. There was not a stain on the silver salt-cellar—the only relic Horace possessed of his disinherited father. It seemed actually to smile—his own phrase—at the slender little statue of the smiling faun in the background. The oil-jug and saucer, the wine-cup and the ladle—all of the plain Campanian ware that he liked—were in the right places; the cheese was from his own dairy; and, in the middle of the table, there was a bronze bowl filled with roses. But the roasted pigeon was growing cold. Could the letter have brought bad news from Rome?

The frog device on the seal that had fastened the outer wrapper was familiar to Davus. He had seen it on the signet ring of Maecenas—a frog crouching on a scarab, very delicately engraved in emerald by some old Etruscan artist. This frog usually brought a smile to the poet's face. It was not the note from Maecenas that had depressed him, but an enclosure in another hand, a letter which had been sealed with a more formidable emblem, the Sphinx. When the eye of Davus was caught by that beautiful little feminine face attached to the body of a wild beast, he drew himself up to attention and stood as motionless as a sentry on guard. He had seen that emblem before, and he knew that it was used by a very tremendous personage. The Sphinx was probably meant to suggest a power that extended to Egypt, and beyond; but it also aptly symbolized its owner's character—frank and open in the face, but cold and crafty at heart. In fact, the three seals Augustus used in the course of his life curiously illustrated its progress: the first, a

Sphinx; the second, a head of Alexander the Great; and the third, a very handsome head indeed, his own.

As a rule, when there were no guests, Horace would talk briskly and cheerfully with Davus; or, if silent, he would drink in the beauty of the landscape framed between the slender stone pillars of the portico. His eyes would seem to enjoy everything he looked upon—the walled garden sloping to the south; the clouds of grey-green olive trees on either side; the fish-pond in the center, with its drowsily plashing fountain; the box hedges that bordered the paths; the beds of roses that he grew for festal occasions; and, at the end of the garden, like motionless black flames, those two tall emblematic cypresses. In the niche between those dark remembrances, there was one slender white figure—a Bacchante, perhaps, with vine leaves in her hair. At this distance he could not see her features distinctly; so, if he wished, she might be Chloe, or Cinara, or Tyndaris, or any of those other charming Greek imaginations; but if the music of a poem can tell us anything about it, perhaps it more often reminded him of Lalage,

> *dulce ridentem . . .*
> *dulce loquentem.*

Lalage of the low sweet voice and happy laughter. She was only a child, as he tells us in another poem. But whether it was memory or imagination, that music had once brought him very good luck on the Sabine hills.

Looking southward, he could see far beyond the garden; for the house stood on a pleasant knoll in the center of the valley. A few oaks and ilexes to east and west sheltered it from the winds. The great hills on either side were near enough to defend it from storms, but not so near as to intercept the sun which flooded the whole farm from early morning till evening. He celebrated this pleasant fact in one of his poems, for, though he liked the shade of the trees in the right place, he was a great lover of the sun:

continui montes, ni dissocientur opaca
valle, sed ut veniens dextrum latus aspiciat sol,
laevum discedens curru fugiente vaporet.

A mass of hills unbroken, except by one valley in which, although it is shaded by trees, the rising sun may look upon the western slopes, and the evening sun warm it on the east.

The hillock in the center possessed the sun all day. From where he sat, he could see on his right hand the wooded slopes of the great hill Lucretilis; and on the left, the bare tawny shoulder of the hill which was then called Ustica (sunburnt) and, in our own time, has been rechristened Rustica. Between the vast ranges to which these hills belonged, the happy valley with its broken river sparkling against moss-grown rocks, or winding under tall poplars and deprecating willows, broadened away southward.

Immediately beyond and below the garden there was a warm belt of glowing color—a cornfield, ripe and yellow. The stream curved around it like a slender sickle moon today, but at certain seasons it would threaten to overflow that sunlit field (*pratum apricum*), and his bailiff would be running around like a hen whose foster-children have begun to use their web-feet. This afternoon the river was chuckling along its proper channel. Alive with light where the stones broke the surface, it streamed down the valley as if it were irresistibly drawn in the direction of Rome, twenty-eight miles beyond the horizon. He could follow it with his eye, in gleams and flashes almost as far as that great hill in the middle distance. Rocca Giovane, this hill is called today, and it has a grey hill-town, like a fortress, clamped into its rocky crest.

In the time of Horace, there was no hill-town on the height, but only a ruined temple, which made the hill look older and lonelier than it does today. It seemed farther away than it really was, for he often walked up to that ruined shrine. It was there, lying on the close-cropt thyme and listening to the goat-bells, that he had composed a brief and charming poem to a friend at Rome, telling him how much was lost by living in a city. It was the sight of a herd of deer on the way up, that had reminded him of the fable of the horse and the stag. He had incorporated this into his poem to drive home his doctrine of the happy life. The stag was defeated but remained free, while the horse purchased his victory by surrendering his back to a rider. "You may gain wealth," he wrote, "but wealth is either a slave or a tyrannical master. I live and reign as soon as I have left behind me all that the chattering throng so praises to the skies. I am like the pontiff's fugitive slave. It is bread that I need, not cakes made with honey. Is the water that tries to burst your leaden pipes in the city any purer than my running brooks? You may drive out nature with a pitchfork, but she will very quickly return, and quietly wreck the perversities of human pride."

It appeared to be almost as impossible to keep the city from invading the country; for that was exactly what this troublesome letter had done. He reread it several times, and Davus decided that it must have brought him very bad news indeed from Rome. It was difficult to suppose that anything could permanently disturb the peace of the Sabine Farm. Horace had passed through arduous times in his youth, of course, and his hair was already touched with grey. But he had almost everything that he wanted now. He was recognized by all good judges as one of the foremost poets of his age. Virgil had been among the first to recognize him, and he knew—he had always known—that to be numbered with that lyrical company was to

gain the land of matters unforgot. He had no other ambition:

> *quodsi me lyricis vatibus inseris,*
> *sublimi feriam sidera vertice.*

For the rest he was content with the mortality of which he was
ever conscious. With a poet of the nineteenth century, he might
ask the question—

> Ah, why should Love, like men in drinking-songs,
> Spice his fair banquet with the dust of death?

But he would probably have agreed with Tennyson in his
answer. It added to the poignancy of all lovely things on earth
that they were so brief; and every evening, every hour, he
looked his last upon them, not so much with regret as with that
strange Roman *gravitas* and *simplicitas* which accepted the certain end as a condition of their being, and was thankful for
what the inevitable law allowed. His sadness, as a rule, was the
deep and philosophic sadness of a naturally happy man.

In one of the most famous of his poems he had written:
"This was what I had prayed for, a few acres of land, a garden,
a spring of water flowing near the house and, above and behind
these, a patch of woodland. The gods have given me all this
and more. It is well. I have nothing more to ask, except that
these things may be mine as long as I live."

Like his father before him he had known what it meant to be
dispossessed; but it did seem that now at last the son of the
"manumitted slave" was to be free to do the work and live the
life he loved. Today, however, something had happened that
imperilled his peace and might alter his whole way of life, not
by dispossessing him, in the ordinary sense, but by throwing
open all the gates of ambition. It was nothing less than an
invitation from Octavian, the future Augustus and, even now,

the Ruler of the World, to become his confidential secretary, personal friend, and a member of his household.

The invitation had been conveyed in a letter to Maecenas, who had sent it on to Horace. The emperor apparently had no doubt that his offer would be accepted. This was implied in every phrase of his message:

Hitherto, I was able to write my own letters to friends, but I am now very busy, and not in good health, and I should like to take our Horace away from you. He shall come from that parasite table of yours to this royal one, and help me in writing my letters.

The message was in execrable taste, of course, but emperors will be emperors. Maecenas had made no comment in his covering note; but with a touch of impishness which, even now, twitched the poet's lips to a wry little smile of reminiscence, he had simply added the letters S.V.B.E.V., which Cicero had sometimes used in letters to his friends. Maecenas, of course, used them ironically. They might be translated "And now I hope you are feeling well. I am just beginning to sit up and take nourishment":

Si valeas bene est, valeo.

Maecenas did not ordinarily use greetings of that kind, and it suggested a possible way out to Horace. His health had never been strong.

Octavian was not blind to the existence of other realms than his own. His dominion extended in space to the frontiers of the civilized world. Already, in some parts of it, he was a demi-god. In Rome, he was tactful and would not allow himself to be deified in any obvious way, but in every indirect way possible the upward movement was encouraged. His choice of the name Augustus a year or two later was as carefully calculated as the high heels he wore to increase his stature. He could rely on the sculptors and the historians to do the rest. Incidentally, he intended to write a personal record of his own achievements. It would simplify matters if, instead of using a stylus with his own hand, he could use a stylist like Horace as his secretary. His house at Rome was not ostentatious, as emperors' houses go; but, a few years later, he took care that his new Temple of Apollo should actually adjoin it—a perfect illustration of a familiar method of compromise. There was another realm, he knew, of an intellectual kind which extended through the ages and, in fact, the proposal he made to Horace was more of a tribute than it might seem. The real purpose was certainly not to rescue Horace from the parasite table of Maecenas. Octavian was not an altruist. The Ruler of the World was following the invariable law of all political potentates—the advantage of his own régime. He wished to strengthen that régime by appearing to incorporate what was left of the Republican tradition in a system which inevitably developed into an autocracy; and, in accordance with that policy, he wished to draw the Republican spirit of Roman literature into his own service. This does not mean that he appreciated the real and permanent values of that literature. Far from it; for he complained in a later letter that the poems of Horace, so exquisite in their form and content, had hitherto neglected the most important subject in the world—Augustus himself.

It is clear from other letters, quoted by Suetonius, that the emperor intended not only to make Horace his confidential secretary, but to draw him into at least an appearance of the closest personal friendship. "Treat me quite freely," he wrote, "as if you were my intimate friend. You will be quite correct in this, and not at all presumptuous, since I myself have wished this to be your attitude toward me, *if it can be done with due regard to your welfare.*" (The italicized clause sounds like something he had picked up in a conversation with Maecenas, who would naturally be concerned with the threatened loss to literature. It doesn't fit the context.) He actually offers evidence of his friendly feeling: "You may hear from our Septimius also what a regard I have for you, as I spoke of you in his presence. Even if you are so proud as to reject our friendship, we were not haughty about it in return." These messages are important because they completely shatter any suggestion that Horace sought the favor of Augustus. The sturdy independence of the poet has been recognized by most historians, but historians are not always consistent, and they have sometimes attributed their own inconsistencies to Horace himself. Some of the literary critics have been even more muddled in their conclusions. Swinburne, for instance, carried away by his own alliterative genius, his own Republicanism, and an echo of what Shakespeare's Cleopatra said on "the shouting varletry of Rome," called Horace "the valet-souled varlet of Venusia," a verdict on which we shall have something more to say later. It is enough here to say that Swinburne once wrote a really glorious ode to Walt Whitman, and followed it by a prose essay in which he compared Whitman with a "drunken apple-woman sprawling in the gutter." Horace did not write nonsense about "the blood-bright splendor of Brutus," but he had been a friend of Brutus. At first sight it might seem that Octavian was displaying a high-souled magnanimity in ignoring the fact that Horace had served under Brutus at Philippi and that he had never publicly recanted, or paid any tribute to the new régime. But it must be remembered that, while he was only a pawn, from the emperor's point of view, in a very much larger plan, the plan itself was calculated. On his way to its fulfillment, it was the emperor with all his worldly power, and not the comparatively helpless poet, who did most of the changing and all the fawning. There is one sentence, curiously self-revealing in a later letter from Augustus: "*Why is it that you avoid address-*

*ing me of all men in your poems? Is it that you are afraid pos-
terity will think the worse of you for having been a friend of
mine?"*

It is a curious fact that, while the rulers of the world are
allowed to compromise on every principle, and are even praised
by historians for doing so, the poet or philosopher, no matter
how resolute and independent he may be, is often accused of
inconsistency if he ventures merely to accept the change which
has taken place, not in himself, but in those rulers. If Horace
had actually accepted the apparent change in the mind of
Augustus, he would have had ample justification. He was a
man of practical wisdom. He hated strife and bloodshed. If
the new order promised not only an end to the internecine
wars of Italy, but actually a return to some of the principles
of Republican government in which he had always believed, he
was justified in acquiescence. But he was not easily carried into
the devotion which Virgil gave to the future autocrat. Octavian
probably intended to be a little ironical in his allusion to posterity, but he came nearer the truth than he realized. The poet,
who already saw his name engraved on something more durable
than bronze, may really have cared for consistency. Perhaps
he remembered that Octavian in earlier days had written ingrati-
ating letters to that older representative of Roman literature,
Cicero; that he had affectionately called him "father"; and
that very shortly afterwards he had made a sordid bargain with
his colleagues in the triumvirate that Cicero should be mur-
dered. The son of Cicero had been a fellow-student with
Horace at what may be called the University of Athens, and in
the same Republican set. The memory of that murder must have
left its mark on the mind of the young poet.

Modern historians in their treatment of Octavian as a benefi-
cent patron of Roman literature have a curious way of sliding
over the grim fact that he consented to the murder of one of

the greatest figures in that literature. The eulogists of Augustus ask us to remember the moral standards of the time; but Plutarch had no illusions about that grim bargain:

The terms of their mutual concessions were these: that Caesar should desert Cicero; that Lepidus should abandon his brother Paulus; and that Antony should give up Lucius Caesar, his uncle by his mother's side. Thus they let their anger and fury rob them of humanity, and demonstrated that no beast is more savage than man when possessed of power equal to his rage.

Horace knew all about the ghastly spectacle when the severed head and right hand of Cicero were fastened up over the rostrum, where the orators—and Cicero himself—used to speak. "It was a sight," says Plutarch, "which the Roman people shuddered to behold; for they believed they saw there, not the face of Cicero, but the image of Antony's own soul."

In his mind's eye Horace might well have seen there the image of the soul of Octavian; for Antony and Cicero had long been enemies, while Cicero and Octavian had been friends.

At the present day, when the world seems to be slowly awakening to the hideous connection all through the ages between crime and political power, we may well refuse to follow the historians who speak as though murder and loathsome treachery in high places were insignificant spots on the sun of worldly grandeur. There has been a time-lag among historians which has continued the old falsification of values into a period where it has become infinitely dangerous. Our modern world boasts of its freedom from worship of place and power, and demands a new moral standard for kings and governments as well as for private individuals; but the historians continue the old evil into the new age. With a strange, unconscious snobbery, they make obeisance before the blood-stained throne of a Caesar and whisper with awe the grandiose name *Augustus*, forgetting that he bestowed it on himself after careful consideration of its semi-divine significance, a proceeding which they would view with contempt in anyone not endowed with worldly grandeur.

Some of these historians might take a lesson from Maecenas, whom they sometimes depreciate as a dilettante. His devotion to literature and the things of the mind was genuine and of inestimable value to his age and to posterity. He has been ridiculed for no better reason than that the emperor spoke of the "perfumed locks" of his verses. But the emperor also spoke of his "parasite table." Neither phrase meant anything more than the usual jibe of the Philistine in power who is prepared to patronize the things of the mind as long as they minister to his own importance, but will dismiss them with a lordly facetiousness if they develop an importance of their own. Maecenas had a difficult task, and he had to be discreet if he wished to use his influence with the emperor in his country's interest.

On one occasion, however, he had the courage to speak very plainly indeed to Octavian. It was during the "purge," as it would be called today—that dreadful scene of blood with which the future autocrat inaugurated his rule. He had been sentencing men to death with the gruesome rapidity of a twentieth-century totalitarian. Maecenas could not reach him through the crowd, but he wrote upon his tablets, *"Surge tandem, Carnifex"*—"Break off, butcher"—and flung the message into the lap of Caesar. Apparently it was effective, for the disconcerted potentate immediately left the judgment-seat.

Time had passed since then. Octavian had quarreled with Antony and emerged victorious. In the eyes of the Republican set, to which Horace belonged, Antony had been the chief enemy; so that Octavian, in defeating him, had to this extent been fighting their battle. When Antony, with the help of Cleopatra, went down in ruin, there would be nothing inconsistent, therefore, in any Republican who should echo the words in which Horace celebrated that defeat—*"Nunc est bibendum."*

To many a man in the worldly position of Horace the emperor's invitation might have presented a tempting opportunity. An obscure poet had been offered a post which would have marked him out as one of the most prominent figures in the world.

It was not easy in those days to withstand the personal wishes of a Roman emperor; but freedom meant everything to Horace. He valued it so much that, on another occasion, when Maecenas himself had endeavored to make him return to Rome earlier than he wished, he had replied with an offer to surrender the gift of his beloved Sabine farm rather than let it be regarded as the price of his liberty.

All these things were passing through his mind as he sat in the portico. At last, after hastily swallowing a few morsels and drinking a cup of wine, he rose from the table and went into the house. It was not one of those luxurious villas to which the rich men of Rome escaped from the summer heat. There was no great marble pool in the dining-room around which the guests might recline, using its rim as a table, and picking their dainties from dishes afloat on the water like miniature swans or ships. There was no ivory or gold about it. The tessellated floor of the atrium pleased the eye, but its plain mosaic would have been far too simple for Pliny. In fact, when Horace accepted the gift from Maecenas, he had looked upon it as a restitution of his father's little farm at Venusia.

In his library, he picked up the writing tablets which he used for rough drafts of his letters, and went out by a door on the north side of the house, which opened into a kitchen garden. Three or four sunburnt peasants, at work with hoes on the terraced vineyard, looked up as he went by and glanced after him, a little surprised that his greeting had been so curt. He went on by the footpath up the valley, skirting a rocky stream till he reached a small mountain pasture where cattle were grazing. A great red rock looked down upon the pasture, and on its summit a long-horned goat stood etched against the sky. A little above and beyond the pasture, Horace reached a tiny glen half-surrounded by tall ilex trees with their roots firmly planted among the crags. Here the stream seemed to flow out of the cavities in the rock, a miniature cascade of cold and very clear water. It was an enchanted place—a place that nobody in later centuries has been able to find with any certainty, but we know a good deal about it. Ferns among wet boulders have not changed much in two thousand years, nor has the sound of flowing water, or the color of cyclamen in the shadow, or the fragrance of wild strawberries in the sun. He threw himself down on the turf at the stream's edge, and the words that welled up into his mind were surely those which open one of his most famous poems—*"O fons Bandusiae."* This, too, was both a fountain and a memory. Some of his readers have wondered whether his Fountain of Bandusia was to be found at the home of his boyhood rather than in the neighborhood of the Sabine farm. He answers this question himself by telling us that a water-spring was among the things he had prayed for, and that it had been granted. He could hardly have been praying for anything but the repetition of a happy memory.

Almost anybody who ever moved from one house in the country to another will understand that desire. There is no reason why a spring of cold and clear water should not have played its happy part in both places. Sacrifice had been made to both, and the song of a brook is the same wherever it flows. Listening to it there, he finally made up his mind. The emperor's invitation must be refused. Perhaps ironically, but not the less tactfully, he drafted an admirable excuse on his writing tablets. It was precisely the excuse which the emperor had made for his letter to Maecenas. His health would not allow him to perform the work adequately.

We may imagine Horace lying at full length on the turf and making a cup of his hands to drink from that cold, clear stream, the fountain of Bandusia, the symbolic source of his poetry, which he was to make more famous than Hippocrene itself. We can picture him rising briskly to return and send off his polite letter of refusal; glancing, as he went, with a new affection at all the familiar haunts and leafy nooks to which he would bring his Greek poets on a summer afternoon. Perhaps on this very walk there came to him some of the great music which was to live in the memory of twenty centuries, and make the Sabine farm a second home to many a thoughtful mind in other lands, long after the Roman Empire had passed away. *Fuge magna!* Fly from what this world calls "great affairs," or, as the English poet [1] echoed it in *The Scholar Gypsy*.

> But fly our paths, our feverish contact fly.

These Italian fields around him were the *arva beata* for which he had prayed, not in a mood of lotus-eating idleness, but as one who found more and more happiness in them because they brought him into a right relation with the powers, or Power, manifested in the universe, and this indeed might be his own definition of religion. He had no more desire for luxurious ease in the country than for Indian gold or ivory in the town. He was not even sure that he could grow good grapevines on the somewhat stony soil of the Sabine farm. His steward—after the way of stewards—told him that he might as well try to grow oriental frankincense. But corn he could grow, and olives and beans, which he humorously called the brethren of Pythagoras,

[1] Matthew Arnold.

because that philosopher's argument for the transmigration of souls led Horace to the conclusion that some of the adherents of Pythagoras had become beans. He would be content, however, if his farm yielded him the simplest fare—olive, and endive, and mallow:

> . . . *me pascunt olivae,*
> *me cichorea levesque malvae.*

It was a reasonable prayer that he addressed to the god of light and song, when Augustus made the new temple of Apollo an adjunct to the imperial library. Perhaps it was in this library that Horace would have done his secretarial work if he had accepted the invitation. Is it too fanciful to suppose that his prayer to Apollo on that occasion has a direct reference in its closing stanza to his refusal?

Son of Latona, let me enjoy what I have with a sound mind and body. I have only one other prayer—let me not be lacking in honor or bereft of song when I grow old.

It is difficult to render this poem in the original metre, but I have attempted to do it, not only because I believe with Quiller-Couch that the effect of the classical metres can be reproduced in English much more successfully than is supposed, but because —if the difficulty is overcome—the rendering really does bring the English reader nearer to Horace:

PRAYER TO APOLLO

(Book I, Ode 31)

What prayers have I, O glory of Helicon?
The throngs go up, far hence, to the Palatine!
   New wine for old! Thy poet asks not
     More than the good that thine own hand gave him.

Not glossiest herds from sunny Calabria;
Not India's gold or intricate ivory;
   Not ripening fields whose banks the Liris
     Washes away with her soundless waters.

Let those whose vineyards flourish abundantly
Prune hard, prune well, and hoard their Falernian.
   Rich merchants wait, with costly wine-cups
     Thirsting to finish the world's best vintage.

Much favored they who, sailing to Syria,
Heap wealth on wealth, or daring the hurricane,
   Four times a year, unwrecked, go westward
     Getting more gold (how the gods must love them!)

Grant me no more than olives and chicory;
Thy murmuring flow, deep-valleyed Digentia;
   Old age serene, not all unhonored;
     Books; and my friends, and—the Nine still near me.

This hope is reechoed in the opening line of Austin Dobson's beautiful tribute to a great American poet:

     Not to be tuneless in old age.

It is in substance the prayer of Keats:

     Mother of Hermes! and still youthful Maia!
       May I sing to thee
     As thou wast hymnèd on the shores of Baiae?
       Or may I woo thee
     In earlier Sicilian? or thy smiles
     Seek as they once were sought, in Grecian isles,
     By bards who died content on pleasant sward,
       Leaving great verse unto a little clan?
     O, give me their old vigor, and unheard
       Save of the quiet Primrose, and the span
        Of heaven and few ears,

Rounded by thee, my song should die away
Content as theirs,
Rich in the simple worship of a day.

The verse of the English poet has a slower and less resilient movement than that of the Roman. It is an adagio, but it comes from a symphony with a single meaning, to which many generations have contributed. Horace was not writing a mere plea for poetry or for a place in the sun in which to write it. He was advocating a philosophy and a way of life, in right relation with the powers that rule the universe. This he believed to be the way to happiness. He thought that pleasure of the right kind was a good thing. In fact, he believed that the right kind of primrose path led, not to the everlasting bonfire, but to the abodes of light. It must be remembered that at least half his pleasure was derived from a fine asceticism. He hated every kind of excess. He gave warning after warning that the Roman world was in danger of losing the way to the good and happy life; and, for all the difference in idiom, his cry was that of the philosophic Lake poet:

The world is too much with us; late and soon,
Getting and spending, we lay waste our powers.

In many ways his refusal of the emperor's invitation was the big decision of his life. It is a part (though only a small part) of the overwhelmingly conclusive evidence available against the suggestion that Horace abandoned his principles in his relations with Augustus. There are many ways in which he strongly resembled that lyrical rebel Béranger. It is strange that Swinburne, of all people, should have forgotten how many great spirits, hundreds of years after the death of Horace, have drawn strength and sustenance from him, and not only in pleasant places. Almost every nation has translated into its own

tongue, and every generation into its own idiom, some of those
noble passages in Horace, which have accompanied men to the
scaffold and the rack. English poets of the seventeenth century,
for instance, translated him into their own characteristic form.
It is a form far less splendid than the Greek rhythms and interlocking golden phrases of the original; but it was the spirit of
Horace that carried Wotton's paraphrase into Palgrave's
Golden Treasury, as one of the outstanding expressions (in
English poetry) of the passion for peace and true freedom [1]:

> How happy is he born and taught
>   That serveth not another's will;
> Whose armour is his honest thought
>   And simple truth his utmost skill!
>
> Whose passions not his masters are,
>   Whose soul is still prepared for death,
> Untied unto the world by care
>   Of public fame, or private breath;
>
> Who envies none that chance doth raise
>   Nor vice; who never understood
> How deepest wounds are given by praise;
>   Nor rules of state, but rules of good.
>   .   .   .   .   .   .
>
> —This man is freed from servile bands
>   Of hope to rise, or fear to fall;
> Lord of himself, though not of lands;
>   And having nothing, yet hath all.

[1] *The Character of a Happy Life.*

II

THE CHILDHOOD OF HORACE

THE INCIDENT RECORDED IN THE FIRST CHAPTER PLUNGED US into the middle of the story, as Horace advised in his *Art of Poetry*. An amusing exposition of this Horatian method is given by Byron in *Don Juan:*

> Most epic poets plunge "in medias res"
>   (Horace makes this the heroic turnpike road),
> And then your hero tells, whene'er you please,
>   What went before—by way of episode,
> While seated after dinner at his ease,
>   Beside his mistress in some soft abode,
> Palace, or garden, paradise, or cavern,
> Which serves the happy couple for a tavern.

We must now, therefore, go back to the beginning.

The poet who had refused Octavian's tempting offer was born on the 8th of December, 65 B.C. He was the son of a freedman, or "manumitted slave." This probably strengthened his sense of the value of freedom and his own sturdy independence of spirit. The district in which he was born had the same effect on him. It was a kind of frontier settlement close to the borders of Apulia and Lucania; and was constantly alert against any invasion of its liberties from those two provinces. The elder Horace may have been taken there as a prisoner of war; or, after saving a little money and securing his freedom, he may have settled there because its independent spirit appealed to him. Horace himself says he is not sure whether he is an Apulian or a Lucanian, so that his father may have been captured during a raid from one of these provinces. In any case, the only explanation of how he came to be a "slave" is that he had been taken prisoner either during the civil commotions in Italy, or by pirates at sea. In the latter case he may have been of Greek descent—and incidentally, so much Greek was spoken at Venusia, that the district has been described as bilingual. The name Horatius was adopted from the patrician clan to which, as a slave, he belonged.

It must be remembered that slaves in ancient Italy, for the reasons already mentioned, might include men of considerably higher cultivation than their masters. In earlier days the poet Terence had been a slave. The eminent physician of Augustus was originally a slave; and so, considerably later, was Epictetus, the Stoic philosopher.

The farm at Venusia was a perfect setting for the childhood of a poet. It had only a few acres of land, and they were not very productve. But it was from this very fact that Horace drew some of the grist for his poetic mill. It was here, for instance, that he learned how character without principles may be likened to a neglected field, which is speedily overrun by bracken and will have to be cleansed by fire. It was here that he found the little parable of the bill-hook which cuts down the good with the bad. Here also he saw the dangerous bull with the hay on its horns, as in his third satire. It was here, in the farmyard, that he saw the hound barking at the horns and empty skin of a deer. It was here, probably, that he heard his father refuting that notion of the Stoics that all sins are equally wicked. The theft of his fresh young cabbages did not matter so much as that of his *Lares* (the little images of his household gods). It was here, certainly, that he learned something about plain living and high thinking. Moreover, there was a world of beauty around him— mountain and rushing river and murmuring forest; and, within his own narrow borders, the boy possessed one immense tract which is often forgotten. He owned absolutely everything, from where the seeds were sown up to the sky, and that is a considerable kingdom.

In one of his poems there is a delightful little fairy tale which must have been founded on a real episode. He tells how he escaped from his nurse and, stealing away from the cottage to which he was taken in the hot weather, got lost on the mountainside. When he was tired out, the birds came and covered him with leaves of myrtle and laurel to protect him from bears and adders; and so, eventually, he was found, smiling in his sleep and unconscious of his danger. The story is told lightly, fancifully, and with a touch of humor, but this does not destroy its underlying seriousness. In several other poems he conveys his constant sense of an overruling and protecting power that accompanied him throughout his life.

It has been observed that in men of genius memories of childhood and boyhood often survive with unusual strength. Sometimes they form a kind of Aladdin's garden into which the mature man may tiptoe throughout his life and return with unexpected treasure. Modern psychologists have specialized in drawing monstrosities from the depths of the subconscious mind, but there is also a forgotten wealth of good and beautiful things. A lost Paradise is hidden away in almost every human being. The man of genius sometimes has the key.

There are many instances in English literature; and, curiously enough, even when the child was apparently unhappy, the mature man often owes the happiest parts of his work to it. The happiest scenes in *Great Expectations* are those in which the little boy is at home with Joe Gargery; and, for David Copperfield, there was no haven in later life so snug and cheerful as the fireside by which he sat, reading about crocodiles with faithful old Peggotty. The surroundings may be no better than Mr. Peggotty's old boat on the beach, but the little windows are perpetually alight with welcome. Among many of the greater poets this early freshness of vision touches their mature pages with an enchanted light. In his *Intimations of Immortality* Wordsworth thought he was recollecting a former existence in heaven; but he was really describing the things he had seen in the earthly Paradise of his own childhood. There is a profound significance in that old idea of the Greeks that, while the god of light was the father of the Muses, the mother of them all was Memory.

In the classic poets of Greece and Rome the influence was not so obvious as in the Romantic poets of England. But in many subtle ways it is there; and when it does manifest itself openly, the effect is often of incomparable beauty. We find it in the return of Odysseus to Ithaca, when the wanderer proves his identity to his old father Laertes by his childhood memories:

Come and I will even tell thee the trees through all the terraced garden which thou gavest me, once, for mine own; and I was begging of thee this and that, being but a little child and following thee through the garden. Through these very trees we were going, and thou didst tell me the names of each of them. Pear trees, thirteen thou gavest me, and ten apple trees, and figs two score, and as we went, thou didst name the fifty rows of vines thou didst give me.[1]

In the fourth eclogue of Virgil again it transfuses with magic one of the most exquisite lines in Latin poetry:

Incipe, parve puer, risu cognoscere matrem.

"Begin, little lad, with a smile to know the fond face
    of thy mother";

but the charm of the line can be conveyed only by its original

[1] Lang's translation.

music. It owes all its beauty to the light on a remembered face. The finest passages in the *Aeneid* are also expressions of filial devotion; and the green valley in which Aeneas meets the shade of his father Anchises enshrines the noblest of them all.

It was on the farm at Venusia that, as English children learn about Puck, Horace became acquainted with Faunus, the friendly spirit of the countryside, who protected flocks and herds. As a child, he had seen the peasants, in their gayest holiday colors, bringing gifts of flowers and fruit, or sacrificing a firstling of the flock. He had seen the smoke rising from the little altar of Faunus at the field's edge, while the great white oxen, relieved of the yoke, lay breathing at ease in the shadow of the dark ilex, and the village girls clapped their hands for the ploughmen dancing in time on an earth no longer rebellious, and all the meadows around them made ready for Spring. This was a memory that came to life many years later in one of the most beautiful of his poems, the prayer to Faunus, which is so instinct with the feeling of the old Italian piety. There is gaiety in it, but there is also seriousness, and a note which is not often found in Horace—a note of tenderness. It was induced here, surely, by the memory of his native fields and the associations of his boyhood. I have attempted to render it in the original Sapphic metre; and, though only four words are given to the exultation of the ploughman over his old enemy ("ploughmen dance, on earth!") they may be nearer to the intention of Horace than the eight or ten with which prose translations have sometimes replaced the terse Latin. It is often said that the effect of Latin quantitative verse cannot be reproduced in English. But I think it can, on one condition. It cannot be done by ignoring the difference between quantity and stress; but it can be done by an order of words in which the natural stress of English falls where, in the Latin metre, the long quantitative syllable would demand it and, so far as possible, choosing words in which those stressed syllables are also "long":

PRAYER TO FAUNUS

(Book III, Ode 18)

Faunus, fleet-foot lover of flying wood-nymphs,
Turn, on tiptoe; enter my sunlit farmland;
Look, oh gently look on my flock enfolded
    Here, with its firstlings.

Bless, and gently go. On thy boisterous feast-day,
Cyprian wine shall flow, where the chosen victim
Stains the fresh-cut turf, and thine ancient altar
    Smokes with our incense.

Goat and kid shall frisk in the flowering grasses,
Ploughmen dance!—on earth!—while the festal village
Claps its hands in time, and the unyoked oxen
    Rest where the streams flow.

There the wolf shall stray, and the flock not fear him,
There, while all the slaves of the land go singing,
Autumn beech-leaves, flying in gold and crimson,
    Fall, at thy feet, Faun.

No rendering in verse could be true to the original, if it aimed at being literal. Incidentally, the order of the last two stanzas is here inverted. The natural "curve" of the poem, in English, seemed to take that form; and I thought it best to obey.

It was on the farm at Venusia that the poet's father, whose days were bound each to each by the old Roman *pietas*, told him about the Lar, the guardian spirit of the household, whose little statue watched over the hearth. At one time the Lar, like Faunus, had been a spirit of the open fields. The Lares used to dwell on the boundaries between farms. Shrines were built for them, with as many faces as there were adjoining farms, each face containing an altar and a little statue of a Lar. On certain days all the households, with all the slaves who worked in the fields, would gather around this shrine, each group worshiping at its own altar, but all united in recognizing their dependence on a divine Power. "It was the only rite," his father would say, lowering his voice a little, "the only worship in which the slaves at that time could join with the other members of the family."

But when the owner of the farm was away, the Lar would sometimes be brought into the house; perhaps as a safeguard against his being stolen. It was then the duty of the head man's wife, the *vilica*, to arrange the ceremony on feast days, and all the slaves would attend as usual. The Lar thus led the way into the house, and eventually the slaves came in to worship him with the rest of the family even when the *paterfamilias* was at home. Thus the Lar of the fields became in time the *Lar familiaris*, the guardian spirit of the whole household, and the family hearth became his altar. The statuette above the hearth was garlanded on festal days; and when the boy's mother, who died in his childhood, first came to the house and took off her bridal wreath of rose and myrtle, she laid it on the altar of the Lar, where it remained until it withered. Every morning and every night before the family meal, his father made an offering to the Lar. It might be only a little salted cake, or a sprig of sweet-smelling vervain or rosemary flung into the living flame on the hearth; but it was always a recognition of man's dependence on powers above and beyond his own.

In some houses, perhaps, the divine inhabitant was looked upon as a kind of ancestral deity, the original founder of the family; but this was no mere ancestor worship. It arose from a sense of tradition, and the fact that the Lar was the guardian, not of one generation, but of all. In the house of the manumitted slave, therefore, the Lar may have had a special significance as the representative of something older and greater than any human tradition.

It was from all these things that the boy derived that understanding of the old religion of the Italian countryside which he showed later in many of his poems. From the very first he instinctively felt that this old religion was groping toward a deeper philosophical meaning behind the forms in which the divine powers were personified; and so, when he became a man, it was not by a mere poetic convention that he appeared to accept these forms. He was not a Lucian. He would not shake the belief of the simplest peasant who accepted these personifications as the reality. The man who rises beyond the forms into the reality does not behave like a minor intellectual or a shallow sceptic. He does not believe less, but a great deal more. Perhaps Horace learned this, too, from his father. That thoughtful old man, who had lived a life of self-sacrifice and toil, close to Nature and the powers behind Nature, may have been more truly philosophical than any of the sceptics in the sophisticated capital. It was at Venusia, in fact, that Horace acquired from his environment and from his father, a rich hoard of memories upon which he could draw for some of his finest poetry throughout the rest of his life.

The personal recollections are concentrated on his father. It is probable that his mother died before he was old enough to remember her. The reference to the nurse in the little fairy tale of his childhood, when he was lost in the hills, tends to confirm this; and he seems to have been an only child. The bond between the boy and his father was unusually strong, and the father was determined to do everything in his power for his son. A freedman belonged to what would be called today the "underprivileged classes." An obscure contemporary, speaking, of course, *de haut en bas*, declared that he had actually seen the elder Horace wiping his nose on his sleeve in the market-place, in the days when he had been a coactor, or collector of payments at auctions. The foolish taunt does not seem very devastating in a world that was to see a Nero enthroned and deified; but it is curious to find the snobbery that invented it in a remote age unconsciously perpetuated in nineteenth-century England. "The Roman poets of the Augustan and pre-Augustan period, unlike Horace, were all well-born," says Sir Theodore Martin; "Catullus and Calvus were men of old and noble families. Virgil was the son of a man of good property."

These sentences are typical of the confusion of values which then prevailed. There is a perfectly logical cause for pride in a certain kind of ancestry. There is none whatever for pride in mere property, nor is the temporary occupation of one individual (even if he did wipe the sweat from his brow) necessarily an infallible guide to the stock from which he sprung. There was a time when Virgil himself was deprived of his property. Once, his life was endangered in the process. It might have required a very slight change in the circumstances of the time for his father to have been made a prisoner and a slave. In this case, the well-born Virgil would have ceased to be well-born. There is ample evidence that, in character as well as in their works, both Virgil and Horace were far better bred than most of the politically exalted personages of their time. They probably did not frequent the gladiatorial shows with the rank and fashion of Rome; but neither of them could have written the crude letter of Octavian, quoted in the opening chapter. How this finer quality of mind came about is a different question. One fact is certain —Horace for many centuries has been regarded as the very type of the cultivated and civilized man.

"He has been taken more closely even than Virgil to the heart of the world," says Mackail. "His *Odes* became a sort of psalter of secular life; his *Satires* and *Epistles* have been, for the whole European world, the great handbook of good sense, good temper, and practical wisdom. No one has done more to spread and fix and make attractive that spirit of 'humanity' which, like its name, is of Latin creation. He gave mankind the type of the man of the world and the gentleman; he showed how it is attainable without birth or wealth, without anxiety or ambition, without either high intellectual gifts or unattainable saintliness of life."

Horace himself, of course, had very high intellectual gifts indeed; but what Mackail says is none the less true. Sainte-Beuve, the best of all French critics, anticipating Mackail's phrase about the "psalter of secular life," says:

"In the modern world, particularly in France, the works of Horace have become a kind of breviary of good taste, of poetry, of practical and worldly wisdom"—"*un bréviaire de goût, de poésie, de sagesse pratique et mondaine.*"

It is impossible to suppose that a character of this kind owed nothing to its early environment and education. It has been the fashion in recent years for "intellectuals" of various kinds to write books ridiculing the lives to which they owe their very existence. The fact that age or the grave precludes a reply has no restraining influence. The sixth satire of the first book, the great poem in which Horace expresses his gratitude to his father, has a good deal to teach them here. Those who think of Horace merely as an exquisite artist, celebrating the pleasures of life, and untouched by any deep affection, will find their answer in this poem. He addresses it to Maecenas; for it was apparently his friendship with "the descendant of Etruscan kings" that roused the envy of certain upstarts in Rome, and caused them to taunt the poet with his origin. His reply, therefore, was not made directly to those who attacked him, but over their heads, as to an equal:

They pretend to attack me for being the son of a freedman

father, but it is really because they envy me your friendship, just as in former days they envied me because I commanded a Roman legion.

It will be noticed that Horace boldly reminds his reader that he had fought against Octavian:

I did not win your friendship by mere good luck. It was Virgil, the best of men, who told you about me. When I first met you I stammered out a few words, for I was tongue-tied and embarrassed. I did not try to make you think that I was the son of a distinguished father, or that I rode about my fields at home on a fine horse. I told you what I was. I went away, and it was nine months before you invited me again and made me one of your friends. I am proud of the fact that I pleased a man like you, who can discriminate between what is really disgraceful and what is honorable, looking not to the eminence of a father, but to his clean heart and honorable life. Moreover, if my vices are comparatively few, in an otherwise sound disposition; if no one can truly accuse me of avarice or base conduct or wrong-doing; if I dare to say of myself that my own life is clean and harmless, and that I am loved by my friends, I owe all this to my father. He was poor, and had only a very small farm, but he would not send me to the local school of Flavius, although rich boys, the sons of high and mighty centurions, used to go there, with their slates and satchels hung over their arms, and their eight pennies in their hands on pay-day. No,—he boldly took his boy off to Rome to be taught what any man of equestrian rank, or indeed any senator, would have his own children taught. If any one in so big a city noticed the way I was dressed, and the slaves who took care of me, he would have thought that some great ancestral estate must have defrayed the expenses of it all. Further, he himself,—the faithfulest of all guardians—went with me to all my teachers. Why should I say more? he kept me chaste, which is the first grace of manhood; he kept me not only from wrong-doing, but even away from the breath of it. He was not afraid that any one would twist it to his discredit if some day I should follow a humble occupation like his own. Nor should I have complained; but now I owe him all the more praise and all the more gratitude. Never while I retain my reason could I regret having such a father. I will not defend myself as many might who say it is not their fault that their parents were not freeborn or distinguished. I say a very different thing from that. For if, after a great space of time, Nature should order us to live our lives over again, and to choose any parents that our pride might prefer, I should decline to choose them from the ranks of the consuls and praetors, and should be content with my own.

This passage has been praised by a thousand critics, but sometimes they unconsciously perpetuate the very snobbery against which Horace is protesting. Even the fact that the elder Horace personally took his boy to school has been treated in this way. Mr. T. R. Glover, for instance, in an otherwise delightful little book (*Horace: A Return to Allegiance*), writes that the father of the poet attended him at his lectures "as a footman." This last phrase illustrates the incorrigible English habit of using a caste system as a kind of social irritant, a mustard plaster, to be applied indiscriminately both to the living and the dead. It happens also to be inaccurate; for the poem makes it quite clear that the actual circumstances were almost the reverse of this. The fact that the older Horace accompanied his little boy to school and looked after him in so many loving ways, hardly justifies the suggestion that he attended him as a "footman."

The schoolmaster at Rome was a well-known grammarian named Orbilius Pupillus, who apparently rivaled the famous Doctor Busby in his use of the rod. It may be conjectured that Horace, being a tiny little boy, exceedingly intelligent, and accompanied by his father, escaped the worst.

One of the most valuable parts of his education at this time

was the way in which his father used to talk to him about the
various characters they met or saw in Rome. He would point
out the effect of their words and actions on other people, in a
shrewdly humorous way as a guide or a warning for the boy's
own behavior. The early satires of Horace owe a great deal to
this habit of direct observation which he acquired from his
father. The satires of Lucilius may have contributed to their
form and technique, but the characters themselves are certainly
living and contemporary, though their idiosyncrasies may be
recognized in every age. Crispinus himself—the button-holing
and indefatigable bore with the hide of a hippopotomus—may
still be found lumbering along Pall Mall or Fifth Avenue!

It is pleasant to picture the elder Horace escorting his little
son up the *Via Sacra* in Rome, and making his comments, with
a twinkling eye, on what they heard and saw in that exciting
scene. They would thread their way through the crowd as it
flowed along the stately colonnades of the fashionable quarter.
Women with braided hair and brightly-colored sandals would
alight from sumptuous litters to look at those new silver hand-
mirrors which the Greek merchants were now displaying; or,
still more interesting, those little chests of carved ivory, the
cistae mysticae, so neatly fitted with the latest manicure set;
the rouge-box, the *vasa unguentaria,* and other absolute neces-
sities. Syrian slaves in crimson liveries would wait behind
them to carry their purchases; and the old sunburnt farmer
would perhaps whisper to his boy: "Do you know what that
little ivory box contains, my chick? [1] It contains three worships,
the swords and shields of an entire legion, and half the cattle
in Venusia."

Bareheaded men, most of them in white togas, walking as
though they owned the world, would pass on their way to the

[1] *"appellat . . . pater . . . pullum, male parvus si cui filius est . . ."* Sat. I,
3, 45.

thermae, those luxurious baths which have left their own ruins to astonish the modern world. Father and son would make a quiet little game of their own, picking out the various types and characters—the grave senator with the broad purple stripe on his tunic; or the dandy with his amethystine mantle, so carelessly flung over his right shoulder and fastened there with a golden clasp. "They confiscated three farms to pay for that," the old man would whisper again. "See how that one struts; how he pushes people aside; how even the women have to make way for him; and how angrily they look back at him. It is not wealth that makes the thoroughbred." This last remark would appear, later on, transmuted into verse, *Fortuna non mutat genus.*

And the little boy would squeeze his father's hand as if he understood, neither of them knowing in the least what the effect of these words and the picture would be later on. It was his father's teaching, however, his father's words, his father's memory that, years later, flashed into those fiery phrases against a certain arrogant and treacherous blackguard who had won the favor of Augustus and become a tribune:

> *licet superbus ambules pecunia,*
> *Fortuna non mutat genus.*

What use was it to send the beaked ships against the pirates, if Rome were to make tribunes of men like this:

> *hoc, hoc tribuno militum?*

It was the bookshops, however, that interested them most. They would often look in at them, not to buy, for the books displayed there were very costly. But merely to look at them was a delight. All the honey of Helicon was distilled, and all the witcheries of the island of Circe were inscribed on those exquisite scrolls of Egyptian papyrus, so smoothly pumiced and so compactly rolled upon their cedar rods, with the ivory knobs or painted cornua at each end, and the rich dyes of their parchment wrappers, and the labels bearing the titles in bright crimson lettering. In some of them the portrait of the author would be painted on the first page; and when the bookseller's back was turned, father and son would unroll a little of that volume to see the face of Theocritus, or Catullus, or Alcaeus (some of whose work Horace had learned at school), or old blind Homer, the father of them all. Occasionally, if the bookseller was really occupied, they would steal a look at the text, so beautifully written in brown sepia-juice, or in a deep black ink, like that which the Chinese use.

There was a certain irony in all this, for the books being too costly for most book-lovers, they were commonly bought by collectors who gave large sums for them, and put them into cedar chests for fear that moths and worms might eat them. But these *cognoscenti*, having locked them up on their library shelves, never looked at them again. Both the boy and his father had a curious premonition that one day the works of a young poet from Venusia would be added to that treasure-house. How it came to them nobody could explain; but the boy had already composed a few lines of Greek verse. One of his earliest recollections, of course, was that episode when he was lost as a child on the hillside. The leaves of wild laurel and myrtle with which he was covered when they found him might have been blown there by the wind, if realistic explanations are required. But it was the wind of which no one could say whence it comes or whither it goes. His father, coming upon some Greek verses among the boy's school exercises, may have said quietly, as though to the unseen mother who had died so young, "It may come true, that fable!" If he did not say it in words, he certainly said it in deeds. The boy's promise was the cause of the father's extraordinary desire to open all the doors of opportunity for his little son, and enable him, when school-days in Rome were ended, to continue his studies at the distant university of Athens. It was not the birds or the winds of Venusia that had covered the child with those prophetic laurel leaves. Nor was it the emperor Augustus that brought the prophecy to fulfilment. It was the devotion and self-sacrifice of a manumitted slave.

III

HORACE AT ATHENS

THE LIFE OF HORACE AT ATHENS CAN BE PICTURED WITH A closer approximation to actual facts than is usually admitted. Exact details are missing. We do not possess a diary; but we know something of his friends, and a great deal of what he saw and experienced there, though much of it has to be reconstructed from casual words and phrases.

Athens was still the great finishing-school for young men of distinguished families in the Roman world. Sons of the Roman aristocracy, or of men distinguished by their achievements, thronged its lecture halls. They met and talked and dined together. They debated art and politics. They discussed poetry and their own love-affairs. Many of them were ardent Republicans, the son of Cicero among them.

It must have been an intoxicating experience for the young son of the freedman, the country lad from Venusia, to be thrown among these young "heirs of all the ages." We must picture him, at this time, as a slender, dark-haired youth, his brown eyes glowing with life, and glancing with a humor that immediately made him popular among his contemporaries. We must picture him walking to the lectures of Theomnestus, the Academic, and Cratippus, the Peripatetic; but, certainly, with his poet's imagination, he would draw more from the great memories and associations by which he was surrounded in the City of the Violet Crown than from anything his professors could tell him. We know exactly what he saw when he stood gazing at the Parthenon. We know how the words of Sophocles must have haunted his imagination when he wandered into the theatre of Dionysus, hewn out of the rock of the Acropolis; and how those white temples on the hill-tops, so sacred to Apollo and the Muses, must have stirred his heart under the burning sapphire sky.

To be young and a poet, at the university of Athens, in the days when Virgil was beginning to write, and so many tremendous events were happening in the world—what imaginable destiny could be more glorious? And, when the sun went down and the dreaming city began to grow cooler under the moon and stars, he must often have laid down his books and gone out to one of those convivial suppers about which the scapegrace son of Cicero writes.

It was life that interested him; but, for this very reason, books interested him also. Books to Horace were not dead things on a shelf; they were his never-failing friends. Plato was first among the prose writers; not the Plato who banished the poets from his Republic, but the Plato who argued so pleasantly under a plane-tree by a flowing stream, the Plato who understood beauty, and love, and death. It was from this Plato, I think, that he caught certain delightful touches of humor and philosophy in the dialogue of some of those early satires, which he was to write in Rome. But at this time he concentrated more on experiments in Greek lyric verse. He actually formed the idea of becoming a poet in Greek, and trying to rival Alcaeus in his own language. Fortunately, this was only a temporary ambition; but it was an admirable training for his future life-work.

Occasionally, perhaps, he would dine with Cratippus, that merry old professor who could sometimes forget his Aristotle and treat his students as younger brothers. The son of Cicero—scapegrace though he was—succeeded in getting Cratippus to dinner, partly because he wanted his father to hear what good company he was keeping; but he found the philosopher more entertaining than he expected. The young Cicero had far too large an allowance for a college student, and he was able to give big dinner parties. Horace probably did not care for him so much as for the friends whom he mentions in his poems, like Messalla. But they were all in the same set, and shortly afterwards they were all fellow-officers in the army of Brutus. Horace undoubtedly, therefore, may be pictured at some of these dinner parties, where the guests wore chaplets of roses, and drank Chian wine, and sang students' songs till the small hours of the morning.

There was a dramatic excitement in the air, an excitement tense as anything aroused in the Greek theater; and we certainly know that the youthful Horace must have shared in this. His early biographers have not exercised much imagination in reconstructing this part of his life from the historical facts which must have quickened the pulse of the young poet. We can picture the day, for instance, when the news of the assassination of Julius Caesar reached these Republican students at Athens. We can picture the lecture halls emptying, the knots and clusters of young men, breathlessly discussing that tremendous scene. Many of them, like Messalla, came from great Roman houses, where the leading figures in the drama were familiar guests, and some of the students were personal friends of Brutus.

We can picture, too, with certainty, the dramatic moment when a crowd of students went down to the harbor at Athens, and met a certain mysterious ship which, it was rumored, was bringing a new and very remarkable student indeed to complete his studies in their company. We can surely hear their shouts as that student walked down the gangplank and was found to be none other than Brutus himself. Whether the poet was in the crowd at the harbor or not, we cannot tell; but quite certainly he heard and saw the tumult in the streets of Athens as the young men brought their hero to his house. A Republican

himself, Horace could not fail to be affected by the wave of
hero worship that swept through the university. Young idealists who hated bloodshed talked of the killing of Caesar, not as
assassination, but as "tyrannicide," an act of the highest patriotism. The reception of Brutus in Athens was overwhelming, and
it was even proposed to set up his statue with those of Harmo-
dius and Aristogeiton.

We can picture the enthusiasm for lectures on Greek philosophy when the students found that Brutus was attending the
courses on Plato and Aristotle. It makes a strange contrast with
the violent drama of which they had all heard. The serenity
with which the older student—their hero, Brutus—having
shaken the Roman world from end to end, now turned to his
books and sat on the same benches with them, must have made
his influence all the more compelling, and endowed him, in the
eyes of his young companions, with almost superhuman self-
mastery. Brutus had a real love of literature and philosophy.
Perhaps it was his tragedy that by nature he was more an
"ideologist," as it is called today, than a man of action. He had
been egged on by men who knew how to make use of his convictions; and his visit to Athens was not merely to disguise his
military plans, though it coincided with them. During his quiet
and scholarly occupations, he made many friends among the
students. Messalla was particularly intimate with him, and he
singled out Messalla's friend, Horace, for high promotion a
little later.

The poet and his young contemporaries regarded Brutus
with something of that idealistic fervor which inspired the
young disciples of Mazzini at English universities in the nineteenth century. The "blood-bright splendor of Brutus" was
invoked by the hero-worshipping poet of the later struggle;
and, different as the circumstances were, the underlying motive
was the same. Often as the name of Freedom has been misused

for base political purposes, young and generous hearts are quickly stirred by that clarion-call; and, unhappily, almost as often they have found themselves in a trap set by the enemies of Freedom.

> Once again the sickening game,
> Freedom free to slay herself, and dying while they shout her name!

But the appeal owes its power to the supreme value of true Freedom, and this value can no more be destroyed by its political profanation than the reality of God can be destroyed by blasphemy. It was a sincere idealism that roused the young men of Athens to follow Brutus. It was not a materialistic war between the "have nots" and the "haves." The son of the manumitted slave had a passion of his own for Freedom; but many of his fellow students belonged to the Roman aristocracy. The Republican party was, in fact, the aristocratic party. The young men at Athens dreamed of a renascent Republic, endowed with the traditional virtues of an ideal Rome, a city not made with hands, which had never actually existed, but continually haunted the mind, either as a memory of something lost, or as a hope of something yet to be born.

A vision of the kind that possessed the young students at Athens was possible to idealistic minds on both sides of the political conflict. It is not on the ultimate goal, but on the means of attaining it, that such men are divided. Virgil, at Rome, could persuade himself that his ideal was attainable under the rule of Octavian. Perhaps he was less troubled about the things that were so rapidly becoming Caesar's, because his own treasure and his own heart were so constantly elsewhere. But for the young students at Athens the blood-red star of Brutus had a direct appeal, all the more potent because it allowed of no compromise. The personal character of Brutus, his curiously hypnotic way of suggesting a high destiny, a power above and beyond his own, using him as an instrument, with complete indifference to his own personal fortunes—all these things helped to make his appeal to youth almost irresistible. Plutarch tells us that, at a banquet, when Brutus was drinking success to his military enterprise, he was moved by something beyond his own will to quote a line of verse which apparently foretold his doom. Possibly he deceived himself by his own self-dramatization. Shakespeare, in a striking passage, has vividly illustrated this rather theatrical doom-fraught sense in Brutus. It is a curious passage, for it raises the question whether Shakespeare was alluding to the old Roman idea of the Genius, the spiritual double that accompanied every man through life and perhaps might be regarded as his immortal part:

> Between the acting of a fearful thing
> And the first motion, all the interim is
> Like a phantasma or a hideous dream:
> The Genius and the moral instruments
> Are then in council, and the state of man,
> Like to a little kingdom, suffers then
> The nature of an insurrection.

But this apparent transcendence of the ordinary motives of success and failure made him a man apart in the eyes of the young—a man of destiny, with all the magnetism of a heroic self-immolation. The abrupt, laconic sentences which he affected—another characteristic which Shakespeare, following the record in Plutarch, has again vividly reproduced with an almost uncanny skill—cast their own spell. They were like the tricks of speech with which a tragic actor has been known to grip his audience; but, although they were tricks of speech, they were used by a man who had driven his own dagger into the heart of Caesar.

There is another characteristic of Brutus which has not been noted in connection with the "favoritism" which he was accused of displaying toward Horace, a favoritism sufficiently marked to arouse considerable jealousy when the freedman's son was made a military tribune. There were six of these tribunes to a legion, and they took it in turns to command. This is what Horace meant when he said he had been placed in command of a legion. Many modern commentators have expressed their own surprise at the appointment, for it was against all the traditions of the Roman legions and the military caste. Horace himself refers to the envy which it aroused, and the taunts to which he was subjected; not, of course, from men like Messalla, who remained his friend for life, but from the ill-bred and ill-natured who thought themselves slighted or "passed over." The poems of Horace throw no light on the "favor" shown to him. There are not many references to Brutus himself, for Brutus died before Horace had really begun to write for publication, and by that time Horace had out-lived the magnetism. But he did write to his fellow-student Messalla, as an intimate friend; and Messalla had been a close friend of Brutus. There is ample evidence that Horace was in the set of students who knew Brutus best in Athens; but it was certainly not on military grounds that Brutus formed his "high opinion" of him. The Roman world was not so highly specialized as the world of today. Statesmen and philosophers turned from the council chamber or the library to the battle-field as if they were merely passing from one room to another. Moreover, Brutus was not what is commonly called a "practical man." He was interested, as we have seen, not only in philosophy, but in literature; and, while he personally affected an epigrammatic terseness of speech, his mind had been nourished upon the master-poets of Greece, the subject in which his fellow-student, Horace, was most deeply interested. Brutus was constantly quoting the Greek poets, and Horace would have been delighted to exchange quotations with him. In the three crises of his life Brutus expressed his feelings through the words of the Greek poets. When he parted from his wife Portia, one of his friends quoted the passage from Homer in which Andromache is parting from Hector, and Brutus instantly replied with another verse, but said that he must not answer Portia as Hector answered Andromache. At the banquet already mentioned, on the eve of his fatal campaign, he foretold his own death at the hands of Apollo, in another verse from the Greek. Defying the omen of the words, which seem to have been spoken despite himself, his watchword to his army at Philippi was *Apollo;* and, when the worst had happened and he was preparing to kill himself with his own sword, almost his last recorded words are two verses of Greek poetry. This is how Plutarch records the incident:

Brutus had now passed a little brook, running among trees and under steep rocks, and, it being night, would go no further, but sat down in a hollow place with a great rock projecting before it, and a few of his officers and friends about him. At first, looking up to heaven, that was then full of stars, he repeated two verses, one of which was:
"Punish, great Jove, the author of these ills."

Translation, of course, mars the spirit of the scene; but it is clear that Brutus was one of those men to whom great books and fine poetry are not dead things, but a means of communion with other minds, and a source of intellectual life or philosophical resignation.

Those who know what a bond the knowledge and love of literature can be, in the fellowship of any two students, will not find it at all unlikely that it had something to do with the "high opinion" that Brutus formed of Horace. At any rate, no better or more reasonable ground has been suggested for what must otherwise remain a mystery. A wide and vital acquaintance with

the masters of his own mind would be quite enough to arouse
an unusual regard for the genius of that witty little fellow-
student from Venusia, who sometimes sat near him in the lecture hall, and could cap his quotations with an inimitable grace.
Moreover, it may not have been so impractical as it appears.
Brutus was short of officers, and all these young men were at
least intelligent. It might even be said that Horace had been
at a semi-military school at Rome; for Orbilius, his schoolmaster, was a veteran soldier. Horace—in one or two poems—
shows a certain pride in his appointment and in the good opinion
that he won during the campaign from those who were entitled
to judge. But this pride was not evinced on military grounds,
and it was free from the slighest touch of vanity. It appeared
only once or twice when he was subjected to those ill-natured
taunts about his birth, by men who on any scientific classification
must have been rated his inferiors in every characteristic and
quality of *homo sapiens*. He was able to make a joke about the
loss of his shield in the rout at Philippi; for, like all brave men,
he was able to laugh at his own misadventures and hairbreadth
escapes; but, when he was taunted with being the son of a manumitted slave, he replied, in effect: "Yes, and I am proud of it;
for Brutus entrusted me with the command of a legion."

CAMPAIGNING WITH BRUTUS

THE CAMPAIGN WAS AN ARDUOUS ONE, AND HORACE SERVED IN the army of Brutus for nearly two years. His boyhood on the farm probably stood him in good stead here, for he knew how to ride, and a good rider knows how to spare both himself and his horse. Otherwise, the long marches, often through wild and difficult country, would have exhausted a body so small and frail.

In later years his own remarks about his riding on a bob-tailed mule are sometimes taken to imply that he was not a good horseman. On many occasions commentators have been sadly misled by his jests at his own expense. Perhaps he was plumper as he jogged along the high road from Rome to Tarentum. But if we are curious to know how he survived the marches that almost killed Brutus himself, we may suppose that a lad from the farm—probably as light as a jockey in those days—would have certain advantages; and it would not be a bob-tailed mule that he rode through Thessaly and Macedonia in command of a legion.

Few incidents of the campaign are recorded in his poems. There is the famous reference to the flight from Philippi and the loss of his shield. Another, apparently more trivial, but treated more elaborately in what is perhaps the earliest of his satires, was a lawsuit which took place near Smyrna, between a rich Greek merchant and a bull-headed officer on the staff of Brutus. Outwardly it appears to be a piece of sheer buffoonery, such as war cartoonists have delighted to illustrate in our own time. But it has a curious biographical interest of more importance than would appear at first sight. Commentators, each echoing another, often tell us that the "only point of the poem is a somewhat flat pun." But its real interest is of an almost startling kind. The joke—a somewhat savage one—turns merely on the fact that the bull-headed officer's name was Rex, and that Brutus, before whom the case was tried, had recently driven his dagger into a more important Rex.

> Even at the base of Pompey's statua,
> Which all the while ran blood.

Now it is all very well, two thousand years after the event, for critics to find a "joke" on that subject amusing or flippant, or to dismiss it with the remark that the "only point of the satire appears to be a somewhat flat pun." But the world was still quivering with the shock of that assassination. Something must have been happening in the mind of Horace to make it possible for him to treat that particular subject in that disrespectful way, under the flag of Brutus. According to the best accounts, Brutus looked upon the assassination of his former friend Caesar as the most tragic necessity of his life, and we are told that Horace made a "joke" of it under his very nose. The two litigants are depicted as abusing one another in court. The officer, Rex, begins to use the scurrilous language which Horace remembered a vine-dresser using at Venusia, when a village boy had shouted "cuckoo" at him—a common taunt for the lazy folk who did not begin to prune their vines before the cuckoo came. The Greek merchant, who is half-drunk, retaliates with an appeal to Brutus. "Killing kings," he cries, "is very much in your line. Why don't you cut the throat of this other Rex?"—"*cur non hunc Regem jugulas?*"

There is more than a trivial play on words in this. It is unfortunate that the critics whose eyes were riveted on the word "*Regem*" could not move them a fraction to the right and consider the savagery of the word *"jugulas."* As St. Augustine said, in a passage of wide and deep application, the meaning is not complete till the last syllable is sounded! It is only in the twentieth century that throat-cutting has become a commonplace; and the punning in that line may be compared with the fiercest word-play in the Greek poets. Ajax, in Sophocles, is made to play upon his own name, after the slaughter of the cattle. Horace was not writing with a feather; he was writing with a stylus; and when a stylus becomes a stiletto, it is funny only at a distance. The real point of the story, as well as of the stiletto, has not been noticed at all. It tells us quite plainly that, only half way through the campaign, in his own mind, Horace had pricked the heroic bubble on both sides of that internecine war. This one little "jest" sets Horace at an immense distance from the heroics of Brutus, as depicted, for instance, by Plutarch, and made familiar to the world by Shakespeare.

The war, in fact, seen at close quarters, was having its effect on Horace, and there are many touches in his early satires which remind us of Swift. It is perhaps significant that, despite the glamor with which Brutus tried to invest his campaign, its effect on Horace was one of disillusionment.

The army of Brutus (says Plutarch) was less in number than that of Caesar, but in the splendor of the men's arms and the richness of their equipage it wonderfully exceeded; for most of their arms were of gold and silver, which Brutus had lavishly bestowed among them, . . . he thought that the riches which soldiers carried . . . would add something of spirit to those who desired glory, and would make those who were covetous . . . fight the more valiantly to preserve the arms which were their estate.

This may be exaggerated; but it has a basis of truth. The display would have delighted Marlowe; but it merely disillusioned Horace, and the appeal to covetousness would have disgusted him. It may even be that he caught a glimpse of the Brutus who had lent money, according to Cicero, at exorbitant interest, and imprisoned the defaulters without food until they died. It is certain that Horace must have discovered that, in politics, "blood-bright splendors" are a delusion.

It is significant, perhaps, that the only hint of glamor which the poetry of Horace extracted from the campaign is in the magical use which he makes of certain place-names. These form almost the only record of the scenes through which he passed. They are a sure indication of the subject in which his mind found refuge; for they were almost all of them associated with the great poetry of the world. Horace never dramatized himself; but neither Childe Harold nor Byron could have known a more exciting moment than that in which the young poet arrived with his legion on the shores of the Hellespont, and saw the unaltering waters flow between the towers of Hero and Leander—

an freta vicinas intercurrentia turres.

What would Byron not have given to be able to picture himself riding behind the glittering eagles of Brutus across the plains of Troy, with "Freedom" for a watchword; or, as night fell, encountering the mighty shade of Hector in a stillness only deepened by the murmur of the distant camp, while the watch-fires, not of Agamemnon, but of the Roman legions, flashed upon golden helmets, and the horses of the Roman cavalry crunched their golden grain under the old unchanging stars?

For Horace it was enough that the names of Priam and Achilles, Hector and Paris, move to music across his pages. He uses place-names, too, like hieroglyphics, knowing that his readers will recognize the golden ore of poetry with which they are loaded. He did not need to tell the story any more than Milton did when, speaking of the death of Proserpine, he added simply,

> Which cost Ceres all that pain
> To seek her through the world.

The entire pilgrimage is in the three words, "all that pain." In Horace the names are almost all that we get, but they are interwoven in such a way with the cadence of the verse that we need no more:

> *quid tibi visa Chios, Bullati, notaque Lesbos,*
> *quid concinna Samos, quid Croesi regia Sardis?*

The question is addressed to his friend Bullatius; but what did Horace himself think of those Aegean Isles at which, according to the Dryasdusts, he had probably gazed only from the mainland? This dull suggestion may surely be refuted by a phrase or two in one of his poems to be quoted presently; but, on general grounds, if poets are poets, it is likely that he would have seized the opportunity of visiting at least one of those islands, though only for a few hours, rather than stand gazing across a narrow strip of water at the shores that Alcaeus and Sappho had made so famous. Lesbos, after all, was the fountainhead of the Greek poetry that he loved most. He must surely have caught a glimpse there of the "white implacable Aphrodite" and the doves that drew her,

> Looking always, looking with necks reverted
> Back to Lesbos, back to the hills whereunder
> Shone Mitylene.

There is a school of biographers and historians which appears to regard the most natural actions and events as utterly incredible, if they happen to please the imagination. The motive is worthy. They quite rightly desire not to invest their subject with any false glamor. Fortunately, in this particular case,

49

Horace not only provides the evidence, but deliberately divests it of any false sentiment. In an epistle of the first book (the eleventh), written many years after the event, he makes it clear that he prefers the Sabine farm to any of these places. The climate of Mitylene, he says, is unbearable. It affects one like wearing a heavy overcoat in summer or flimsy athletic attire in winter. He says it with a personal feeling that is unmistakable. It does not arise from "hearsay"; for, from the days of Orpheus to the days of Swinburne, Lesbos has been hymned by the poets and praised by the historians, not only for its natural beauty, but for its climate. In Tacitus it is *"insula nobilis et amoena."*

Poets have idealized a thousand places that they never visited; but there is probably not a single instance in which a poet has taken the trouble to contradict the common notion about the climate of a particular city in a foreign land, unless he had visited it. Poets will use generalities, but they do not invent so personally felt a phrase for the stuffiness of a particular atmosphere as that remark about the heavy overcoat.

Some of the closest parallels in literature to the use of place-names in Horace may be found in Tennyson. His poem to Edward Lear, for instance, on his travels in Greece, might be described as a Horatian Epistle in English:

> Illyrian woodlands, echoing falls
> Of water, sheets of summer glass,
> The long divine Peneian pass,
> The vast Akrokeraunian walls,
>
> Tomohrit, Athens, all things fair,
> With such a pencil, such a pen,
> You shadow forth to distant men,
> I read, and felt that I was there.

It covers a great deal of the country through which Horace himself was passing: but for all the exquisite art with which

Tennyson summons up the vision of that old poetic ground, the glistening torrents, the "broad-limbed gods at random thrown by fountain-urns," and all that pencil and brush could bring before us, we could not be sure whether Tennyson had been there himself or not. In another poem, however, which is also one of the most Horatian epistles in English, we can be quite sure—at least in the second stanza quoted below—that Tennyson is describing a personal experience:

> What Roman strength Turbía showed
> In ruin, by the mountain-road;
>   How like a gem, beneath, the city
> Of little Monaco, basking, glowed . . .
>
> But, when we crossed the Lombard plain,
> Remember what a plague of rain;
>   Of rain at Reggio, rain at Parma,
> At Lodi, rain, Piacenza, rain.

We may hope that the weather at Mitylene was as exceptional an experience as that at Parma, and that Alcaeus and Sappho were more fortunate; but we can hardly doubt that it was an experience. It is not necessary to suppose that Horace visited Mitylene in winter as well as summer, in order to discover that it was guilty of the extremes which—in all things—he detested. He would only have to remark upon the one to be informed of the other. But it seems quite likely that he gave it a second trial in the cooler weather if he was in the neighborhood, and that he met with a second disappointment. He was enthusiastic enough to be drawn to the haunts of his favorite poets; but, all through his life, his frail physique made him sensitive to climate. Looking back on his travels from the pleasant haven of the Sabine farm, he came in later years to the conclusion of Emerson that the best journeys are those that are made at home by the mind, not those that are made in distant lands by the body. But he had tried both methods.

One of the place-names, however, he mentions with a peculiar feeling which occurs more often in Horace than would be allowed by the cheerful commentator who described him as a "typical club-man." There will be more to say about this when we come to his life on the Sabine farm. But we are concerned here with his vivid reminiscence of the little lonely town on the coast of Ionia named Lebedus. It had been destroyed in war three hundred years earlier, and had never recovered. Its population had been deported almost as ruthlessly as if they had been living in the twentieth century; and it was now hardly more than a fishing village haunted by a memory of

> Old, unhappy, far-off things,
> And battles long ago.

Its loneliness, its outlook on a wild sea, and—perhaps—its speechless commentary on those far-off things made an impression on Horace which brings him, for a moment, into touch with the romantic spirit of the early nineteenth-century poets in France and England. It even seems to share, though again only for a breath, the Byronic disillusionment which found a melancholy pleasure in the beauty of desolation. In effect, this is what he says:

Heartsick of all your wanderings over the seas and the long roads of the world, perhaps you will find, as I did, something to praise in Lebedus. You know what Lebedus is, more deserted than Fidenae, which also was destroyed four hundred years ago, and never rose again. Lebedus is even more lonely, and yet I could wish to live there, forgetting my own folk and utterly forgotten by them; there, safe on shore for a little while to watch far off the raging of that untameable sea.

Most of this he actually says; but he suggests the rest and more, in the music of his verse. Some extremely prosaic interpretations have been placed on this passage by one or two editors who suggest that Horace is merely writing to a friend who is afraid of being seasick, and warning him that while he may prefer to remain safely on the shore at Lebedus, he will one day desire to come home. They also suggest that the beautiful lines about Lebedus are really a quotation from the friend to whom he is writing and that Horace is criticizing his sentiments. This interpretation can only be maintained by calling in the aid of the printer and quotation marks. For those who have ears to hear the music of poetry, it is hardly worth discussing. Horace is writing some years after he had passed that way, and he is telling his friend how he once felt, not quoting somebody else. Poetry glances with many colors; but there is a world of profound sadness in the music of a line like:

oblitusque meorum, obliviscendus et illis.

This is perhaps the most memorable line in the passage about Lebedus. It was borrowed by Pope, who translated it into an English pentameter, not in his more flippant imitations of Horace, but in the most romantic of his poems—the Epistle of Eloisa to Abelard—a strang sublimation, indeed, if the line had been originally addressed to a gentleman who had exiled himself for fear of seasickness. The line has become almost proverbial in its application to the disillusioned who turn to the healing solitudes of Nature, or the cloister, in which the inhumanities and falsities of the world are renounced or left out of sight and sound:

The world forgetting, by the world forgot.

But there is far more than this in the deep emotional throb of that Latin phrase, *oblitusque meorum*—forgetful, even of my own. It is the remembered cry of a wounded spirit. There is far deeper feeling in it, for instance, than in the opening lines of the second satire of Juvenal, in which he would like to fly from a hypocritical world to some region beyond Sarmatia and the Arctic Sea. It is not so very far from the mood of a nineteenth-century wanderer who, in his own disillusionment, cried,

O that the desert were my dwelling-place.

Curiously enough, that line in *Childe Harold* occurs just two stanzas after his reference to the Sabine farm and the retreat at Tusculum where "Tully reposed from Rome."

In Horace, the mood was brief; and he never would have been carried into extremes by it; but, for this very reason, it was more sincere than that of Byron. He is able to smile at it now, for he has found a more pleasant haven. It is this self-criticism which has misled some of his commentators. He is writing to a friend, of course, to warn him that he had better not sell his ship on the other side of the sea, for one day he will want to come home. But he is warning that friend, quite definitely, out of his own experience. That is why he tells him, with a certain sympathy, that there was a time when he himself could have wished to live at Lebedus; but the wider bearings of the passage are indicated by the obvious reference to the famous passage in Lucretius:

Suave, mari magno turbantibus aequora ventis,
e terra magnum alterius spectare laborem.

It was not merely physical hardships that caused the disillusionment of Horace with the stormy seas of political conflict and civil war.

In addition to all this, he had certainly discovered what soldier-poets, no matter how loyal and patriotic, have discovered in almost every age—the tragic and soul-shattering ironies whereby in war the innocent suffer for the guilty. In our own day, almost every man will have discovered some of these ironies for himself, and there is no need to dwell upon them. It was too early, perhaps, for him to discover what the world has just begun to realize; and his disillusionment did not extend to every kind of war. He served with honor in the campaign, and won the praise of the best of his fellow-officers. But it was a fratricidal conflict, and he began to look with horror upon the civil wars of Italy. Perhaps one day it would be recognized that all wars are fratricidal.

There is a question which might be recommended to the attention of those critics who are unable to believe that Horace actually visited the places which he mentions. It is quite certain that he passed through a great many places during the campaign with Brutus, and that he passed through the neighborhood of the places with which we are concerned. Are we to suppose that he carefully abstained from mentioning all the places he had visited, and mentioned only the places he had not visited? That is what some of the critics imply. It does not seem very sensible. It is merely an example of that conventional caution which makes a certain type of sceptic shudder at the bare suggestion that Seneca had ever heard of St. Paul, although one of the most famous incidents in the life of St. Paul was his trial before Gallio, the brother of Seneca.

We may well believe that Horace not only went to Lebedus, but went there in the disillusioned mood that he describes in his epistle. This epistle was written from the safe haven of the Sabine farm, where he had long outlived the mood which he described. But the very fact that in his happier surroundings he no longer wants to live forgotten by his friends, emphasizes this other fact—that he is remembering an earlier disillusionment.

Horace was a sensitive young man, setting out on what he

believed to be a high adventure in the glorious name of Freedom, and in a cause so clear that all the wrong was on the enemies' side, and all the right on the side of his friends. He discovers, first of all, that there may be injustice on both sides. He discovers that men may serve the right cause for bad motives; and perhaps he finds the idealized commander making use of those bad motives, and appealing to covetousness, a vice which Horace abhorred. At the next stage he is confronted by an even more ironical event. To a man like Horace, the idea of killing an enemy is tolerable only if you have a bad opinion of him. It is so with all decent men. But at a critical moment in this campaign, when Brutus fell seriously ill, the inhabitants of the city which he was besieging behaved with a generosity which illustrates the precepts of the New Testament. This is how Plutarch describes it:

Brutus growing very faint, and there being none in the whole army that had anything for him to eat, his servants were forced to have recourse to the enemy, and, going as far as the gates of the city, begged bread of the sentinels that were upon duty. As soon as they heard of the condition of Brutus, they came themselves, and brought both meat and drink along with them; in return for which, Brutus, when he took the city, showed the greatest kindness, not to them only, but to all the inhabitants, for their sakes.

Most of the really great poets have had a golden logic of their own, moving with the precision of music to its inevitable conclusions. Horace would be forced by events of that kind to think that the Civil War had been imposed on people who really did not want it at all. These people would have been able to live in peace and happiness with their neighbors but for the madness artificially aroused in their minds by little groups of men who were bent on their own political ends. Those ends, in their real significance, were entirely hidden from most of those who suffered and died for them. It may be that, after seeing a few men killed, he began to dislike the idea of assassination, even when it was called tyrannicide.

At present Horace was engaged in war as a soldier. By nature he was imbued with the truest kind of patriotism. In one of his later poems he gives the final and perfect expression to the noblest spirit of the soldier-patriot—*"Dulce et decorum est pro patria mori."* It is the perfect tribute to the *sacramentum supremum* of the dying soldier; and no one but Horace could have used those words for a death on the battle-field, words so full of a tender grace, so instinct with the Roman sense of order, and the beauty of what is right and fitting; so exquisitely temperate and restrained, and yet as moving as the smile on a young face, content, with all its earthly duties done. *"Dulce at decorum est . . ."* Who could suppose that words so gentle and restrained were destined to have such a long history. For twenty centuries they have been the epitaph of the young in every country of Europe. In recent years they have been printed thousands of times in the memorial columns of English newspapers as a last farewell to some boy who died in a foreign land "With the last darkness in his eyes, and *domum* in his heart."

Our brave new world, it is sometimes said, has little use for the enduring words of the classics. But if those words have sunk deep into the English mind, and helped it to endure both in victory and in defeat, we may as well remember that it was neither the schoolmasters nor the playing fields of Eton that originated them. The son of a poor farmer in Italy had something to do with it.

Proud, high-spirited, and on fire with his first enthusiasm for the cause of Freedom, this young poet, who was not only capable of giving to Europe what Mackail calls "the very type of the gentleman," but also of giving it the very pattern of the ideal soldier, suddenly makes an ironic discovery. A cold and mean, but quite implacable, cause of disillusionment struck him unexpectedly, like the unclean missile flung over the hedge into the face of Jude the Obscure.

In the youthful society and university life of Athens he had perhaps been tempted to forget his "unprivileged" status in the Roman world. He had been accepted as a friend on equal terms by those young men of good breeding. He belonged to their set: Brutus had accepted him on the same footing; and thus unconsciously violated the traditions of the military caste. But it would hardly have occurred to Horace to raise any such objection to himself, on the eve of a war against tyranny. The best of his young friends would have thought it ridiculous if he had done so; and some of them might have thought it cowardly. But the objection did occur to a brass-hat on the staff of Brutus, and he proceeded to make himself offensive about the parentage of the young tribune. The scholiasts say that it was Rupilius Rex, the bull-headed officer of the lawsuit, who began the attack; and they say that this was the real explanation of the fierce satire in which Horace asked why Brutus—the killer of kings—did not cut the throat of this Rex also. This gives us a clue, perhaps, to what has been called the "flippant" treatment of Brutus himself. "Flippant" is hardly the word for that question: *"Cur non hunc Regem jugulas?"* It sounds more like the harsh laugh with which the bitterly hurt spirit of the young man disguised his real feelings. It is possible that Brutus may have received the complaints of Rupilius Rex with more complaisance than Horace liked. Brutus may even have been annoyed at his own mistake, and as he would not be anxious to alienate the brass-hats, his manner in public may have altered a little toward the young commander of a legion. The man who had killed Caesar in the name of freedom may not have been too pleased to find that he had been treating the son of a freedman as if he were actually free. This would be quite enough to account for the disillusionment so clearly indicated in the satire on the lawsuit. Between a free man and a freedman there was a vast difference in those days. A freedman was by no means a free man; and the son of a freedman would not only be debarred from military promotion. The best of the careers which opened so delightfully before his companions at the university would all be closed to him. It is easy to pass these things over as insignificant, but even in democratic America the young student who is debarred merely from some of the college clubs has been known to suffer keenly. And this was something that could not be remedied. From the cradle to the grave, and all through time it would be there.

The young soldier of freedom must have realized with some bitterness that—no matter who won the war—the legend: "Son of a manumitted slave" must be branded upon him as remorselessly as if he had been a thief. It would be recommended to the derision of his associates. The statement of the scholiasts that Rupilius Rex made a particular point of doing this is confirmed by the statement of Horace himself in another poem, though he mentions no name.

The essential facts are known with certainty; but it is the habit of modern commentators to pass them over too lightly. If we are to obtain a true portrait of Horace, we must try to imagine what he undoubtedly felt. This feeling would not be limited to the rare moments when he expressed it. His critics may be grandly indifferent to it, but that is not the point. As Mr. Kipling once told us:

> The toad beneath the harrow knows
> Exactly where each toothpoint goes.
> The butterfly upon the road
> Preaches contentment to that toad.

The derogatory brand that was set upon his mind and heart

affected him not only during his life. It has affected, sometimes quite unconsciously, the critics of our own day. One distinguished editor of Persius, for instance, quite unaware of the absurd snobbery of his words, actually remarks that the exquisite style of Horace was probably due to the fact that, being of low origin, he was afraid to write with the careless ease of a man of quality.

V

HORACE AND THE FORTUNATE ISLES

THE AMNESTY PROCLAIMED AFTER PHILIPPI ENABLED HORACE to return to Rome; but his position was precarious. Amnesties after a conflict of this kind are always probationary. His freedom, his life even, might depend on what he said and did. The hopeless Republican struggle was still going on in some regions. If it became too troublesome, it might lead to another proscription. A word, or a malicious twisting of a word, would be enough to implicate him; and, when the blood-soaked sacks of severed heads were next carted up to the Forum, the head of the young writer who had commanded a legion under Brutus, and now commanded a witty and satirical pen, might very well be among them.

The wise old father was no longer there to advise. He must have been carrying a heavy burden of anxiety during the last years of his life, and he had probably succumbed under it. Among the familiar sights and sounds of Rome where they had done so much together, the boy—for he was little more—must often have missed that wrinkled old sunburnt face with the kind eyes.

The farm at Venusia had been confiscated; and the son whose welfare had been the object of so much toil and thrift was flung upon Rome to fend for himself as best he might. "With my wings clipped," he wrote, "humiliated, deprived of my father's estate, and the Lar that watched over his hearth":

> *decisis humilem pennis inopemque paterni*
> *et laris et fundi.*

This last phrase (*et laris et fundi*) in the Italian countryside really did mean something more than the mere property into which the modern world would sink its richer significance. It may sometimes have been used conventionally, but Horace was a supreme artist in words; and when in another poem he said that the sin of stealing a man's cabbages was not so heinous as carrying off his household gods (*Lares*), he meant exactly what he said. Possibly it was this very confiscation of the farm at Venusia that revived the comparison. Something had been taken from him which was precious in its associations.

Hungry as the lad from Venusia may have been for his *arva beata*, he was not to find them yet. He obtained a clerkship in the quaestor's office, which gave him enough to live on, and for nearly ten years after his return from the campaign with Brutus, his lot was cast in Rome. Probably it was the best thing that could have happened to him at the time and in the circumstances. Rome was the recognized center for the free-lance in literature; and Horace was very much of a free-lance when he began to write. Our knowledge of the life of ancient Rome would be immeasurably less vivid if it had not been depicted in that wonderful little series of satires which have justly been compared with the pictures of eighteenth-century characters in Addison, though they might find a closer resemblance in the seventeenth-century characters of La Bruyère, who has more of the Horatian humor and lightness of touch. Something they owe in outward form to the earlier satires of Lucilius; but the proof of their real originality is their immense autobiographical value. They allow us actually to see and hear Horace himself as clearly as if we were engaged in conversation with him. He tells us about all the details of his life in the capital, not out of egoism, but to illustrate his constant theme—the nature of the happy life, the follies and vices that interfere with it, and the value of individual freedom. Not political freedom only, but freedom from vanity, freedom from avarice, and freedom from worldly cares. He finds his own lot happier than that of the seekers after place and power, and he is able to tell us this without appearing to be self-satisfied, for he is always ready to reveal and to laugh at his own frailties:

If I were in the place of so-and-so, I should have to keep more servants and horses and have a huge train of baggage-wagons following me whenever I went to the country. As it is, I can jog along on my bob-tailed mule, all the way to Tarentum if I like, with my saddle-bags galling his sides and the rider bruising his withers. Nobody will talk of my meanness, as they do of yours, my dear praetor, when you take the Tibur road with only five slaves following you to carry your cooking-pot and your wine-basket. In thousands of ways I can live a great deal more comfortably than you, my noble friend.

Whenever I please I can wander about alone in the city. I ask the price of vegetables and wheat-flour; or if it is in the evening, I wander round the Circus Maximus, where there are so many interesting swindlers. I stroll past the Forum and sometimes stand in the crowd to watch the fortune-tellers. Then I go home to my supper of leeks and peas and fritters. I have three slaves to wait on me. I have two drinking-cups with a ladle, a cheap salt-cellar, an oil-jug, and a saucer of Campanian earthen ware laid out on my white stone table. After supper I go to bed, not worrying about what is to come on the morrow. . . . Sometimes I lie in bed till ten. Then I go for a stroll, or read or write something from which I get a great deal of quiet pleasure. After this, I anoint myself with real olive oil, not the stuff that vile Natta steals from the lamps. When the sun grows hotter and tells me it is time to go to the baths, I prefer to do that rather than go to the Campus Martius. After a light lunch, I take a siesta; and I comfort myself by thinking that in all these ways I live far more pleasantly than if my grandfather had been a questor and my father and uncles questors into the bargain.

It required considerable courage, however, for Horace to go straight back to Rome, as he did, making no attempt to court the victorious government of Octavian; and indeed beginning almost at once to write with the utmost independence. So much is generally agreed. There was no capitulation of any kind in those days, when he was stripped of everything and comparatively friendless. The ill-natured charges of inconsistency brought against him by a few critics will be examined in a later chapter. It is enough here to emphasize a point already mentioned—that Octavian himself, as time went on, did appear to change his policy in many ways. The patron of letters who, to cement a temporary alliance with an enemy, consented to the murder of his friend Cicero, developed into a strange, inscrutable being whose complex character only Gibbon, perhaps, has fathomed. Gibbon had no compunction in describing him as an "artful tyrant." A famous incident recorded by Plutarch vividly illustrates the change in Octavian. Many years after the murder of Cicero, the emperor found one of his grandsons with a book of that author in his hand. The boy was afraid, and tried to hide it under his gown. The emperor noticed it, however, and taking the book from him, stood there lost in thought and turning over many of its pages. Finally, giving it back to the boy, he said, "My child, this was a learned man, and a lover of his country."

Was the true Octavian revealed when the head and right hand of the man who loved his country were nailed up over the rostrum? Or was he revealed in this later scene? And are we to accept his words in the later scene naively, as a sincere expression of sorrow for what he had inflicted upon one of the chief glories of European culture; or, with Gibbon, are we to regard him as a "crafty hypocrite" who with immense political adaptability had drawn his opponents into alliance with him, and now was satisfied because, having irreparably destroyed the liberty of the people, he had concentrated all power in his own hands under forms that merely disguised it? If he was sincere in his change, was there any reason why Horace should not have accepted it? On the other hand, if we think that Gibbon is the only historian who has really analyzed the mind of Augustus, it must still be remarked that it was the emperor, and not the poet, who wore the mask.

One thing is quite certain: Horace from the beginning of his writings to the end never changed the principles for which he contended. He never disguised his views and, when he came back to Rome, he displayed considerable courage in expressing them. He was disillusioned about the political conflict. The leader of the Republican cause had committed suicide; and for a time Horace despaired of his native land. But it was not the defeat at Philippi that made him despair. The campaign, as we have seen, had taught him a great deal about the ironies of war, and especially of civil war. He had seen how bad men may fight, with the wrong motive, in a cause far too good for them. Perhaps he had learned that the best of leaders was not good enough to be entrusted with powers of life and death over so many innocent people whose only desire was for a peaceful life in their native fields; and when the threat of a new outbreak of fratricidal bloodshed darkened the horizon, he uttered a cry that might well have found an echo in millions of minds throughout Europe in our own day:

Another generation is now being ground to dust by civil war. That great city which neither the Marsians . . . nor brutal Germany with its blue-eyed youth had the strength to destroy, will be brought down in utter ruin by ourselves and our own wrong-doing.

Like all young idealists, he had dreamed of a better world. The hope of it in Italy was apparently beyond realization. But he could not abandon that vision. He tried to transfer it to a world elsewhere.

In one of the finest of his early poems (the sixteenth epode) he looked westward. Thousands before him, millions after him, have heard that sea-wind whispering, "All good things are in the west." Plutarch tells us how Sertorius, after his defeats in Spain, met certain seamen recently arrived from those Atlantic Isles which are called the Islands of the Blest, and were celebrated by Homer. Sertorius, he says, was seized with a wonderful passion for those Islands, and had an extreme desire to go and live there in peace and quietness, free from oppression and unending wars. It was not a mere poetic dream. It has launched many a ship since then, and taken many a pilgrim beyond the sunset.

Just as the fourth eclogue of Virgil was touched with a certain mystical light from a spiritual world beyond his horizon, so this poem of Horace was an instinctive anticipation of things yet to be discovered on earth and beyond the seas. It is an expression of the same instinct, the same longing, as that which led the early voyagers across the Atlantic. That strange westering movement was summed up for the eighteenth century in Bishop Berkeley's line, so familiar to the beautiful university campus on which he lived, and which now bears his name in California:

Westward the course of empire takes its way.

More prosaically, but more laconically, it was summed up in the advice of a famous American: "Go west, young man, go west." Instincts and impulses prompted that movement, perhaps as far back as the *Odyssey*, long before its real significance disclosed itself. But only a generation later than Horace, the idea took a remarkably definite form in the prophetic and strangely beautiful lines of Seneca:

> *Venient annis saecula seris*
> *Quibus Oceanus vincula rerum*
> *Laxet, et ingens pateat tellus*

Horace and the Fortunate Isles

Tethysque novos detegat orbes
Nec sit terris ultima Thule.[1]

The impulse behind the poem of Horace was even more like
that of later centuries. The old world was soaked in blood. Age
after age, generation after generation, it would continue to be
soaked in blood. He turns then to a new world beyond the horizon. He pictures a migration, not of great numbers, but of the
few who really desire to build a better world. There was no
better plan than this. They would have to be pilgrims. "They
must go wherever their feet might take them, or wherever the
winds might carry them over the seas. *Quid moramur?* Why
linger? It was the old cry, so ancient and so new, for something
more than the eyes could yet see. It pulsed through many a
passage in Shelley:

> Why linger? Why turn back? Why shrink, my heart?
> Thy hopes have gone before; from all things here
> They have departed; thou should'st now depart.

Byron had known it, as our own day knows it, and he looked in
the same direction:

> Can tyrants but by tyrants conquered be
> And freedom find no champion and no child?

There was bitterness in it, for Horace as for Byron. His voyagers into that sunset would not return. *"Redire sit nefas"*—it
would be a sin to return. Stones would sooner rise from the
depth of the sea and swim upon the surface. *"Sed juremus in
haec"*—let us swear an oath. It reminds us in some ways of the
cry of Tennyson's voyagers, in which the "equal mind" is also
Horatian:

[1] "An age will come, in the fullness of time, when Ocean shall unloose the
bonds of things, and the whole huge earth shall be discovered, and Tethys shall
unveil new worlds, and Thule shall no longer be the remotest of lands."

67

Let us swear an oath and keep it with an equal mind.

Never should their sails be set for home till the dove should mate with the hawk, and the lowing herd lie down with the lion.

Strange hints of things to come, strange echoes of old prophecies, haunted the Roman world in that age. Virgil and Horace, each after his own fashion, caught them in the subconscious network of their sensitive minds, and translated them into music:

Us the immense and wild world-wandering ocean awaiteth.

And beyond it, there were the Islands of the Blest. There the unlaborious earth yielded its corn, the unpruned vine was loaded with grapes, and the olives never failed. There the dark figs ripened on the bough in peace, and honey flowed from the hollow oak, and the herd found its own way home to the milking shed.

It was a vision that has haunted many generations of poets. To the nineteenth-century disciple of Mazzini the sea-wind brought a beautiful rumor of it:

From the bountiful infinite west, from the happy memorial places,
   Full of the stately repose, and the lordly delight of the dead,
Where the Fortunate Islands are lit with the light of ineffable faces,
   And the sound of a sea without wind is about them and sunset is red.

But this was the dream of a world beyond death, in which the neo-pagan Swinburne was really borrowing something from the Christian heaven of the Italian painters. The "ineffable faces" belonged to the realm of Christian art, though Swinburne was apparently quite unconscious of what he borrowed from Christendom to bestow upon the ancient world.

Both Horace and Virgil were thinking primarily of this earth, though Virgil constantly idealized his subject. In the fourth eclogue, for instance, he appeared to be prophesying a millennium, the return of a Golden Age to a glorified Italy; while Horace was thinking of an actual and immediate migration to isles across the sea, where it would be possible to live a happier and more peaceful life. Virgil, in some of his poems, appears to be conducting a debate between the two points of view. Tityrus remains happily piping under his beech-tree, and declares that a god has given him this blissful existence, while Meliboeus cries: "We must fly from our fatherland and these beloved fields"—"*et dulcia linquimus arva.*"

In the same way Horace often passes from his own realm into that of Virgil, and touches his subject with a gleam of the ideal. But speaking broadly, Virgil was the idealist, and Horace the realist. That is also true of their pictures of the country life. Virgil idealizes it, and Horace looks at it more directly, as he looked at it in the days of his boyhood. But they are both far nearer to the mood of Tennyson in his *Ulysses* than to that of Swinburne. Tennyson used the fable of the Happy Islands to shadow forth the hope of a better world actually attainable, although it was beyond the sight of the eyes and the grasp of the mind:

> Come, my friends,
> 'Tis not too late to seek a newer world.
> Push out, and sitting well in order, smite
> The sounding furrows, for my purpose holds
> To sail beyond the sunset and the baths
> Of all the western stars, until I die.
> It may be that the gulfs will wash us down;
> It may be we shall touch the Happy Isles,
> And see the great Achilles, whom we knew.

Tennyson wrote his poem with direct reference to the new conditions which the science and philosophy of the nineteenth century appeared to be bringing about. There is precisely the same merging of this world into the next which we find in varying degrees both in Horace and Virgil. But Tennyson was thinking of the intellectual voyage through strange seas in the age of modern agnosticism, while Horace was thinking of a real voyage to a better country. At the same time the imagination of the Roman poet, who was able to believe in the reality of the Fortunate Islands, is touched with religion in his picture of their perfection. "In that happy place," he says, "there is still more to engage our wonder"—*"pluraque felices mirabimur."* All the operations of Nature are in harmony there. The rain does not spoil the harvest, nor does the sun burn up the seeds before they come to fruition This, like the fourth eclogue of Virgil, is really a symbolic picture of the kingdom where God's will is done on earth as it is in heaven. Horace actually comes nearer to saying it than Virgil does; for when he tells us, in the sixteenth epode, that these harmonious conditions are brought about by the King of heaven (*rege temperante caelitum*), the most exacting literalist can hardly pretend that he means Augustus.

There is another and an extremely important element in what he says of that happy and harmonious country, and that is its dependence for those happy conditions upon a right relation, an ethical relation, with the supreme power manifesting itself in the universe. It is often forgotten by those who think of Horace merely as an apostle of pleasant living that he is profoundly interested in the right conduct of life. In the sixteenth epode, it was the King of the heavenly powers who had set these Happy Isles apart, "midmost the beating of the steely sea." The poet tells us that only one kind of voyager will be enabled to find them. They were not to be found, unless the right conditions were fulfilled, by any winged pines, in fable or history.

Non huc Argoo contendit remige pinus.

Not Jason's *Argo* with all those urgent oars; nor the seamen of Sidonia; nor Ulysses himself (*nec cohors Ulixei*) could ever make that haven. But it might be found by the upright of heart and the innocent, and those who love justice. For the King of heaven, he says, had hidden those happy shores away as a refuge for those who truly serve him—*illa piae secrevit litora genti*. He had set it apart for a righteous people (*piis fuga datur*) from that far-off time when the Golden Age of peace and innocence broke down first into the Age of Bronze, and then into the Age of Iron. This, after all, in its own pagan terms, is not far from the doctrine of Christendom.

Sellar suggests that the sixteenth epode expresses the feelings of the losing side before the peace of Brundisium; while Virgil, in the fourth eclogue, expresses those of the winning side after its conclusion. Two important inferences, in that case, would certainly follow. The first is as obvious as it is important— that Horace anticipated Virgil in the subject of a very famous poem. The treatment of the subject is different; but in varying degrees both combine the real and the ideal. A second inference is perhaps only a probability, but it seems to me almost certain that the later poem was written in answer to the earlier. Horace had said, in effect, "Our only hope is to seek elsewhere for that better country of the poets and prophets"; and Virgil had replied that "The Golden Age, so beautifully described by Horace, was now dawning in Italy itself." It will be noted that Horace was actually expressing a feeling of hopelessness about the régime of Octavian, while Virgil was just as definitely defending that régime. I cannot help thinking that it was this interchange of ideas that brought the two poets together. Perhaps in conversation, and certainly in his own mind, Horace must have discovered that Virgil, without knowing it, was really writing of that ideal country which is the common ground of all the great poets, though it may have little relation to the

temporal politics of the world in which they live. It was the
world envisaged by Shelley when he wrote:

> The world's great age begins anew.
> The Golden Years return.
> The earth doth, like a snake, renew
> Her winter weeds outworn.
> Heaven smiles and faiths and empires gleam
> Like wrecks of a dissolving dream.

Horace knew that country of the heart very well. He knew
also that it had very little to do with Octavian, and he had the
courage to say so. At the same time, he could not fail to recognize in Virgil one of the great prophets of that transcendent
and ideal kingdom; and it was surely this recognition that made
him describe Virgil as the other half of his own soul. For his
own part he was concerned with more immediate things. It is
curious to reflect that Virgil, setting out to glorify the possibilities of the new imperial order, was carried far beyond it, on the
wings of his own music, into something like an apocalyptic
vision; while Horace, proposing to abandon his native land
altogether, becomes the poet of the real Italian countryside,
and "the very Rome." It is a beautiful picture that he paints of
those Happy Islands; but when we consider it in detail, we discover that, like many other voyagers, he has rounded the world
in order to return home. For it is Italy, after all, that he is
painting. Grapevine, and grey-green olive, and dark fig—far
away as he pretends to find them, Italy still enfolds him:

> Free in her heart, ere yet her soul be free,
> And lovelier than her loveliest robe of air.

In that happy place there was no arena for the entertainment
of the brute in man. It was Italy as she might have been, and
yet might be, if man could be more merciful to his own kind;

Italy of the quiet country places, the little patches of corn, and the hill-tops crowned with temples. There, in that Italy, were his happy fields, his *arva beata*, on the little farm at Venusia, where earth was not unlaborious, but where the sunburnt peasants went to their work with a song, and the little household gods had been so good to him in his childhood. They had taken care of him when he had wandered away and was lost on the hills. Perhaps, not for his own merits, but through the prayers of an old manumitted slave somewhere on the other side of Lethe, they would take care of him, even now, in Rome.

VI

THE SHIP OF STATE

IT SEEMED ALMOST TOO GOOD TO BE TRUE THAT POETS LIKE Horace and Virgil, each the complement of the other, should have been brought together in Rome at this time. It was like something planned by a supreme artist that the two halves of so great a whole should thus be made fast in friendship. Virgil was five years older than Horace, and was already a friend of Maecenas, with whom he must have discussed the literature of the day. It may have been on the ground of the two poems which we have been discussing that Virgil first talked to Maecenas about the young Republican poet. The plan—an "appeasement plan," as it is called today—of drawing the Republican partizans into accord with the new régime was already being developed. Neither Horace nor Virgil, perhaps, would have realized this. But Maecenas was not merely an advocate of that political plan. He was also a true lover of art and letters. He expressed a wish to meet the young firebrand, and Virgil arranged it.

The first interview between Horace and Maecenas, as we were told in the sixth satire, quoted above, was brief. Apparently, no further overtures were made on either side at the time; Maecenas liked him, and nine months later he drew Horace into the circle of his intimate friends. This meant that the ball was at the poet's feet, if he wished to play it, for Maecenas was the most trusted councillor of the man who then ruled the world, and that man now desired to have the literature of the world on his side. As we have seen, however, the poet maintained his independence. It was literature only that bound him to Maecenas, and on all political matters he was still in opposition to the new régime. Again and again he ranges himself with the followers of Brutus. He calls the attention of Maecenas to the fact, and he writes in praise of friend after friend who shared his opinions at Athens. It should be emphasized that his disillusionment during the campaign with Brutus does not mean in the least that he had better hopes of the new régime. He paid no tribute of any kind to it at this time. His only political concern was to oppose with everything that was in him any new outbreak of civil war. He undoubtedly irritated Octavian by his deliberate abstention from mentioning him at a time when it was almost customary for writers to pay a formal literary tribute to Caesar. The fierce pessimism of the sixteenth epode could hardly be regarded as flattering the prospects of the new régime. It has been suggested that great credit is due to Octavian himself for the magnanimity with which he overlooked such things; but it must again be remembered that his policy—so largely influenced by the advice of Maecenas, with his enthusiasm for literature—was to draw the opposite faction into his own administrative system. He was a very skillful exponent of that art of political compromise which has played so immense a part in modern times—the art which in contemporary politics has so often silenced an enemy by making him a minister of the government.

The new war of which Horace speaks in his epode on the Fortunate Islands makes it possible to date that poem. It was probably written in 41 B.C., when the Perusian War began. Horace was then twenty-four years old. The epodes were not published as a volume until nine years later; but it is generally agreed that some of the poems, including the sixteenth, were the work of those earlier days. The poem on the Fortunate Islands was certainly the work of a young man; and, as we have seen, there is good reason to suppose that it was the first

point at which the work of Horace and Virgil came into con-
tact. Virgil was precisely what Horace called him, the complement of his own soul. Horace is often thought to be lacking in
certain qualities which Virgil possessed. Perhaps he did not have
that depth of tenderness, that deep sense of tears in mortal
things, that intuitive perception of a mysterious meaning in the
tragedy and pathos of human life; or, if he possessed them, he
did not express them in his verse. Newman, however, coupled
him with Homer, for the "sad earnestness" of some of his
phrases, and their power of piercing the heart in the later life
of his readers. It may be said moreover that possession and expression are two very different things, a fact often forgotten by
the literary critic. The poet who prefers to pass over certain
depths on the wings of a jest may be a better and clearer thinker
than many a solemn writer without a smile. The apparently
lighter poet may be, in his own character, a far deeper man. He
may prefer to keep certain matters locked up in that "sacred
silence" of which Horace speaks in one of his most familiar
phrases. It is significant, perhaps, that Horace recognized this,
but it is more important for us to note his awareness of the fact
that, at the point where he ended, Virgil began to fill up what
was lacking. It shows a very remarkable power of self-criticism,
and what is perhaps the rarest of all critical gifts—the power to
appreciate a point of view that was different from and transcended his own. It must be remembered, on the other hand, that
there are qualities in the work of Horace which are lacking in
that of Virgil—the lightness of touch, the irony, a certain close-
ness to immediate realities, a metrical variety, and that lyrical
gift in which Quintilian placed him first among the poets of
Rome. Perhaps Horace was aware of this, too, when he spoke of
Virgil as "the other half of his soul." There was one half which
was entirely his own.

Virgil, announcing a Golden Age in Italy, was saved from

being a "court-poet" because his music unconsciously carried him far beyond his chosen subject into the depths of the spiritual world. His idealization of the past and future of Rome lifted him into the *Civitas Dei*. There and there alone, in the light of that spiritual city, his noblest lines revealed their full significance. Horace, on the other hand, discovers that what he had really prayed for was a small piece of land in Italy with a garden and a water-spring near the house, and a patch of woodland behind it. But he wanted these things because they would enable him to lead the life he loved, devoting himself first to poetry, and then to philosophy. He actually experienced the feelings of both the characters in Virgil's first eclogue, the Meliboeus who lamented that he must leave the fatherland and the pleasant fields of home, and the Tityrus who lay piping under his beech tree. The sixteenth epode, in fact, anticipated the lament of Meliboeus,

> *Nos patriae fines et dulcia linquimus arva.*
> *Nos patriam fugimus . . .*

And in later poems at the Sabine farm, he really deepened the reply of Tityrus:

> *O Meliboee, deus nobis haec otia fecit.*

In the clear cool mind of Horace there was no confusion possible between *deus* and Augustus, or between earth and heaven, nor, it may be added, is there any of that literary confusion of the sexes which we seem to get in the eclogues—the girl masquerading as a Theocritean shepherd, or the Theocritean shepherd as a girl. The songs of Horace, *virginibus puerisque*, are as clear-cut in their tones as the two choirs that sang the *Carmen Saeculare*.

We have no details of the first meeting between the poet of the defeated Republic and the poet whose "ocean roll of rhythm sounds forever of imperial Rome." We know only that it took place, and that Virgil, wishing to help his fellow-poet, arranged for him to meet Maecenas. In some ways it must have been embarrassing for the young wing-clipped Republican poet to meet the confidential friend of Octavian. Horace tells us, as we noted earlier, that he was almost tongue-tied. It is said that in one of his satires he had actually ridiculed Maecenas. The passage in question is quite inoffensive. It is concerned merely with the different ways in which two characters wear the toga. One of them, walking in the street, held it too high, and the other allowed it to trail. The second was supposed to represent Maecenas. The memory of this, quite apart from the adventures with Brutus, would be enough to embarrass the young man. It can only have been through Virgil's insistence that Horace accepted the first invitation to the house of Maecenas, and Virgil must have emphasized the real enthusiasm of Maecenas for literature.

Politically, Horace was in the opposite camp to Virgil; but Virgil, nevertheless, offered him a perfect meeting ground. Horace admired him as a poet, and he must have recognized that his poetry completely transcended his politics. They had both suffered the confiscation of their estates after Philippi; for whole districts had been subjected to seizure without the slightest consideration for individual differences. In fact, Virgil had suffered two confiscations, and in one of them his life had been threatened. Whether he felt it or not, he showed no animosity against the central government on this account, but came to Rome, where, through the influence of his friends, Pollio and Varius, he had recovered his estate. The shepherd, in the first eclogue, when asked what had taken him to Rome, replied, *Libertas;* and he meant just that freedom of the individual to live his own life, for which Horace was hungering and thirsting. Liberty in this sense was equally dear to Virgil; and, to all outward appearance, Virgil had succeeded in obtaining it. His friend Varius was in high favor with the ruling party for his epic on Julius Caesar. It is said that Octavian gave him a million sesterces for his drama *Thyestes*, but we may suppose that it was really for his Caesarean sympathies. In any case nobody could have made a better liaison officer in bringing Maecenas and Virgil together. Horace tells us that Varius also helped Virgil to arrange his own meeting with Maecenas. The works of Varius have been lost; but he seems to have been a good poet, and both Virgil and Horace praised his work, which had a reputation based, not on politics, but on its poetic value. The importance of this is obvious. It was not politics but poetry that brought Horace into touch with Maecenas. And there was not the slightest sign of any change in the political principles of anyone concerned. In fact Horace continually, and even a little defiantly, reasserted his principles, at this very time; and, even in the circle of Maecenas, provoked the Emperor to remonstrance by his aloofness.

It is quite clear from the sixth satire that Horace neither asked for any favors nor concealed anything. He reminds Maecenas of this, as part of his defense, when ill-natured tongues were once more at work.

The famous poem on the Ship of State (*Odes*, Book I, 14) was probably written about the same time as the poem on the Fortunate Islands. Sellar thinks it was coincident with the seventh epode, which was probably written in 38 B.C., when a new civil war was threatened. If so, the poem on the Ship of State would be three years later than that on the Fortunate Islands; and this is confirmed by the poet's declaration that a certain change had taken place in him. The state of Rome, which had so lately been a source of utter weariness to him, had now became the object of a longing (*desiderium*) and the anxiety of a filial patriotism.

It seems to me almost certain that the poem on the Fortunate Islands had not only aroused the interest of Virgil, who replied to it in the fourth eclogue; but that it had led to a discussion of the "Ship of State" with Maecenas who used the same figurative language in an address to Octavian. The figure of "the Ship of State" is a familiar one today; but Horace was two thousand years nearer to its original use. Two of his favorite Greeks had used it before him—Alcaeus in a slighter way, and Plato, to illustrate the very problems of government which the new régime was raising in all thoughtful minds. If one may hazard a guess, it seems possible that Maecenas, in one of their discussions, reminded Horace of Plato's parable of the Ship of State. Its anti-democratic aspects would not be emphasized; but the figure of the ship at sea and the necessity for an authoritative steersman might easily be used by the persuasive friend of Octavian, to justify the methods of the new régime. It would not be surprising if this argument and this figure, so plausibly used by Plato, were the real source of the ode by Horace, and were also the beginning of his acquiescence in the new régime, which at least seemed to promise a period of peace. There are certain striking omissions in the poem which confirm this and suggest that Horace was by no means wholly convinced. He omits all reference to the main point of Plato's argument. He says nothing about the steersman or any controlling human power; but he does refer to something even more important, which he says is lacking. It is interesting to compare the two passages. Plato in the *Republic* begins his parable by saying:

I must have recourse to fiction and put together a figure made up of many things, like the fabulous unions of goats and stags which are found in pictures.

We may note, in passing, that this is the very kind of picture which Horace satirizes in the first paragraph of his *Art of Poetry*.

Imagine a ship (Plato continues) in which there is a captain who is taller and stronger than any of the crew, but he is a little deaf and weak in sight and has a limited knowledge of navigation. The sailors are quarreling—everyone is of the opinion that he has a right to steer, though he knows nothing at all of navigation, and indeed will assert that it cannot be taught, and is ready to cut in pieces anyone who says it can. They throng about the captain begging him to entrust the helm to them. If others are preferred, they kill them or throw them overboard. They mutiny; take possession of the ship; and make free with the stores. Thus, eating and drinking, they continue their voyage as might be expected. The man who chiefly aided them in their plot, they compliment with the name of "pilot" and abuse any one who takes the other side. The fact that a true pilot must pay attention to the sky and stars and winds and many other things, if he is to be really qualified for the command of a ship, and that he must and will be the steerer whether the people like it or not—this union of authority with the pilot's art has never seriously entered their heads.

It is obvious how this famous anti-democratic argument could be used by Maecenas to justify the new régime in any discussion of its methods with Horace.

In an address to Octavian, as recorded by Dio, Maecenas said:

Our city, like a great merchantman full of a crowd of every race, borne without a pilot these many years through rough water, rolls and shoots hither and thither because it is without ballast. Do not, then, allow her to be longer exposed to the tempest; for you see that she is water-logged; and do not let her be split upon a reef; for her timbers are rotten and will not be able to hold out much longer. But since the gods have taken pity on this land and have set you up as her arbiter and chief, do not betray your country.

Through you she has now revived a little; if you are faithful she may live with safety for years to come.

It has been suggested that in this passage Dio is imitating Thucydides (VII, 25); but the passage in Thucydides is not figurative. It deals with a real ship, and it has no bearing at all on the "State." It is surely more reasonable to connect the words of Maecenas with a poem which must have been familiar to him. I have attempted to render this poem also in the original metre:

THE SHIP OF STATE

(Book I, Ode 14)

Wild new tempests, O Ship, whirl thee to war this night,
Oarless bulwarks a-wash, wallowing out to sea!
   Seek not, thus, thy dominion!
     Back, beat back to yon harbor-light!

Blind, bruised, quivering hulk, naked of girding ropes,
Seek no glory out there! Look to thy splintering spars,
   Main-mast cracking, and sails rent.
     Seest thou not? It is *Africus!*

Fire-new paint on thy poop! Ay, but thy gods are gone!
Gods, who knowing our need, once were enshrined in thee!
   All earth's forests avail not,
     Now, nor timbers of Pontic pine.

I, heart-sickened of war, still—as a lover or child—
Filled with longing would cry, "Back from that waste of death!
   Back, beat back to thy haven!
     Tempt not the glittering Cyclades!"

THE JOURNEY TO BRUNDISIUM

IN THE YEAR 37 B.C.——THE MOST PROBABLE DATE——MAECENAS invited Virgil, Horace, and a few other friends, to accompany him on a journey to Brundisium, the modern Brindisi. Horace wrote a delightful account of the expedition in the fifth satire of the first book. The exact occasion of the journey has been a matter of some debate, but there is no doubt that Maecenas was to meet the representatives of Antony, and try, if possible, to prevent a further outbreak of hostilities.

Antony had set sail for Italy with a great fleet of six hundred ships, pretending that he was bent on cooperating with Octavian to crush the Republican forces which were still holding out under Sextus Pompeius in Sicily. Octavian had in fact made overtures to Antony for this purpose; and Antony, with his fleet as a bargaining weapon, seized the opportunity to make a new bid for power. It is said that he tried to come into the harbor at Brundisium, but was prevented by a formidable show of resistance. Negotiations began through envoys, and the fate of innumerable innocent and obscure lives depended on decisions which those lives were powerless to influence for good or for evil. It is an ancient tale, and a modern. The whole tragedy of Western civilization can be summed up in that brief sentence.

The agents of the two "giants," as they would be called today, had been unsuccessful until a quite irrelevant giantess had been brought into the game. Octavia, the sister of Octavian, and wife of Antony, had been able to effect a temporary reconciliation between the Big Two, each of whom wanted to rule the world alone. To complete the picture, it must be remembered that another giantess, Cleopatra, was still the mistress, not only of Egypt, but of Antony; and that Octavian had ruthlessly used his sister for a political purpose which—for herself—could only end in disaster. At the moment, however, a temporary agreement was in sight. Concessions were being made on both sides, and it was to represent Octavian in these negotiations that Maecenas took his famous journey to the great sea-port of the south.

His traveling companions, in addition to Virgil and Horace, were the poet Varius, and a Greek scholar named Heliodorus, of whom we know nothing more than the tribute of Horace to his learning. He is sometimes identified with Apollodorus, the former tutor of Octavian; but the only evidence for this is the similarity of the names. It is sometimes suggested that Maecenas took these friends with him merely because he wanted congenial company on the journey. Not long ago, in a delightful, but not quite accurate essay, a former British diplomat evinced a natural surprise at the choice. Slightly elevating one eyebrow, he remarked: "Mr. Eden does not drag all Bloomsbury with him when he flies to Moscow or Teheran."

It is difficult to imagine anything less like Bloomsbury than Horace and Virgil; but the real reason for taking them was one we have already encountered. Literature, in those days, had not been swamped by cataracts of ephemeral froth. Julius Caesar himself was seriously affected by a brief epigram of Catullus; and Octavian was only following his great uncle's policy in trying to enlist the naked phrase as well as the naked sword on the side of the new régime. This desire was manifest on many occasions, as we have already seen. Maecenas, however, understood the permanent values of literature. Virgil, who was to join the party on the third day of the journey, was probably the bait for Horace. The young Republican poet associated Maecenas with pleasant discussions of art and poetry rather than with the policy of Octavian to absorb the opposition and gather all power into his own control. A little later Virgil discovered to his cost how injurious this might be to literature itself. But, so far as Horace was concerned, either his *genius* or the shade of the old farmer of Venusia must have been continually whispering in his ear, "Put not your trust in princes."

At the outset of the journey, Horace and the Greek scholar Heliodorus set out from Rome along the Appian Way, probably in a four-wheeled carriage drawn by mules. They had a driver and one or two attendants, for we hear of their dining together, a little later. The stone pavement of the Appian Way made it desirable to travel slowly, and they accomplished only sixteen miles on the first day, spending the night at Aricia. This was a little village with a modest inn (*hospitio modico*) near the temple and grove of Diana, on the *Lacus Nemorensis*. We can imagine Horace and his Greek scholar discussing, with a certain awe, the strange custom of former days, whereby the priest of that temple remained in office until he was killed by a more powerful or crafty successor. They would look at the woods surrounding the temple and picture the trepidation with which the old priest must have surveyed them at night-fall, uncertain whether the new priest might not already be lurking there, knife in hand. Macaulay, in his *Lays of Ancient Rome*, describes the sinister associations of the still, glassy lake that sleeps beneath Aricia's trees:

> Those trees in whose dim shadow
> The ghastly priest doth reign,
> The priest who slew the slayer
> And shall himself be slain.

On the next day they reached Appii Forum, twenty-seven miles further south, a place made famous to Christendom a few years later by an incident recorded of St. Paul:

When the brethren heard of us they came to meet us as far as Appii Forum and the three taverns: whom when Paul saw he thanked God and took courage.

Country towns in those days did not change very quickly. It is possible therefore that, with a generation or two intervening, Horace and St. Paul spent a few hours at the same tavern. It is unfortunate, however, that Horace did not anticipate the advice of St. Paul and take a little wine for the good of his stomach. The water at Aricia was poisonous, and the poet was so upset by it that he was unable to dine, while the Greek scholar, the mule-driver, and the attendants ate their fill.

The satire in which Horace gives us a little diary of this journey belongs to a *genre* which may owe something to Lucilius; but, as in other cases, the autobiographical value of the later poem is a sufficient proof that it is no mere imitation. It is more illuminating, perhaps, to discover its kinship with later examples of the same *genre*. It is the miniature prototype, for instance, of certain essays by Stevenson, especially perhaps his *Travels with a Donkey*. In both cases, we have an account of the trivialities, little accidents, and amusing tribulations of a picturesque and picaresque journey, told with apparent artlessness, but really with great artistic skill. The gravity of the mission on which Maecenas was bent is kept entirely in the background. It is never mentioned directly; and this very silence perhaps is part of the satire. We get no political illumination; but we hear that innkeepers are sometimes grasping, and that boatmen get drunk. There is the same pretence of annoyance, and the same fun derived from it, as in several of Stevenson's adventures with Modestine in the Cevennes.

From the Appii Forum, at the beginning of the Pomptine Marshes, sixteen miles of the journey had to be made on a canal-barge. There is a vivid little scene at night when the baggage was being transferred. We hear the mule-drivers and the bargees bawling at one another—*"huc appelle!"*—*"trecentis inseris."* *"Ohe, jam satis est!"* ("Hi! That's enough! You are shoving in three hundred!") The satire breaks into burlesque heroics here, just as Stevenson, or Belloc would have done. "And now the night . . . night with her train of stars." . . . We can hear the very tones of the ironical parodist:

Jam nox includere terris
umbras et caelo diffundere signa parabat.

In three or four lines he makes us feel all the confusion of that delay at the wharf—the shouting, the collecting of the fares, the thumping and bumping of the baggage, the harnessing of the mule that was to tow the barge through the night while, theoretically, the passengers slept. The stars were lit as punctually for Horace as for Stevenson in "God's green caravanserai"; but there was no sleep that night. Instead of sliding through the peaceful darkness, the barge remained at the wharf. Innumerable frogs croaked in the marshes; and, whenever the travelers grew drowsy and tried to use a haversack for a pillow, the whine of the mosquitoes jerked them back to life. To cap everything, the bargee in charge of the mule on the towing-path got drunk, and began to sing about the girl he missed so much (*absentem cantat amicam*), whereupon a passenger—in the same hilarious condition—began a musical contest, and tried to out-bellow him. This lasted until the passenger was exhausted and fell asleep. The tipsy bargee then unhitched his mule, turned it out to graze, and decided to take a nap himself on the bank. At daybreak, when the reeds looked sharp and black against the graying pools, the barge had not moved from the bank; and might have remained there until the fall of the Roman Empire, if another stout-hearted passenger had not leapt ashore and lustily thumped the heads of the sinful bargee and the innocent mule with a knobbled club. The Latin hexameters here reproduce, in an amusing piece of onomatopoeia, the very sound of that lusty walloping:

> *Ac mulae nautaeque caput lumbosque saligno*
> *fuste dolat . . .*

It was ten o'clock before they reached the temple of Feronia, where they were to resume their journey by land. There Horace and his friends washed their hands and faces in a fresh water-spring—"thy stream, Feronia."

> *ora manusque tua lavimus, Feronia, lympha.*

It is pure Stevenson, in the idiom of Rome.

After breakfast, their mule-carriage crawled slowly up the steep road to the hill-town of Anxur, set high among its bright limestone crags. Here Maecenas was to join them, with Cocceius. Horace tells us that they were special envoys on that important mission, the nature of which he never directly mentions. He merely indicates in a single clause that these envoys were well accustomed (*soliti*) to bringing estranged friends together. The estranged friends, of course, were Octavian and Antony; and the remark that the envoys are accustomed to reconciling them is not only an allusion to the earlier occasion at the peace of Brundisium, but a subtle hint, conveyed in hardly more than a faint satirical smile, that these reconciliations are temporary. The commentators appear to have missed the real point of this, and they have surely missed the sly and amusing stroke of satire in the next sentence. Immediately after the quiet observation that the envoys were on their way to reconcile the two estranged friends, Horace adds with apparently artless irrelevance, "Here I daubed my weak eyes with black ointment":

> *Hic oculis ego nigra meis collyria lippus*
> *illinere . . .*

In the very next sentence he goes back to the subject of Maecenas and his companions; and the wicked little interruption about his weak eyes is so very abrupt and brief that it has the effect of an interjected glance of polite scepticism. Horace did have a certain physical trouble with his eyes; but so—for instance—had the late Sir Edmund Gosse, from whom, on sceptical occasions, the Savile Club must have heard many a remark in precisely the same dry tone. Moreover, in the third satire of the same book Horace uses almost exactly the same words for a very similar purpose. Describing a man who doesn't want to see a thing, he says: "*You daub your eyes with ointment to make yourself blind to your own sins*"; and he uses the word *lippus* for that self-blinded condition here, just as he uses it in the later passage.

This interpretation also answers the question of one or two critics who have been puzzled by the fact that the ointment was intended to improve the sight, not to obscure it. It is only the temporary blurring effect, of course, to which Horace is alluding. In the passage about the envoys, it has always been taken as a mere reference to his physical condition. But, in view of the circumstances—his long-standing distrust of those "estranged friends"; and his little dig at the "accustomed" task of reconciliation; his use of the very same words about the blindness and the ointment for a subtler purpose in another and an earlier passage, we can hardly suppose that an artist like Horace, alive to every ambiguity of tone and every shade of significance, was quite as innocent as he looked in his observations about the "estranged friends." A former reconciliation had led to a savage proscription, and the murder of Cicero; a second, at the peace of Brundisium, had led to nothing more than a period of watchful waiting. Wherever one probed the policy of these "giants," it broke beneath the testing finger, and proved to be honeycombed with intrigue and rotten with treachery. The "accustomed" envoys might think they were going to obtain a more satisfying settlement on this occasion. But Horace, in a subtle and polite way, was surely anticipating the method of Nelson, when he ignored the signal ordering him to retire:

> He clapped the glass to his blinded eye,
> And "I'm damned if I see it," he said.

The argument, of course, is not that Horace spoke of the ointment in a merely figurative sense. He did actually use it on his eyes; but, as any satirical writer might, he spoke of it in this case with a double meaning. If the satire is deprived of these flashes of significance, which can be found in what Horace actually says, and sometimes in what he obviously refrains from saying, the apparent trivialities become too trivial for any artistic purpose. In fact, some of the commentators who have taken everything in this satire quite literally do appear to find it a very flat production, "a bare recital," only redeemed by the antiquarian interest of its minor details. But they forget that Horace was not writing for antiquarians in the far future; and since he would then be deprived of the only interest left in the poem, it would have appeared infinitely more flat to himself. He was interested and amused, however, by what he was actually describing at the time; and he was far too intelligent a man to find interest and amusement in anything as flat as the literalists would make it. It is the task of the critic, therefor, to find out exactly what amused him.

The next halt was at Fundi, where the mayor, as he might be called today, came out to meet them with a pompousness which amused Horace immensely. The chief official of Fundi was appointed annually from Rome. In this case, it was a certain Aufidius Luscus whom Horace had last seen as a somewhat crazy scribe in his own office at the Treasury. The appointment to Fundi had apparently gone to the head of Aufidius and turned him into an early edition of Malvolio. Cross-gartered with the black thongs of the senatorial attire (to which he was not entitled), he approached the ambassadorial party in a purple-bordered toga and a tunic with the broad purple stripe, or *"latus clavus,"* which indicated senatorial rank. A pan of burning charcoal was carried before him by a slave. The pan of charcoal might be used for two purposes—warding off infection, and offering up incense. It is not clear which was intended on this occasion; but in view of the distinction of the visitors, one may hope that incense was in the air. Horace was so delighted that he called his old acquaintance "Praetor," which was an even more exalted title than "Senator"; and the party left Fundi in a gale of joyous laughter at the crazy scribe (*insani ridentes praemia scribae*).

Terse as the allusions are to the place at which they slept (*Formiae*), their satirical flavor must again be remarked. We must remember that names which we pass over lightly today were often rich with significance to those who used them two thousand years ago. It was from Formiae that Mamurra came, the rascally favorite of Julius Caesar. Catullus had flayed Mamurra in several savage epigrams. Horace merely calls Formiae the "City of the Mamurrae," using the plural as if he were speaking of a very noble and distinguished clan. The reader of his own day would have been alive to all this. He would probably remember how Julius Caesar himself had tried to stop the attacks of Catullus by interviewing him personally at his father's house in Verona; and how Catullus had merely substituted the nickname Mentula for Mamurra in his future lampoons. The attacks on Mamurra indirectly reflected upon Caesar, of course; but Catullus had never been afraid of attacking him directly. One of his most contemptuous epigrams deals with the expressed wish of Caesar to meet him on this very occasion:

Never a wish have I, O Julius Caesar, to please you!
Nor do I care how you look, whether a black man or white.

Horace achieved his own effect by giving Formiae a new name as if it were a distinction; and then, with the utmost urbanity, he passes quietly on.

The next day brought the joyous reward of the whole journey for Horace. The sun rose in a glory (*Postera lux oritur multo gratissima*) for Plotius and Varius, and Virgil himself, "than whom the whole earth had borne no whiter souls" (*animae, qualis neque candidiores terra tulit*). We can hear and feel the exclamatory excitement in his lines as they meet. We can almost see the demonstrative Italian greeting. "There is no joy like that which the arrival of a friend brings us; nothing that I would compare with it, while I am in my right senses":

> *O qui complexus et gaudia quanta fuerunt!*
> *Nil ego contulerim jucundo sanus amico.*

It is a good saying, and, like all really true things, it can be said afresh in every generation without any fear of its becoming commonplace, when it comes from the heart as it undoubtedly did with Horace. A note of gaiety seems to come into the narrative at this moment. It is difficult for a modern reader to follow all the fun of the contest in ridicule between a servant of Maecenas and Cicirrus, "the game-cock," at the villa of Antony's friend, Cocceius, where they fared somewhat better than at the wayside inns. But the supper was a merry one.

Their misfortunes were equally enjoyable. At Beneventum the innkeeper nearly burned down the house while he was roasting some thrushes for their evening meal. The guests and the panic-stricken slaves helped to put the fire out; and, after this, as the house was full of smoke, they took their evening meal in a green arbor outside. We can picture that scene—the amphora, and the wine cups on the little table; Maecenas, acting as a genial chairman, and turning to Heliodorus, as if he were a Greek encyclopedia, to confirm a fact or complete a quotation;

Varius and Plotius discussing the possibilities of the Roman theater; and, in the real center, wherever they might happen to be sitting, Virgil and Horace. A curious contrast those two. Virgil was a tall and slender young man, with a delicate and sensitive face, and dark glowing eyes like those that look out at us from the face of Saint John in one of Raphael's great religious pictures. It was not merely because he had written pastoral poetry that one could imagine him as a shepherd on the hills, with a crook in his hand, and a lamb in the fold of his arm. He was somewhat awkward in his manner, as though a woodgod or Faunus himself had taken possession of a country shepherd's body and had not learned how to use it yet. Perhaps this was why he was a little dyspeptic. In ordinary conversation, too, there was a slight impediment in his speech; which suggested, not the self-consciousness of the recluse, but the protective shyness of a power that must hide itself. When he warmed to his subject, however, especially in the quotation of poetry, the power shone through, and his voice became as musical as the wind in a pine-wood. Horace, sitting opposite to him, was of much smaller physique, perhaps about the size of the little Scot who wrote *Dear Brutus*; but he was at no disadvantage when they talked, and, curiously enough, one ceased to observe his physical dimensions.

Occasionally—we may be fairly sure—he would rally Virgil a little about his political idealism. We can imagine the discussion that took place at these suppers—the weighing of one style against another, Alexandrian against Atticist, with Virgil all for the deep undertones and the great rolling sea-waves of the hexameter, while Horace, aware and appreciative of both, would put in his word for the Greek lyrical measures, and the use that might be made of them in Latin poetry.

We can hardly doubt that, on some of these occasions, the two poets touched upon ultimate things, discussing Epicurus, and his notion that the gods had no care for mankind; and the Stoics, who believed in a divine Providence, ordering all things from end to end. Horace might incline at first to the Epicurean side; but he would bind himself to no particular school, and he would take what he wanted from any of them. He was far from being a sceptic. He loved the old religion of the Italian countryside. The little gods of the woods and fields were perhaps no more than representations of the different attributes of one supreme God. At this time of his life, if people spoke to him of divine intervention in human affairs, he was inclined to reply *"credat Judaeus Apella, non ego."* "I have learned," he once said, "that the gods lead a carefree life. How can they do that, if they are continually changing the course of Nature?" He said this when they arrived at Gnatia, where somebody tried to persuade him that frankincense melted without fire in the local temple. But, when Virgil gave him some of those lines from the *Georgics,* he listened intently:

> Happy is he who can search out the causes of things,
> For thereby he masters all fear, and is throned above fate.

Still more intently would he listen, if Virgil had continued, as well he might, with some of those magnificent lines which were afterwards incorporated in his epic:

Are not the sky and the earth, and the wild flowing plains of
    the ocean,
Ay, and the moon on her way, and the sun on his chariot of
    splendor,
All sustained from within, by a Spirit, a Mind in the Cosmos,
Moving the blindfold mass . . . *et magno se corpore miscet?* [1]

    Brundisium, he says, came at the end of a long journey. The party broke up; and we hear nothing more of the political conference. But we know that the envoys, so accustomed to recon-

[1] From *The Last Voyage,* by Alfred Noyes.

ciling estranged friends, were able to do it again for a brief
breathing space, and that it all ended in another effusion of
blood on land and sea. But the two poets at least had caught
glimpses of that other city whose walls are built of music; and,
on the way to it, shortly after leaving Beneventum, Horace had
caught sight of certain familiar hills in the distance, the known
and beloved hills of Apulia that once watched over his father's
house:

> *Incipit ex illo montes Apulia notos*
> *ostentare mihi. . . .*

He became moody that evening. They would never have defeated those hills, if it had not been for the little house at which
they halted for the night. The familiar fields, the familiar trees
were round him, the great dark friendly trees. He knew where
that road on the other side of the stream would lead him if he
dared to follow it only a mile or two away. What was the
matter with little Flaccus? He was very silent that night. He
grumbled about the wood they put in the stove. It was green,
and the smoke had made his eyes smart. Green boughs, my
masters, green boughs and crowds of young leaves, as green as
memory. The careless host had stuffed them all into the stove
to crackle together under the pot like a fool's laughter; and
if, next morning, the poor fool (*stultissimus*) was able to make
a crude jest at his own expense, a jest as coarse as the common
talk of the army camps in Macedonia, he had not yet outgrown
the effects of that campaign. On this occasion, moreover, he
really did borrow from Lucilius who, in his own satire on a
similar journey, told the very same crude story. The autobiographical value, therefore, is at least doubtful; and both the
circumstances and the companionship on the later journey made
it doubly so. But, since the incident is somewhat "off-color,"
the twentieth-century neo-pagans will naturally insist that it is

the only bit of the satire which has any autobiographical value at all. Let them have it then. But, in the face of twentieth-century literature, editors must not pretend to be shocked by a sentence in Horace. They might as well be shocked by the youth of St. Augustine, who said equally frank things about himself. By the standards of St. Augustine, Horace was very far indeed from being a saint. He was a pleasure-loving man of the world. But, compared with the twentieth-century neo-pagans, he was at least able to make distinctions between good and ill. He did so in this very passage.

It seems to me that what actually happened was this. When the great hills of that south country rose before him with all their memories, the poet in him could hardly fail to respond. Possibly, on re-reading what he had written, he thought that the response was too sentimental. He therefore cut it out and replaced it by this crude jest from Lucilius, very much as a man might blaspheme to conceal an emotion. He replaced it by something which he knew would bring no daws to peck at his heart.

Virgil might make immortal poetry out of the sense of tears in mortal things; but not Horace. He would only grumble a little about the green boughs in the stove. But there was once a poet who wrote of the Roman as well as of the British soldier. He loved Horace, and he would have found him out that evening. He would understand very well that certain things must not be spoken; and he would simply lay a hand on the little man's shoulder and say quietly, "I think I shall call you Smoke-in-the-eyes."

Horace went back alone by way of Venusia. It is conjectured that he halted there to take his last look at the home of his boyhood. He never returned to it again, and he tells us nothing of this last visit. Only Virgil, perhaps, could have done that. But it is not in poetry only that the memories of a man really crowd together by the River of Oblivion, stretching out their hands in speechless longing to someone on the further shore.

PRAYER FOR VIRGIL

(Book I, Ode 3)

Wave-born Queen of the Cyprian foam,
    Far-famed glittering twins, beautiful pilot-stars;
Thou, too, Father of winds and waves,
    Watch well over that ship, spreading her sail to-night,—

Ship now bearing away from us
    Virgil, half of my soul, over the darkening sea;
Keep her true to her trust, we pray!
    Bring him safe to his goal, yonder in Attica.

Three-fold bronze, indestructible oak,
    Armed that seaman who, first, fearing not Aquilo,
Pushed out into the roaring deep
    Past thy ship-wrecking rocks, Acroceraunia!

Vain, ah vain, was the god's behest;
    His, who sundered the lands, once, by that salt decree.
Man still follows the Titan's road,
    Storms through heaven and, now, thunders at Acheron, too.

Bearing Virgil away from us. . . .
    Ours, all ours, was the sin, sending him hence in vain,
Sin, compelling the lightning flash,
    Wrong, compelling the gods, hesitant long, to smite.

VIII

THE FRIENDS OF HORACE

THE SATIRES OF HORACE WERE USUALLY QUIET AND GOOD-natured studies of character, in the manner of Montaigne rather than of Swift; but the smile made them all the more effective; and it began to be recognized in Roman literary circles that Horace was one of those disconcerting little creatures whom it is not safe to attack, because they not only defend themselves, but are wicked enough to make the world laugh at their enemies. He seems to have been conscious of the growing respect that this power commanded; and it is pleasant to notice how thoroughly he enjoyed using it, in the sixth epode, to protect one of his friends who, apparently, was of a gentler disposition and less able to defend himself. There is a fiercer indignation in it, and it is a more serious poem, but it has a Rabelaisian gusto that reminds one of the lines in which Belloc castigates the don "who dared attack my Chesterton."

Horace calls himself "a friend to shepherds" (*amica vis pastoribus*), and it has been conjectured that the friend he is defending in this poem was none other than Virgil, who was known at this time only by his early pastorals:

Why do you attack innocent strangers, snarling cur that you are? You run quickly enough at the sight of a wolf! Why not attack me, whose teeth are ready for you? I am a friend of shepherds—a trusty hound bred of the Molossian or Spartan kind. I prick up my ears, and drive the wild beast back to his mountain snows. You make the whole forest echo with your terrific barking; but if any one tosses you a scrap, you stop at once to smell the bribe (*projectum odoraris citrum*).

Various attempts have been made to identify the "dog." The most probable guess is that of Ritter, who thinks it was Furius Bibaculus, a bad poet and lampooner to whom Horace pays further attention in his tenth satire. The contemptuous reference to the bribe, or scrap of meat, fits him very well, since, after lampooning Julius Caesar, he was induced not only to desist from barking, but to write an epic on the Gallic war. Professor Tenney Frank identifies him further with the "Bavius" of Virgil, a reasonable conclusion since Bavius means "barker," and his conjecture is supported, if not by direct evidence, at least by a "consilience of inductions." The sixth epode seems like a companion-piece to the tenth, in which Horace deals with Maevius, whom Virgil linked with Bavius in that famous line of the third eclogue—"Let him who hateth not Bavius, admire your music, my Maevius":

qui Bavium non odit, amet tua carmina, Maevi.

The pastoral reference in the sixth epode, and the amusing contrast between the prayer for the shipwreck of Maevius in the tenth, and the prayer for Virgil's safe voyage in the third ode, certainly appear to link the three poems together as incidents in the friendship of Horace and Virgil. Even at this distance of time it is difficult to read the prayer for the shipwreck of Maevius without a chuckle. It has been compared with Swinburne's *Dirae*; but Horace, just as he sometimes amuses himself with mock-heroics, so here, with incomparable artistry, amuses the reader and himself by pretending to be in a terrible fury. If it were entirely in earnest, it would be quite out of proportion to the subject; but there is a good deal of fun in the gusto with which Horace prays that ugly waves may batter the ship of Maevius, and a black wind strew the sea with her broken oars and halliards. If only a delicate morsel could be flung on the beach to feed the cormorants, he promises to sacrifice a goat and a lamb in thanksgiving to the blessed storms that accomplish it. But we know, all the time, that Horace had not the slightest wish for cormorants to pick the bones of Maevius. His worst desire was probably that the poetaster who attacked Virgil should squirm a little when some kind friend sent him the tenth epode to read during that voyage.

The friendship between Horace and Maecenas was resented by the political place-hunters and candidates for office, who fought and snarled like dogs over a bone for the eminent statesman's favor. Maecenas at this time was the fountain of honor and preferment, and some of the place-hunters looked upon Horace as an illegitimate competitor in their own field. They behaved exactly like the "brass-hat" on the staff of Brutus, and eagerly pointed out that Horace was the son of a freedman. Julius Caesar had actually made it possible for freedmen, in certain circumstances to become senators; but the purpose for which he did it had only increased the feeling against them; and Augustus, before very long, was to purge the senate of these undesirable members. The social discrimination against their children had not changed, and, if Horace had entertained any political ambitions, he would have found endless obstacles in his path. Fortunately he had no ambitions of that kind. But his enemies imputed their own desires to him, and they were not above suggesting that Maecenas had been hoodwinked by an upstart. How, otherwise, could Maecenas have treated this "outsider" as a friend, inviting him to his most intimate dinner parties and showing him every mark of fraternal affection, while they—the upholders of tradition and all the correct conventions—had to be content with a careless nod or a brief interview in an anteroom. Horace took the trouble, in the sixth satire of the first book, to answer this charge by giving a detailed account of his introduction to Maecenas by Virgil and Varius. He remarked that the knowledge of his birth had made no difference to the affection of his friend. We can hardly wonder that his answer to enemies of this kind was as contemptuous, though not quite so light-hearted, as the reply of Browning to an invidious attack on the great poets of the nineteenth century:

> While, treading down rose and ranunculus,
> You Tommy-make-room-for-your-Uncle us!
> Troop, all of you—man or homunculus!

It was a curious social comedy—all those dull and insignificant homunculi, as Browning called them, trying to look down their noses at one of the immortals, while hungrily and humbly soliciting the least crumb of favor from his friend "the descendant of Etruscan kings." But Horace actually held the strongest of all positions on this matter; for he wanted nothing. He was not a competitor with homunculi and, if he had been offered all that they thought he wanted, he would have rejected it instantly. He desired no spoils of office and had no wish to change his skin. On the other hand, Maecenas and (through Maecenas) Octavian, already suspected that Horace had something of inestimable value to bestow upon the new régime. They could hardly foresee that seventeen hundred years later a little man at Twickenham-on-Thames would be translating what his Roman predecessor had taught a hundred generations to translate:

> Vain was the chief's, the sage's pride!
> They had no poet and they died.
> In vain they schemed, in vain they bled!
> They had no poet and are dead.

Alexander Pope, the poet of the curiously misnamed "Augustan age" in England did not express, and never could express, the deeper meaning of the Roman poet. It was not in any personal pride that Horace invoked the sacred and prophetic fire. Virgil had already added to the lustre of his generation. History had shown in the past, as she would show again in the future, that where there is no great literature (*carent quia vate sacro*), the memories that knit the generations are buried in a long and very dark night. It would certainly have occurred to Maecenas that Horace might add a further lustre to the new régime. Octavian boasted that he had found Rome brick, and would leave it marble. He would have liked his own name to go down to posterity in the masterpieces of Roman literature, where they were less likely to crumble. Literature in those days was not swamped by the ephemeral, and it was easier for men of discrimination to recognize the work that would endure. Certain values—perfection of form, clarity, depth, radiance, craftsmanship—were as recognizable in a poem as the qualities of a well-cut diamond, and the poem that possessed them was almost instinctively known to be imperishable. The poets themselves knew it, and made predictions at which the world might smile if the predictions had not come true. Horace himself had not yet made the famous prediction of his maturer life—*Exegi monumentum aere perennius*—which Shakespeare turned into his own equally immortal English:

> Not marble, nor the gilded monuments
> Of princes shall outlive this powerful rhyme

But Horace could not help being conscious of his power to express and interpret, in a perfect form, certain ideas and feelings that are of permanent interest to the human spirit. Maecenas had already convinced Octavian of this power, and had thus placed Horace in a position from which he was able to deliver a crushing reply to his enemies. In some ways it was the most complete reply ever made on such a subject. Without the slightest hesitation he reminded his readers of his association with Brutus. It was the boldest and most unanswerable way of demonstrating that he had no desire for political preferment under Octavian; and he made this demonstration in what is nothing less than an open letter to the emperor's chief minister. To the taunts about his ancestry he gave first the ironical reply that any man of the world might give, making a subtle distinction between the unknown and the ignoble; but he treats these answers as merely subsidiary to the one final and absolute answer—the beautiful tribute to his dead father—in which, as we saw earlier, he transcends all worldly considerations. It is amusing, however, to follow the wild-goose chase upon which his argument leads the homunculi. He reminds them, for instance, by a mere allusion that in the olden days one of the kings of Rome had formerly been a slave.

In the famous ode *"Ne sit ancillae"* he uses the same argument, but approaches his conclusion from the opposite end, telling to the lover of the slave-girl that her intrinsic qualities proclaim her queenly lineage. "She who is loved by thee, and is so constant and so free from all base worldliness, was born of no base mother." The homunculi might suppose that this was going to be his line of argument; and, if it had been, it would have given them a glorious opportunity for raillery. But almost at once they find themselves pinned into the opposite corner. "Before that ignoble kingship (*ignobile regnum*) there were many men without ancestry," he says, "who lived uprightly."

Here his enemies would hardly know which was the feint and which was the home-thrust before the point had slipped between their ribs. Were they to answer him on the upright life, or was it the democratic position that he was taking? If they decided upon the latter, the very next sentence would throw them off their balance. "Ancestry," he remarked, "did not help Laevinus, even when the people voted for him. You know what the judgment of the people is worth (*judice, quo nosti, populo*). You know how in their folly they give honor to the unworthy; how they are carried away by mere notoriety and spellbound by titles (*stupet in titulis*). While his opponents are wondering whether they are to defend titles or the proletariat, he takes their breath away by calmly asking Maecenas, the descendant of Etruscan kings, what he and his friend, Quintus Horatius Flaccus, are to do about the snobbish nonsense which these homunculi had been talking! "What are we to do about it—we who are so far above that common crowd?" (*a volgo longe longeque remotos*).

We may conjecture that Maecenas himself suggested that unexpected blow from the son of the freedman. The poem had almost certainly been shown to Maecenas before it was circulated. It would have been ineffective, on that crowd, but for the link with Maecenas. It is too personal to have been made public without consultation, and we can imagine Maecenas making exactly that comment. Possibly his first remark would have been, "Why take any notice of such people? They are too insignificant to hurt you or me." It sounds more like Maecenas than Horace. It is unlike the usual modesty of Horace to make assertions of that kind; and, indeed, when he was criticizing anyone, he usually laughed at himself as well. But he may have seen here something that appealed to his sense of humor. It would have pleased him vastly to picture the discomfiture of the homunculi when they found him so fraternally linked with that exalted personage, the chief minister of the emperor, upon whom all their hopes depended. Maecenas himself, on the other hand, had his own pride in the association with Horace; for he had literary ambitions of his own. He had written a certain amount of poetry, imitations of Catullus in his lighter vein, and he liked to think of himself as one of the little group of writers who were now coming to the front. A little later Maecenas added to the discomfiture of the homunculi by publishing a symposium of his own, in which Virgil, Horace, and Messalla were the chief characters.

For Horace to rank himself so gaily with that company, however, without the backing of Maecenas, might have given the homunculi their opportunity. "Ah! Here we have him," they might think; "he is becoming pretentious." But as Macleane remarks, there is no evidence that Horace was ever spoiled by his good fortune; and in the very next lines Horace affirms that, if he ever became a candidate for political honors, the Censor would quite rightly strike out his name for "not being content with his own skin" (*quoniam in propria non pelle quiessem*). And here he gets a threefold benefit out of the allusion to the Ass in the Lion's skin. He wins the reader's goodwill by laughing at what *might* have happened to himself, if he had been so foolish; he anticipates the possible use of the argument against himself; and, at the same time, he deftly forestalls the derogatory comparison by making it quite clear that he is not in that position at all, since he had no thought of competing either with lions or homunculi, and is quite content with his own skin, even if there are a few moles or beauty spots on it:

> . . . *velut si*
> *egregio inspersos reprehendas corpore naevos.*

At least they are not the spots of avarice or vice. It is vanity that causes the trouble. Vainglorious Ambition drags both the lowly and the lofty behind her glittering car. "What advantage," he asked, "was it to you, Tillius, when you became a tribune and put that broad purple stripe on your tunic? You immediately became the target for Envy."

As for Horace himself, people had been turning up their noses at him, he says, for two reasons. In former times it was because he had been entrusted with the command of a legion under Brutus; now it was because he had become a friend of

Maecenas. On the first charge, he gave the disconcertingly bold and exceedingly shrewd reply that anyone might be justified in envying him that high command. But on the charge that Maecenas had taken him into his friendship, he refused with a subtle irony to regard that as an offence on the part of Maecenas. It was true, of course, that the homunculi could not obtain it themselves; for Maecenas was very careful about the choice of his friends, but the descendant of Etruscan kings had at least the right to choose his own society.

Greenough justly remarks that, in the humor of the satires, Horace bears a closer resemblance to Thackeray than to any other English writer. Like Thackeray, he detested ill-natured snobbery, and in his early sermons, or imaginary conversations in verse, he was really composing a little book of Roman Snobs, with a few Roundabout Papers thrown in. He had felt the sting of snobbery at every stage of his own career, and, as we have seen, he had discussed it, over the heads of his enemies, with Maecenas. He was completely justified in doing this. There was no reason whatever why the snobs should have been allowed to have it all their own way.

It is a little surprising, therefore, to find a real misrepresentation of his character on this very point, in Professor Saintsbury's *History of Criticism*. Saintsbury on many subjects was one of the soundest, if not always the most sensitive, of British critics. He says some exceedingly good things about Horace on many other pages; but he does him a real injustice in his comments on the tenth satire of the first book, where Horace is again defending himself against the homunculi. One cannot help observing with a certain satisfaction that Nemesis immediately overtakes Professor Saintsbury; for, in the very act of treating Horace unkindly, he tumbles headlong into what is probably the only major blunder in all his volumes of history and criticism.

This blunder is well worth examining, for it forms the very core of his misjudgment of Horace. *"With a touch of something not quite alien from snobbishness,"* he says: *"Horace boasts of his intimacy and agreement, not merely with Varius, Virgil, Pollio, Messalla among men of letters, but with Maecenas and Octavius."*

In this sentence Professor Saintsbury takes the name "Octavius" out of its proper place in the poem and couples it with Maecenas, for the obvious reason that he is confusing the "Octavius" of the tenth satire with Octavianus, the future "Augustus." But the Octavius mentioned by Horace was Octavius Musa, a historian and poet and friend of Horace. He was not very well known, so I suppose that even a snob could hardly object to Horace mentioning *him*.

Many English writers have the habit of referring incorrectly to the autocrat of Rome as "Octavius." Professor Bury points out, in one of his notes to Gibbon, that Merivale does this, incorrectly. But no Roman writer would have done it after 43 B.C., unless he intended a deliberate slight. The young Caesar whose name was originally C. Octavius "ceased to be an Octavius and became a Julius when he was adopted as the heir to Julius Caesar. His full name in 44 B.C. was C. Julius Caesar Octavianus." It is amusing to find Cicero, in his letters to Atticus, fighting against the change. In April, 44 B.C., following the assassination of Julius Caesar, Cicero complains that "Octavius" is already being called "Caesar" by his followers. By October, 44 B.C., however, Cicero has acquiesced, and henceforward invariably speaks of the young Caesar as "Octavianus," completely dropping the "Octavius" which he had always used before. Six or seven years later, in the circle of Maecenas, Horace would certainly have given Caesar his correct name. It was not till 27 B.C. that Octavianus became Augustus. Whenever Horace mentioned him in his poems, he called him either

Caesar or Augustus. He does not mention him at all in the satire under discussion.

But the ironical imps of the judgment have not yet finished with the unkind critic. One of them, with a red-hot pitchfork, may well point out that the future Augustus wrote to Horace, as we have already seen, expressing real annoyance that the poet did not mention him in these earlier works. *"Me, of all people,"* he exclaimed. *"Are you afraid that posterity will think the worse of you for having been my friend?"* But this proffered friendship, from which with extraordinary persistence the poet kept himself aloof for so many years, was the very thing which, twenty centuries later, he was accused of boastfully parading. Poor Horace! whatever he did, there was no escape. With great courage he maintained his personal independence against the blandishments, the almost importunate pleading, of the emperor, who had said, "take any liberty with me"—only to be "gorgonized" after two thousand years, by the stony British stare of Professor Saintsbury. It is a pity, for Horace would so thoroughly have enjoyed the "Cellar Book."

It should be observed, incidentally, that Messalla, Pollio, and Maecenas were known in Rome as the central figures around whom the three outstanding schools of contemporary poets were accustomed to gather. It was for this reason that Horace mentioned them, answering attacks upon his own verse by saying that he was content if he was approved by these three circles. Horace, after all, conferred at least as much distinction on those groups as they could confer on him. Virgil was still a young poet at the time in question. He had written neither the *Georgics* nor the *Aeneid.* He was known only to a very small public. He was only five years older than Horace, and he was a personal friend whom Horace had actually defended against the malice of Bavius and Maevius. It is quite unhistorical, therefore, to suggest that Horace was pretentiously claiming acquaintance with a man of universal fame already recognized as *l'altissimo poeta*. Horace, in fact, contributed to that world-wide recognition, and Dante met them together in his grim underworld without any feeling of social embarrassment. The other names in the list were admittedly obscure. One or two of them had been on the side of Brutus, and the association might have done Horace more harm than good from any worldly point of view. But had they been as illustrious as they were obscure, there was no earthly reason why Horace should have gone about in what W. S. Gilbert called "a humble and pottering way," afraid to behave naturally, afraid to mention his friends in his verses as Maecenas in turn mentioned him. It was the universal custom among the poets of that age to address their friends in verse. The friends whom Horace did mention in this satire were introduced as poets or the friends of poetry; moreover, they were introduced in a most modest way, as the judges whose approval he would like to win. What more could be decently required of a master of letters whom Pope called "supreme in judgment as in wit"; and whom Mackail, our best contemporary critic of Latin literature, described as having given to western civilization the perfect type of a well-bred and cultivated man.

IX

HORACE AND THE KNIGHT OF SUESSA

IT WAS NOT THE ARISTOCRATS OR THE PEASANTS, BUT THE plebeians, who went about Rome describing—untruly—how they had seen Horace's father "wiping his nose on his sleeve." As Professor Campbell wittily, though perhaps a little "Jesuitically," observes, "If the end was attained, the method seemed a secondary matter." But it was not so easy for Horace to laugh at the malice that could attack the son through a beloved father.

The statement was, of course, baseless and silly. Even a homunculus was not likely to remember an incident that supposedly took place in Venusia, a decade or two earlier; for he had no reason to anticipate the future fame of the son, or the use that could be made of the incident. If the homunculus was actually in the habit of remembering such things, on the off-chance of using them later, his head must have been *plein de mites*. Horace once said that, if a man starts in the race of life at a disadvantage, he deserves all the more credit for his achievement. It is a sentiment on which the modern world has often prided itself. Horace was far too sensitive to have made that claim on his own behalf. It was extorted from him in answer to his enemies. All through his career he had to contend against the opposite and less sportsmanlike handicap. He says very little about it directly, but there is ample evidence in poem after poem that he felt it keenly. It should be noted that when Horace showed himself willing to admit the suggestion of the contemporary homunculi that Lucilius was his superior in genius as well as in rank, his acquiescence merely led to a further indictment. His quiet, ironical bow, the only way in which a man of good breeding could answer such vulgarity, has been used by some modern critics as if it were a confession of weakness. The stupid reference to his "low origin" has only occasionally affected the criticism of his work in modern times, but it has not yet died out. It has been more common in Germany than in England. In his estimate of the comparative merits of Horace and Lucilius, Professor Saintsbury, unfortunately, follows Mommsen—and Mommsen in his estimate of Lucilius would have made a perfect specimen for Thackeray's *Book of Snobs.* Eminent historian as Mommsen may have been, his literary criticism is sometimes fantastic. His own countrymen, according to Warde Fowler, repudiated his judgment on Cicero, whom he described as the "worst type of journalist." In certain periods, indeed, there has been a depreciation of the great work of Cicero, who practically recreated and gave its definitive form to the Latin tongue. But the depreciation has always come from the men who failed to understand the true function of the literary artist. Cicero ranked with those interpretative artists who, by insight as well as by expressive power, are sometimes more creative than the philosophers whom they interpret. He gave life and vitality and many new relationships to ideas which might otherwise have remained in the quarry. It is a mistake to suppose that the man who hews the marble out of the mountain is always more highly gifted than the man who carves the statue. Even that enemy of Cicero, Julius Caesar, said that he had "advanced the boundaries of the Latin genius." St. Augustine in his *Confessions,* tells us that Cicero's book *Hortensius* entirely changed his feelings in the days of his paganism, *et ad te ipsum, domine, mutavit preces meas.* He is the Roman classic more frequently quoted than any other by St. Thomas Aquinas, who built some of his ideas into the mighty cathedral of the *Summa.* Professor Rand in his *Cicero at the Court of Aquinas* points out that, in this

instance, St. Thomas gives him the victory over Aristotle. If
Cicero had done no more than that, he would still be one of the
great movers and shapers of the world.

But Mommsen surpasses himself in the distinction he draws
between Lucilius, whom he calls, "The Knight of Suessa" and
Terence, whom he calls the "African Slave." If he had done
this to emphasize the genius of Terence in accordance with the
principle of Horace that, when a man starts with a handicap, he
deserves all the more credit, there might have been some faint
justification for the irrelevant antithesis. But Mommsen used
it as part of a critical argument, to crush the better man. In the
same way he tells us that Lucilius was a better poet than Horace
and ignores the verdict of history to do so.

Although Lucilius was born more than a century before
Horace, he owes his place in the textbooks almost entirely to
the younger poet. It is unlikely that he has ever been discussed
in modern times except in relation to Horace, whose name will
be found sprinkled over every page and almost every paragraph
dealing with the older satirist. Only a few fragments of Lucilius
remain—almost all of them uncouth and slipshod in style; and
sometimes absurdly dotted over with Greek words, which stand
out in the viscous lump like raisins in an uncooked pudding. He
was greatly admired in his own day; and as Quintilian remarked, "even in ours." That little word "even" is a delightful
example of the "hedging" with which Quintilian occasionally
made concessions to both sides, while quietly pushing his reader
over to the side he preferred. "Lucilius had wonderful learning," he says. Quintilian does not agree with Horace that the
verse of the elder satirist was a "muddy stream"; but, at the
same time, he thinks Horace immensely superior—"far terser
and purer, and without a rival in his sketches of character."
When to this we add Quintilian's opinion that Horace was the
best of the Roman lyrical poets, and indeed "the only one

worth reading," we can hardly contest the right of Horace to an opinion about the older poet.

Modern scholars are inclined to agree with Horace. Macleane speaks of the "absurd jargon" of Greek and Latin used by Lucilius; and when two men of eminence, like Mommsen and Saintsbury, profess to find Lucilius the greater poet, it is difficult to avoid a suspicion that something "not altogether alien" from a desire to avoid the commonplace truth is affecting their judgment. Some of the arguments they use are quite illegitimate. Mommsen, for instance, takes advantage of what might be called a courtesy phrase in Horace, a note of half-ironical politeness and deference, to suggest that Horace himself had acknowledged his inferiority to Lucilius. Horace was, in fact, answering the critics who complained of his entirely just examination of both the faults and the merits of Lucilius. These critics had accused Horace of a want of respect for the older writer, whom they declared to be the "sole begetter" of what was then called "satire." They thought Lucilius the greatest poet that ever lived. They would have liked the world to understand that Horace was a mere imitator.

It was natural enough for Horace in his reply to acquiesce, with that polite bow, to their contention that Lucilius was his superior in literature, and—as they also nobly contended—in rank; but it is utterly uncritical to take any man's polite bow in those circumstances as evidence of his inferiority. "I never make way for a blackguard," said the lout who met Chesterfield on a narrow sidewalk. "I *always* do," replied Chesterfield; and, with a bow, courteously circumnavigated the ponderous obstacle. Mommsen not only uses the bow of Horace as evidence of inferiority, but he does it in the face of two thousand years of history, which have irrevocably consigned Lucilius to oblivion and Horace to immortality. Moreover, the critics who take so seriously a single ironical phrase in which Horace speaks of

Lucilius as the "original inventor of all satire," completely ignore the really serious and closely reasoned passage of the tenth satire in which Horace had already examined and dismissed the preposterous claim. There, in accordance with the principle that "literature is an organic growth, not a series of disconnected explosions, or unrelated and entirely new inventions," Horace affirms that satire did not begin with Lucilius. The old Greek comedy, he says, represented by Aristophanes and others, would unhesitatingly satirize the scoundrels of their day. On these writers he says in the fourth satire, Lucilius depends entirely (*hinc omnis pendet Lucilius*). These writers Lucilius has followed (*hosce secutus*), changing only the metres of the verse. Even supposing that Horace is wrong in this assertion, how is it possible for any sound critic to take the little ironical bow at the end of the poem literally, as a complete contradiction of the serious argument that preceded it? Yet this is exactly what Mommsen did.

The argument of Saintsbury is even more unsound. Following Mommsen, he refers to the fragment by Lucilius on Virtue (which Mommsen quotes at length) and refuses to accept the verdict of the modern critics whom he calls "our greatest English Latinists." He draws a curious distinction between linguistic and literary merit (for use, apparently, on this occasion only), and then makes this remarkable affirmation: "It (the fragment on Virtue) has a far sincerer, loftier, and more truly poetical tone than anything of the kind in Horace and than most things in Juvenal. And everywhere I see quality, passion, phrase. Here at least I can agree with Cicero."

Highly impressive. It is pleasant to know of that agreement with Cicero in view of the trouncing that Professor Saintsbury gave Horace for the much more modest remark that he would be proud if his verses were approved by his friends, Virgil—who at the time was known only for his eclogues—and Octavius

Musa. Saintsbury was fond of quotation, and in view of the
high place he gives this fragment by Lucilius, it would seem
to be a mistake that he forgot to give his own readers an opportunity of agreeing with Cicero. It is undoubtedly the best of
the surviving fragments of Lucilius:

> *Virtus, Albine, est pretium persolvere verum*
> *quis in versamur, quis vivimus rebus potesse;*
> *virtus est homini scire id quod quaeque habeat res;*
> *virtus scire homini rectum, utile, quid sit honestum,*
> *quae bona, quae mala item, quid inutile, turpe, inhonestum;*
> *virtus, quaerendae finem rei scire modumque:*
> *virtus, divitiis pretium persolvere posse;*
> *virtus, id dare quod re ipsa debetur honori;*
> *hostem esse atque inimicum hominum morumque malorum,*
> *contra defensorem hominum morumque bonorum,*
> *magnificare hos, his bene velle, his vivere amicum;*
> *commoda praeterea patriai prima putare,*
> *deinde parentum, tertia iam postremaque nostra.*[1]

The passage has a certain resemblance to some of the minor
Elizabethans, and Professor Saintsbury himself compares it in
its roughness with Marston. But it is possible to maintain that
any poem dealing with vague generalities about Virtue in a
style no better than that of Marston can be compared with
the work of Horace, even in his early satires, or with that later
poem (picked out by the foremost of French critics as among the

---

[1] "Virtue, Albinus, is to be able to pay the price of the things among which
we move, and by which we live: virtue is to know how each thing turns out for
a man: virtue, to know what is right, useful, honorable, for a man, what things
are good, also what bad, what useless, base, dishonorable; virtue, to know the end
and method of seeking wealth: virtue, to be able to pay the price of riches: virtue,
to give what is really due, to honor; to be the foe and hater of bad men and
customs, but the defender of good men and customs, to esteem these, to wish them
well, to live with them as a friend; moreover, to put first the interests of the
fatherland, next, of parents, then, third and last, our own." *Lucilius Ex libris
incertis.* (Lact. *Inst.* VI, 5, 2.)

finest in all literature) which begins, *"Hoc erat in votis?"* This is what Sainte-Beuve says about it:

Whatever may be the distractions and confusions of modern life, that man will not have renounced the delicate cultivation of the mind, or his intercourse with the Graces, who can spend even a quarter of an hour, in a trench or in the waiting-room of an inn, with his Horace, reading the *"Hoc erat in votis."*

As for what Professor Saintsbury calls "phrase," it is the very quality in which Horace stands supreme. In his *Odes,* as Mackail observed, "every other line has become proverbial." It is by their perfection of "phrase" that they wing their way through centuries.

It should be remembered that Horace was not fighting for his own hand. He was very much in earnest about the necessity for finer workmanship, a closer attention to style and purity of language, if the literature of Rome was to take its place with that of Greece.

There is not a writer in the world who does not owe an immense debt to his predecessors; and the bigger the writer, the bigger the debt. Shakespeare is the outstanding example of this, not only in the subject matter of his work, but even in the plots and the very form of the blank verse in which they are written. The debt of Virgil to Homer has probably been increased by the German discovery that Homer never existed; and the debt of Homer himself to his predecessors is so great that we have at least to admit that they wrote his works. The critics who place his works, in point of art, above those of Dante and Milton are still finding it difficult to explain how a collection of folk-songs should come to be organized into Greek hexameters, in so unified a pattern that, from Horace to Landor, or for that matter to Andrew Lang, extremely well-qualified poets and critics have saluted in their non-existent author the artistic "crown of indivisible supremacy." The fact that Homer "sometimes nods" would not have seemed to Horace a proof that the sleeper of whom he speaks was somebody else. Nor would he have thought that because Spenser wrote his *Faerie Queen* in a language taken from several periods, and certainly not the language of Elizabethan England, that the *Faerie Queen* must have been composed by a committee of ballad singers in the time of Ethelred the Unready. But undoubtedly Spenser could not have obtained either his subject matter, his metrical form, or his curiously composite language, if he had not been able to draw very largely on a great number of predecessors. It is difficult, therefore, to understand the statement of some commentators, that Horace is altogether "crude" and wrong in suggesting that Lucilius owed everything to the old Greek comedy. In the first place, we know very little about the works of Lucilius as a whole. Only fragments survive; and Horace—surely a somewhat considerable man of letters—was familiar with the whole body of his work. These very critics, moreover, admit the close connection between the satires of Lucilius and the earlier satires of Ennius. They enlarge on his debt to Bion, the Borysthenite, and drag in the extremely crude Fescennine verses, as if they were a highly preferable source for the sole begetter of Roman satire. It is all very impressive; but if they prefer these other debts, there is still no reason to suggest that Lucilius was any more original than Ennius. There are differences, of course; but the differences are not so great as the resemblances; and, in point of art, there is more difference between the rough verses of Lucilius and the polished hexameters of Horace than there is between Lucilius and Ennius.

It seems incredible that, in his argument for Lucilius against Horace, Professor Saintsbury should have introduced as part of the indictment the "too famous sneer" of Horace at Catullus and Calvus. This mistake has been corrected a score of times. It is true that their temperaments being so different, Catullus being almost everything in extremes, Horace may have lacked enthusiasm for him, may even have criticized him. If he did, there is nothing wrong about that. But there is no evidence. A "sneer" is a different thing; and all the best authorities agree that there is no suggestion of a "sneer" at Catullus and Calvus. Nor does the text lend the faintest support to the suggestion. What Horace said was that a certain bad musician in Rome, named Hermogenes did nothing but sing Catullus and Calvus. To complain that a boring acquaintance did nothing but declaim Shakespeare would not be to sneer at Shakespeare. There was probably a vague idea in the minds of a few critics that the coupling of Catullus with Calvus was itself a sneer. But nobody in the time of Horace would have thought so. Cicero had praised Calvus very highly indeed. He was frequently coupled with Catullus, exactly as we speak of Keats and Shelley, without the slightest suggestion of anything derogatory. Occasionally the charge is somewhat carelessly repeated by modern writers who quote, out of its context, the single line—"skilled only at singing Calvus and Catullus":

Nil praeter Calvum et doctus cantare Catullum.

"Nothing can sweeten that," says a recent writer who on many other pages shows a fine critical sense. But it would not need to be sweetened if he had only given the rest of the sentence about Hermogenes, the singer. Still less would it be necessary if he had quoted what Horace says in other satires about Hermogenes and his habit of singing the poems which he thumbed over at the bookshops. It would be quite finally unnecessary if the modern critic had looked again at the passage in which Horace objects to Hermogenes singing the poems of no less an author than Quintus Horatius Flaccus himself. It is quite inexplicable that any critic should take part of a sentence out of its context in this way. It is just as misleading as the constant quotation of Byron's too famous line: "Farewell, Horace, whom I hated so." Byron admired Horace; and imitated him in one poem of considerable length which he entitled "Hints from Horace." When the context of his "too famous" lines is given, the effect of his farewell is very different. He is actually imitating Horace again, and echoing the very feeling that Horace himself expressed about the fate of poetry in the schools:

> Then, farewell, Horace, whom I hated so
> Not for thy faults, but mine; it is a curse
> To understand, not feel, thy lyric flow;
> To comprehend, but never love thy verse,
> Although no deeper Moralist rehearse
> Our little life, nor Bard prescribe his art,
> Nor livelier Satirist the conscience pierce,
> Awakening without wounding the touched heart;—
> Yet fare thee well—upon Soracte's ridge we part.

This leads him directly up to that magnificent stanza on "Rome, my country, city of the soul"; and there is a real connection, though he does not state it. Still more interesting, and always overlooked, is the passage preceding the "too famous" line. It alludes to the lines of Horace describing

> The long ridge of Soracte white with snow,
> The straining woods all bowed beneath their load,
> The streams, at winter's touch, all frozen still:

> *Vides ut alta stet nive candidum*
> *Soracte, nec iam sustineant onus*
> *silvae laborantes, geluque*
> *flumina constiterint acuto:*

Byron's answer actually embodies a eulogy of Horace which goes far beyond anything ever said of him by any writer in any language. It begins with a description of the Alps, the new-trodden snow of Jungfrau, and the glaciers of Mont Blanc. He tells us that, although he has seen the Acroceraunian mountains of old time and has watched the eagles flying over Parnassus itself like soaring spirits; and though he has looked on Olympus, Aetna, and Atlas, the Alps made all these hills appear like "things of lesser dignity,

> All, save the lone Soracte's height, display'd
> Not *now* in snow, which asks the lyric Roman's aid
> For our remembrance, and from out the plain
> Heaves like a long-swept wave about to break.

Soracte is a comparatively small hill, but the picture that Horace paints in the ninth ode of the first book could surely have elicited no more tremendous response from the poet who is commonly supposed to have hated him.

X

THE USURER AND THE
COUNTRY LIFE

A FURTHER STAGE IN THE FRIENDSHIP AND WHAT MAY BE
called the conversations in poetry between Horace and Virgil
is marked in the second epode. Just as Virgil's fourth eclogue
appeared to be a reply to the pessimistic poem in which Horace
advocated a migration to the Fortunate Islands, so—in the second epode—Horace appears to be making his own comment on
Virgil's poems advocating a return to the land of Italy.

The *Georgics* were not published in a complete volume till
the year 29 B.C. But Virgil began to write them at least seven
years earlier, and undoubtedly they were discussed among his
friends long before they were given to the copyists for general
publication. The second epode of Horace was probably written
during this time of discussion. It has many characteristics of
his early work; and it appears to bear directly on some passages
in the second book of the *Georgics*, especially that famous one
beginning:

> *O fortunatos nimium, sua si bona norint,*
> *agricolas!*

Sellar calls the second epode "the most poetical and at the same
time the most perplexing in its meaning." His chief reason for
saying this was that the last four lines of the poem may be taken
as a cynical jest at the beautiful rhapsody on the country life
which precedes them. No lines of Horace are more familiar
than what may be called the beautiful part of the poem, beginning:

> *Beatus ille qui procul negotiis,*
> *ut prisca gens mortalium . . .*

"Happy is he who far from this world's busy cares . . ." It is not one of his best poems; but it has probably been translated into verse more often, and into more languages, than any other Latin lyric. It has been made especially familiar to English readers through the juvenile paraphrase by Pope:

> Happy the man whose wish and care
> A few paternal acres bound,
> Content to breathe his native air
> In his own ground.
>
> Whose herds with milk, whose fields with bread,
> Whose flocks supply him with attire,
> Whose trees in summer yield him shade,
> In winter fire.
>
> Blest, who can unconcern'dly find
> Hours, days, and years slide soft away,
> In health of body, peace of mind,
> Quiet by day,
>
> Sound sleep by night; study and ease
> Together mixt; sweet recreation;
> And Innocence, which most does please
> With meditation.
>
> Thus let me live, unseen, unknown,
> Thus unlamented let me die,
> Steal from the world, and not a stone
> Tell where I lie.

But English readers are not so familiar with the four amusing lines which close the original poem, and were not represented in Pope's youthful paraphrase. Horace, in fact, suddenly gives the reader of the Latin poem a humorous jolt by adding: "When the usurer Alfius had said all these fine things, he called in all his money to set himself up in a farm. But a week or two later he was trying to reinvest it in the City."

Many translators have omitted that amusing conclusion, apparently perplexed by the same problem as Sellar, finding it "cynical, or contradictory, or destructive of the beauty of the poem."

But there is no problem here that cannot be solved with a smile. It is a stroke of deliberate art, of course, with a Socratic chuckle in it, very like that with which Horace ends his epistle on the wise man.

"The wise man is second only to Jupiter—rich, free, honored, handsome; in short, a king of kings; and a very sound one, except when he has one of those nasty little colds in his head":

> *Ad summam: sapiens uno minor est Jove, dives,*
> *liber, honoratus, pulcher, rex denique regum,*
> *praecipue sanus, nisi cum pituita molesta est.*

I feel sure that Horace learned this touch from the amusing "asides" which Plato records of Socrates. Many of these were in exactly the tone of the lines about the usurer; and Horace discovered a more definite artistic use for them. They were no longer mere "asides." He found that they could complete a poem with the blessing of surprise. He used the device again and again to give the last masterful touch that brings art full-circle back to nature. He used it sometimes with the happy nonchalance of a man who is always ready to smile at his own enthusiasms, real as they may be. Sometimes it gave a neat epigrammatic conclusion to a conversation which might, in the ordinary course of nature, trail on to an unnecessary length. Sometimes it is like the closing of a little scene in Molière by the entry of another character; or the snap of the couplets which bring down the curtain in some of Shakespeare's comedies. Sometimes, when it appears at first glance to be quite irrelevant, it enhances by a subtle contrast the effect of what went before; or, like the motley-minded sayings of Touchstone, or

Jaques, or even Hamlet, brings the real meaning home, and gives it a sharper point by apparently making light of it or dismissing it.

This second epode is not a jest at Virgil's praise of the country; nor is Horace cynically pricking the bubble of his own rhapsody. What may be called the beautiful part of the poem would be out of character if the ideas are supposed to have originated with the usurer. But the usurer is evidently fascinated by the ideas of somebody else. Perhaps he had been reading Virgil's eclogues, or studying the new propaganda to promote agriculture in Italy. It is not necessary to suppose that the usurer even uttered all those fine sentiments. Editors have chosen to include them all, in a sort of monologue, by putting their own quotation marks at the beginning of the poem. But the usurer's "reactions" might very well begin at the sixty-first line with "*has inter epulas*," where the rich man's ideas introduce a different tone, and instead of the simple peasants described in the earlier and more beautiful part of the poem, we hear the owner of a "wealthy house" beginning to talk about the troops of slaves he will employ to do all the work for him. Moreover, in the forefront of his own praise of the country life, Horace uses one word which would have been impossible to the usurer. The word *paterna* in the third line strikes the keynote, and gives the real significance of the poem. *Paterna rura* (paternal acres), tilled by the men who knew and loved them, were very different from confiscated lands handed over to inexperienced farmers, or purchased by rich usurers from the city. The political side of all that dispossession and replacement had not appealed to Horace. He would not have gone so far, perhaps, as the English yeoman who remarked that the only way to make a success of agriculture was to be born in a manger and marry a dairy-maid. But it must be remembered that Horace was still smarting under the loss of his own paternal acres. Perhaps his visit to Venusia, on his way back from Brundisium, had given him a glimpse of some unsatisfactory new owner of his father's land. However that may be, in this poem he was again displaying his independence and criticizing the new political attitude toward the land. The whole point of the poem is in the contrast between the deeply-rooted life of the true country-man, going peacefully on from generation to generation, and some of the new owners of lands from which the true country-man had been ruthlessly and sometimes quite unreasonably driven out. Virgil himself had been driven out, not because he had been engaged in conflict with the government—he had not been a Republican like Horace—but merely because the whole district in which he lived had been placed under an undiscriminating ban. His estate had been restored eventually, but it is said that he was first offered a confiscated estate belonging to someone else, and that, knowing the distress of the former owner, Virgil refused to take it.

It was the policy of Maecenas to settle the returning soldiers on the land and induce them to become farmers; and in connection with this he was eager to encourage Virgil's famous poem in praise of country life. He certainly aroused the interest of Augustus in the work; and it appealed to the idealism of Virgil to think that swords were now to be beaten into ploughshares, with a great light on the horizon. Like Horace, he hated war, and loved the peaceful ways of the countryside. He wrote the poem sincerely, and there are passages in it which have seldom or never been surpassed in the literature of the world.

But he paid dearly for his innocent cooperation with Augustus; for in the second edition of the poem, the jealous autocrat insisted that Virgil should cut out the praises of his friend Cornelius Gallus with which the fourth book originally culminated. Virgil thereupon inserted the story of Orpheus and Eurydice, beautiful in itself, but artistically quite irrelevant. "A standing proof," Sellar calls it, "of the malign influence which the Imperial despotism exercised on the inspiration of genius, as well as on all sincere feelings."

In the second of the *Georgics*, the passage quoted earlier must have touched Horace to the quick. It was not only beautiful as poetry, but it must have awakened a thousand nostalgic memories of wood and stream and secluded valley in the mind of the younger poet:

How more than happy are those tillers of the soil if they only knew their blessings, for whom, far from the clash of arms, the most righteous earth pours forth from her soil a harvest so easily won.

Virgil, of course, idealized it. He was always in the world of perfection, or, perhaps unconsciously, using the things of this imperfect world to shadow forth a better. Horace, on the other hand—though the cry went to his heart—was more realistic. He could see in his mind's eye an old sunburnt farmer at Venusia shaking a wise head over that word *facilem*. In many passages Virgil painted the constant struggle with Nature, and the hard-working life of the peasant; but over it all he cast the light of a world elsewhere. Sometimes with exquisite art he melted his native landscape into the glens and mountain pastures of Sicily. If the sun beat down too strongly, he would lead you at a step into the cool valley of Tempe; and before you came to the end of it, he would dissolve those mountain walls again into the snakeless meadows of the Golden Age. He wrote of his native land with so much idealism that he became the poet of an unknown Paradise; but he and his friend, that other half of his soul, were still on earth; and Horace, who had few illusions, became the poet of the Italy he knew.

Virgil, of course, had a deep understanding of the old country life and customs of Italy. It was probably in accordance with the tactful suggestions of Maecenas that he appears so often to be addressing the new owners, unacquainted with the land. He tells them that they must learn about the different soils, and how to use the pruning-hook, and how to plant trees; and what a happy life they will have. He omitted to mention a great many hard facts; but he was absolutely sincere. His poem was one of those rare conjunctions where propaganda and inspiration can cooperate.

But Horace disliked the government project, for he probably knew that certain Roman circles were fostering a great deal of false sentiment about this new love of the country. If we examine what I have called the beautiful part of Horace's poem, we find that it deals with generalities which—while they appeal to the real lover of the country, are of just the kind that would be used by the sentimentalists—the warbling of birds; the shade of the trees; the logs for the winter fire. If we take it that the usurer really uttered all those fine thoughts, there is still nothing perplexing about it. Indeed, there is an additional touch of real humor in his rapturous allusion to "paternal acres." Sellar is one of the best interpreters of the more serious passages in Horace, and certainly one of the most distinguished scholars of his day; but—unlike the Matthew Arnold of Max Beerbohm's cartoon—he was always "wholly serious." In all the pages—those really beautiful pages—that Sellar devotes to the poetry of Horace, there is not the faintest trace of a smile. He would have found less perplexity, perhaps, in this famous little poem, *Beatus ille*, if he had read some of Mr. Belloc's writings; or studied with care some of the highly finished poems in *Punch*. A certain book entitled *Horace at Cambridge*, and another, *Anni Fugaces*, both by writers on the editorial staff of that periodical in the nineteenth century, reproduce exactly the same mixture of true sentiment, and irony at its misuse, which we find in the second epode.

Pope in his paraphrase emphasizes the idea of the deeply rooted country life by adding the phrase "native air" and "his own ground." As a rule, the eighteenth century could not really recapture the charm of the Augustan poetry. It conveys a sense of the compact interlocking phrases and the precision of the Latin idiom; but as a rule, it offers you the reproduction as if it were an amber snuff-box. The forms of speech, so natural to the Latin, become a sophisticated gesture, almost an affectation, disguising the authentic voice of poetry. The villa at Twickenham is a very long way from the Sabine farm, and farther still from Venusia. But Pope wrote his paraphrase long before he had seen Twickenham, and when he was too young to wear a powdered wig. Perhaps for this reason his little poem, which he called *Ode on Solitude*, is by far his best imitation of the form, and certainly his most successful attempt to convey the poetry, of Horace. He is said to have written it when he was twelve years old. If so, I think he must have touched it up later. But it has hardly a trace of that true knowledge and love of the country which shines through the irony of the original. Nor is there a trace of the irony itself, or even of the realism which, if we read the Latin poem carefully, brings the thought of the usurer into the opening lines, so that the conclusion need not be such a jolt after all. *Procul negotiis,* far from the business of the city, is not quite the same thing as the reference to *care* in the first line of the paraphrase.

Scores of famous poets have attempted to translate that brief epode. Desportes, in his poem beginning, *"O bien heureux qui peut passer sa vie"*; Ben Jonson in *The Forest*; Dryden and Cowley—all tried their hands at it. Curiously enough, none of them could render more than a slight part of its beauty or its humor, and usually the humor was omitted entirely. The poet who came nearest, perhaps, to suggesting the real feeling for the country was Herrick in his poem *On the*

Country Life, which diverges widely and is much longer, but has many suggestions from both Horace and Virgil. Herrick comes nearest in his feeling for the country because he was deeply rooted to it in his own way.

It is not impossible that the circulation of the second epode in Rome, and the discussion which would naturally be aroused by its ironical treatment of a sentiment which the government wished to encourage, may have led directly to a very important event in the life of Horace. This is only a conjecture, but it would be the most likely thing in the world that Maecenas should have said in conversation with Virgil,

"What does your friend Flaccus mean by this poem about the usurer and the paternal acres?"
And nothing is more likely than that Virgil should have replied,

"I am afraid he is rather unhappy about his own paternal acres at Venusia. You see, he has been somewhat in the position of my Meliboeus, "*Nos patriam fugimus, et dulcia linquimus arva.*" To which Maecenas would reply,

"I wonder if we couldn't find a little farm somewhere else that would suit him better."

XI

THE SABINE FARM

THE SABINE FARM WAS BESTOWED UPON HORACE IN THE YEAR 32 B.C., after he had made his headquarters in Rome for nearly a decade. Virgil had already recovered his original property; and, though Horace obtained another and—in many ways—a more desirable abode than the "poor farm" which had been taken away from his father, it was none the less an act of restitution, not of patronage. Maecenas had the disposal of many properties that had been taken over by the State, and it cost him nothing personally to instal Horace in one of them. The State had taken away and the State had made restitution. There are writers who apparently do not like to see any great man escaping the humiliation of dependence upon the whim of a patron. These writers demur strongly to the idea of restitution; but they give no reason for their objection to the clear-cut argument on the other side. This does not in the least detract from the part played by Maecenas. It rather heightens it, and allows us to concentrate our attention on the really fine discrimination with which he picked out Virgil and Horace, long before they had written their most important works. Horace was naturally grateful to Maecenas; but he was grateful to a friend and lover of poetry, not to a patron. As we have seen, Horace offered to return the gift rather than let it be regarded as the price of his independence. He made it quite clear that this was his point of view in accepting the gift. If Maecenas himself could have agreed with those writers who would make the poet more subservient, we do actually have the terms which Horace definitely laid down in his own writings, and that is all that concerns us here.

It was one of the most fortunate gifts in literature; for it made Maecenas immortal, and it brought Horace back, like a prodigal son, to something that resembled his father's house. It might almost seem that the kind old farmer of Venusia was still watching over his son from another world, quietly leading him home to the hills and woods and stream and the familiar sights and sounds of the farm that was his boyhood's Paradise. We can imagine his first entry upon his own land in that peaceful valley: a lonely little man with greying hair, catching his breath for sheer pleasure as he stood gazing at the sun-flooded farm-house on the knoll above the river. Most of the things that he saw and heard and loved have not altered in the two thousand years between his time and ours; the sound of the flowing river; the lowing of the herd in the pasture; the murmur of the bees in the walled garden, say exactly the same thing to us as they did to him; and to Horace they were memories of something well-nigh lost in those crowded years at Rome—

> Where each man strives nor knows for what he strives,
> And each half lives a hundred different lives.

We can picture him exploring every nook and corner of his new property; walking first, perhaps, to the farmyard behind the *villa rustica,* as the back portion of the house, in which the eight farm servants lived, was called. It was a spacious walled farmyard with a big stone drinking pool, in the center, for the cattle. In the northeastern corner there was a sheep-fold where the shepherd was already securing his flock, for his day's work was nearly done; and, although it was fine Spring weather, the flock could not be left on the hill-side in those days. There were too many wolves for that. He would greet Horace with a friendly grin, and they would talk for a while, leaning on the wall of the sheep-fold. Then, perhaps, they went together to look at the hen-house and the *aviarium* which held several hundred plump missel-thrushes, black-birds, and quail, for the delectation of future guests. There seemed to be a great number of them, but four-and-twenty black-birds do not make a very large pie. Above them, in the center of the north wall, rose the turret-shaped *columbarium* or pigeon-house. It was painted white because it was thought that pigeons had a great liking for that color. There were scores of pigeons, too, some of them bowing and spreading their tails like fans on the roof of the barn, others sunning themselves or cooing to their mates on the farm-house roof, while others were circling in the air high above it. Horace had already made a friend of his shepherd, and they crossed to the northwest corner to look at the goat pens. Everything was in remarkably good order. The barns and store-sheds ranged against the wall on either side, between the house and the pens for the live-stock, were all well-stocked and well-kept. Perhaps Maecenas had told the bailiff that the new owner of the farm would prefer beauty and order to profit.

The scent of wood-smoke greeted him on the threshold of the large kitchen, where the *vilica* was already superintending the preparations for the evening meal, in which, as a kind of housewarming feast, the whole establishment might share on this occasion. It was rather dark in the kitchen except for the blaze on the hearth. In one of the solid stone walls Horace saw something that carried him straight back to Venusia—a broad opening through which the oxen in the adjoining cattle-stalls could look at the fire. The Italian peasants in those days believed that the pleasure of looking at the fire, especially on long winter nights, improved the coats of the oxen and induced the cows to give better milk. The opening had only a half-door, as high as a man's waist. The cattle sometimes laid their heads across it, while the cooking went on; and, at all times after dusk, many friendly glances were exchanged between the dark glowing eyes on either side of the barrier.

It was not what the modern world would call hygienic; but the cattle were out most of the day on the clean dry hill-side; fresh wheat-straw was plentiful for their bedding, and nothing could have been healthier than those peasant faces in the firelight. They looked pleased to see the new owner of the farm and he amused the *vilica* hugely by describing to her a puzzle-banquet which he had recently attended in Rome.

The corridor led him from the kitchen across the broad porticos that separated the *villa rustica* from the front section of the house, the *villa urbana,* where his furniture and his books had already been installed. On his right as he entered there was the heating apparatus, the *tepidarium* and the bath, all very simple by Roman standards, but more elaborate than anything known in Europe between the fall of Rome and the nineteenth century. Beyond this, on his right, were three or four small bedrooms, all spotless, with one or two delicate paintings on the walls, and mosaic floors in a very simple pattern. Beyond these again was the summer dining-room with the couches made by Archias; and immediately opposite, across the central *atrium,* was another dining-room for winter. Behind this was the library and several more bedrooms. The house was a little larger than a lonely bachelor might require; but it was good to know that he had plenty of room for his friends. The furniture in the house was far too plain to please an Albius. Horace had none of those precious tables with ivory pedestals for which Cicero had paid so many thousands of sesterces. Like the lecti, most of his furniture was made by Archias, who worked in cedar-wood and was just as good a craftsman in his day as Hepplewhite in our own eighteenth century.

Going into his library he found that his books, so neatly rolled on their cedar rods, had acquired a new charm from their surroundings. There were all his beloved Greek poets in one section. His Roman poets occupied another, beginning with Ennius and Lucilius, and coming down through Lucretius and Virgil to none other than Quintus Horatius Flaccus himself. He had some good editions now; and as he looked at them, he remembered, perhaps, with a slight dryness in the throat, a day in Rome when a very little boy and his father had entered a book-shop together and, deciding that the books were too costly, had stolen a glimpse or two at the portraits painted on the first pages.

There was another section which, in some ways, was becoming more important to him now than his poets. Perhaps it was natural for this other interest to develop as his hair grew grey. It was not that he loved his poets less, but that his mind had begun to hunger for more light on man's destiny, and perhaps his own relationship to the Power or powers manifested in the universe. He had never ranged himself with any school of philosophy. He had taken what he thought he required from all of them. He could smile at himself, a little whimsically, for taking up that subject now; for he knew that the search was unending and that life was very short. But one of the great joys of this new-found peace in the country would be the opportunity it gave him of really getting to know what his philosophers could tell about the great secret. They were all there. Plato and Aristotle, with their commentators, occupied two very noble cedar chests, in places of honor; but, curiously enough, the Epicureans whom he had chiefly affected in his youth had been promoted to an upper shelf from which it would be rather more difficult to take them down; and the Stoics were placed more conveniently to his hand. Cicero was probably within easy reach, with his book *De Republica* and one or two other volumes.

In many ways his life at the Sabine Farm may be pictured almost as clearly as that of Pope at Twickenham, or Tennyson in the Isle of Wight. The old adage that a happy country has no history is grimly true if it be taken as an ironical comment on history itself, or on the usual conception of it. Otherwise, it would be a remark worthy of the Fat Boy in *Pickwick Papers* who was never happy unless, in the intervals between his profound slumbers and almost academic snores, he was able to make your flesh creep. The quiet and sensitive records of art and literature—as the best modern historians increasingly testify—have a far greater value than those blood-stained footprints of bogus giants on the sands of oblivion from which the young have so long been expected to learn the history of their civilization and its glorious progress from the Roman catapult to the atomic bomb.

Certain kinds of biography and autobiography are often the best historical sources. Plato, in his account of the last days of Socrates; Tacitus, in his little masterpiece on Agricola; St. Augustine, in his confessions; these, and others like them, give us a better understanding of their times than any formal history.

Poetry, when it is a really personal expression, often fulfils the same function. It should be remarked that this is largely due to the perfection, the exquisite precision, of its metrical and musical form, which in its finest examples reflects every inflection of thought and feeling, so that they come to us exactly as they left the poet. The restrictions to which he submitted, the discipline of line and measure, are more than compensated by the fact that when the thing said falls into its "inevitable" and perfect form, and is therefore said perfectly, it will continue to speak perfectly to others for endless generations. It becomes indestructible and acquires the authority of a natural law.

The Roman poets—especially Horace—interpret their period to us as only the living personal voice can do it. In the best of their poetry we are indeed listening to a living voice. Every note of it, every cadence, every pulse and tremor of the living, breathing human being can reach us through their words as intimately as if they were in the same room with us. The metrical form gives to every syllable the precision of a note in music.

But it is not in the tumultuous setting of Rome that we really come to know Horace and his times best, but in the quiet retreat among the Sabine hills. He continued to visit Rome at certain seasons of the year; but his visits became less and less frequent. His life in the country was extremely peaceful and in some ways surprisingly lonely. If poetry, as Wordsworth said, "is emotion recollected in tranquillity," the Sabine Farm gave him every opportunity for writing it. Part of his pleasure in the place was the contrast of its wholesome fare and plain living with the repulsive materialism, the greed and gormandizing of Rome. But though he grew to love the place more and more, there is no evidence at all that he had any constant companionship there. The life was pleasant, but half the pleasure was in its fine asceticism. Nothing could be further from the truth than the popular picture of a Horace continually chapleted with roses, drinking endless cups of wine, and, like Chesterton's glorious heathen, filling his life with love-affairs, his house with dancing-girls. Tyndaris, if she is not a figment of the imagination, seems to have required some persuading to bring her music into that lonely valley. Young women of that vivacious kind do not often wish to leave the gaiety of the metropolis to entertain a middle-aged bachelor at an isolated farm, thirty miles from any excitement, and with only a horse or a mule to carry them there. Horace had occasional visitors—Maecenas among them—and perhaps on those occasions Tyndaris, or someone else with vine-leaves in her hair, brought her music to entertain the guests. But—if he really wanted her society—he would have to find it in Rome; and, more and more, as his aims in poetry became clearer to him, he preferred to concentrate on his nine-years-pondered lays, and to live with memory as the great companion.

A few commentators have maintained that his early satires in which he depicts his life at Rome are his most valuable contributions to literature. The sixth satire of the first book, in which he pays that beautiful tribute to his father, stands by itself. It is possible that he wrote it at the Sabine Farm, for it is addressed to Maecenas in terms of a well-established friendship, and memory plays a great part in it. But the earlier satires and some of the epodes which he wrote in Rome can hardly be compared with the best of his later poems. The critics who think otherwise usually have no ear for poetry. Horace himself drew a firm line between his poetry and what he called his verse. The satires, he said, could have been printed as prose without very much loss. He said this partly because he was criticizing Lucilius, of whom he said the same thing; and he did not want to say it of Lucilius with any appearance of self-assertion. But it is true if we disregard the epigrammatic point which verse alone could give to some of the sentences. This is probably why Pope and Swift could quite successfully imitate the satires, but failed completely even to suggest the beauty of the more lyrical work— the prayer for the safety of Virgil, for instance, on his voyage to Attica, or the exquisite little ode beginning "*O fons Bandusiae.*"

The famous character in Molière, who had used prose all his life without knowing it, has his counterpart in a certain kind of modern critic who will deliver judgment on the masterpieces of poetry without the slightest idea that he really cares for nothing but prose. It may be very good prose that he likes; but such a critic confuses all the values by his unconscious demand that poetry shall become something else, and aim at the effects of prose. He would prefer to call it "realism," perhaps. But the music of the songs of Shakespeare in *The Tempest,* and the metrical technique of Horace would mean comparatively nothing to him. A single crudely "realistic" word would give him more pleasure than all the choruses in *Samson Agonistes*. It never occurs to him that he could get everything that he really likes from any vivid bit of ephemeral reporting in a newspaper. Critics of this kind are almost certain to appear, before long, with the theory that the two youthful epodes which are omitted from many editions of Horace are his masterpieces. Particular attention would then be called to their "splendid brutality." The savage point and the Swiftian moral would of course be overlooked. The more immature satires would be selected as the next best; and the other poems would follow in an order inverse to their real merit. The most important, original, and highly finished poems would be described as conventional in form; and, if they gave the final and most perfect expression to some fragment of eternal truth, they would be described as commonplace.

Horace, however, has set that kind of criticism a real problem, by producing all these varieties of work in the wrong order as he advances from immaturity to maturity. Such a critic would have to picture him moving steadily backwards from the "splendidly brutal" epodes of his youth to the disgracefully beautiful order and proportion of that exquisite ode which begins, *"Diffugere nives."* It is the same problem which, if our literature continues on its present happy road to the everlasting bonfire, will confront some of the critics of Tennyson, when they discover that the work which he discarded altogether, or never dreamed of publishing, comes infinitely nearer to their strange new standards of perfection than the work upon which he lavished all the resources of his mature art. He wrote the *Devil and the Lady* when he was only eleven years old, and who can deny that from a certain "modern" point of view the *Devil and the Lady* has none of the conventional merits of *Oenone*, or the effete beauty of that vale in Ida . . . lovelier than all the valleys of Ionian hills. Possibly, if we had some work written by Tennyson in his cradle, we might find that he was a great poet after all.

Nothing could have been more tactful, however, than the announcement by Horace that his early satires were not poetry, but "verse." He does not say that verse was to be despised; for Horace knew as well as any man that the art of verse could give wings to words, and make it certain that they would reach the land of matters unforgot. Verse could do certain things with words that prose could never do. It would be impossible to turn some of the couplets of Pope into prose with anything like the point and sparkle of the original. But when Horace called his satires "verse" and his epodes "iambics," the most jealous of his rivals could hardly accuse him of pretentiousness. In making no claim at present to the great name of poetry, he was following a modest policy of conciliation. It did not save him from the attacks of the less competent; but as Macleane remarked: "There is not the least appearance in any of his writings of his having been spoiled by his good fortune, and probably malignancy never attacked anyone less deserving of attack than Horace."

The assumption by a great many modern writers that all the young women mentioned in the poems of Horace are figments of the imagination is perhaps only less curious than the equally unsatisfactory attempt to suggest that epodes five and seventeen refer to an actual love-affair with the Sorceress Canidia, who seems to be a direct ancestress of the witches in Macbeth, and in some ways even more horrible. But it has had a salutary effect in restraining impossible attempts to identify his more charming feminine characters and to invent love-affairs for Horace on insufficient evidence. The ninth ode of the third book is obviously an imaginary dialogue; I have tried to translate it isometrically:

Horace

He

Once, ah, when I was loved by thee,
  No young impudent arm, over thy shoulder flung,
Found thee whiter than woodland snow.
  Persian demi-gods, then, never were happy as I.

She

Ah, but others thou hadst not sought!
  I, the first of thy loves, ever was first with thee.
Proud as Chloë was Lydia then.
  Ilia, mother of Rome, never was proud as I.

He

Thracian Chloë can sing and sway!
  Who so artful in song, deft in touching the lyre?
I would die for her; gladly, too;
  If by death I could bring—life to a life more dear.

She

Me, too, Love with a torch more true
  Leads ere long to a youth—son of a far-off King.
Die? Yea, laugh at the Fates, could Death
  Fling my love at his feet, light as a flower in Spring.

He

Ah, but what if the old, old love
  Woke, like Spring in the heart, seedlings we thought had died?
What if Chloë, her songs all done,
  Went her way through the night? what if the door stood wide?

She

Ah, then, then, though the stranger's love
  Shone like a star, and thine—thine is a stormy sea;
Tempest-torn, to thy love turn I,
  Once more, living to love; loving, to die, with thee.

Some of these feminine characters may have been drawn from life without being involved in a love-affair with the poet. They have been compared sometimes with those early poems in which Tennyson celebrates Claribel, Eleanore, Isabel, and others whom critics have assumed to be as imaginary as the Lady of Shalott. Unfortunately for this theory, Tennyson was actually paying a tribute to a very real person indeed under the fictitious name of Isabel; and there is no reason to suppose that others in his gallery of portraits were not drawn from real life. It is not necessary for an artist to be in love with his originals. The main point is that we cannot identify the feminine characters named in Horace.

There is little logic, however, in the usual critical assumption that all the masculine characters refer to real persons while none of the feminine characters (except Cinara and the horrible Sorceress, and the wife of Maecenas) can possibly represent anybody at all. There is a sense of life in some of the feminine portraits, even when hardly more than a phrase or two is given to them. It is very difficult to suppose that Horace had no living, breathing human being in his mind when he wrote,

> *dulce ridentem Lalagen amabo,*
> *dulce loquentem.*

It is impossible to translate those phrases without losing something of the quiet music with which some personal memory seems to have endowed them; but, as I once ventured to make an imaginary poet say in one of my *Tales of the Mermaid Tavern:*

> *Dulce ridentem*—laughing through the ages,
> *Dulce loquentem*—O fairer far to me,
> Rarer than the wisdom of all his golden pages
> Floats the happy laughter of his vanished Lalage.

Dulce loquentem—we hear it and we know it.
  Dulce ridentem—so musical and low.
"Mightier than marble is my song!" But did the poet
  Know why little Lalage was mightier even so?

Dulce ridentem—through all the years that sever,
  Clear as o'er yon hawthorn hedge we heard her passing by—
Lalagen amabo—a song may live forever.
  Dulce loquentem—but Lalage must die.

Lalage, as we shall see later, and as Horace himself tells us, was only a child, too young to think of love, or courtship or marriage and, in Italy, that meant very young indeed. Probably she was the child of the *vilica*, or of one of the tenant farmers, a happy little figure, dancing in the sunlight of the poet's rather lonely estate.

Cinara, on the other hand, the good, though "greedy Cinara," was obviously a memory of the earlier days in Rome, after the amnesty. She was known to the circle of Maecenas. Horace writes to him as if she were known to them both. Possibly, like Tyndaris, she was a singer who came to entertain his dinner parties. But—unlike Tyndaris—and despite her greed, she apparently became the penniless poet's mistress for a time. It was all quite open, and—in the pagan codes of the time—it would not have seemed *contra bonos mores*.

Some of the critics who are most certain that the feminine characters in Horace are completely fictitious provide excellent entertainment, for those who enjoy unconscious humor. Sir Theodore Martin, the venerable biographer of Queen Victoria, is quite certain that they never existed, but he also persistently calls them "ladies of a certain class." He quotes with great deference the opinion of Lord Lytton that Glycera was undoubtedly a real lady of that class; and that Horace, definitely, was not in love with her. "Great weight must be attached to the

opinions of so experienced an observer of the female heart,"
says Sir Theodore. It would be far indeed from the mind of Sir
Theodore to suggest that so wide and conclusive a knowledge
had been derived from anything more than "observation" from
a commanding height. He forgets that all we know of the
"female heart" in question is what Horace tells us; for Horace,
though he was nearer to the scene by two thousand years, was not
in a position to observe the "female heart" so comprehensively.
He really knew it chiefly through a series of fictitious characters
which he had created himself. At the same time Sir Theodore's
enthusiasm for these phantoms of delight whom he describes also
as "members of the demi-monde," is as amusing as it is unexpected. He says they were always beautiful and might be seen
"courting the admiration of the wealthy loungers of Rome by
dashing along the Appian Way behind a team of spirited ponies
driven by themselves." According to the unobservant Horace
(in his account of the journey to Brundisium) you had to drive
very slowly along the Appian Way unless you wanted to be
jolted to death; and one cannot help wondering whether the
eyes of Sir Theodore had been going astray after some of the
princely favorites in Hyde Park. In any case the "splendor that
out-vied the Roman matrons" hardly sounds like the plain
living of the Sabine farm. It is with reluctance that one sprinkles
the cold clear water of Bandusia's fountain in the rosy faces of
these venerable and vicarious roués; but in the interests of historical accuracy, it has to be done. It may even be enlightening
to examine what Horace himself said about some of these feminine characters.

Sir Theodore is quite sure that the non-existent Lalage belonged to what he calls the "demi-monde," but what exactly does
Horace tell us about her? She is mentioned in only two of the
odes. In one of them, Horace describes how he was wandering
alone through the woods, singing a song about Lalage; and,

because he was free of wrong-doing (*Integer vitae scelerisque purus*) he escaped from being molested by a wolf. He goes on to say that, for this reason, he will continue to love his sweetly smiling, sweetly speaking Lalage,

> *dulce ridentem Lalagen amabo,*
> *dulce loquentem.*

That is absolutely all. In the other ode, Horace tells us quite clearly that Lalage is a child, too young to think of courtship or marriage, but that one day she will be more interested in such things. That again is absolutely all; and, on that evidence and that alone, the biographer of Queen Victoria calls her "a lady of a certain class" and tries to stick a scarlet letter on her innocent little forehead. In two other cases he does exactly the same thing with a youngster about whom Horace wrote in the spirit of Burns' poem:

> I'm ower young to marry yet.

Horace does it more objectively, and without that touch of the "sly dog" which occasionally creeps into the work of the Scottish poet.

There is not the slightest doubt that Horace followed the custom of the time which saw nothing "*contra bonos mores*" in those light love-affairs outside marriage. But it really is necessary to discriminate. Cinara was really not Lalage; nor was either of them in the least like the field-woman, Phidyle, in whose case there was no question of a love affair at all.

Sir Theodore Martin gives us the pleasure and excitement of a few more discoveries, however. The heart of Horace, he says, was never really touched. At the same time, Horace experienced "the infinite torture a charming and coquettish woman has it in her power to inflict." This is eating your cake and having it with a vengeance. Horace was attached with "infinite pain," and he was not attached at all. Sir Theodore gives an almost complete list of the feminine characters in the poems and, having dismissed them all as mere imaginations, and at the same time members of the demi-monde, he says (a) that Horace was quite unable to appreciate the possibilities of marriage, and (b) that nevertheless he "revered the marriage tie." "Horace did his best to forward the policy of Augustus in his effort to arrest the decay of morals by enforcing the duty of marriage." There is some truth in the second of these statements. Horace never played fast and loose with the marriage-tie. That, in his view, was where the offence against morals lay; and his code was certainly more honest that that of the treacherous neo-pagans of the "modern" world. Horace and Maecenas were convinced that laws *"sine moribus"* were futile; and it seems likely that this was one of the reasons why Horace distrusted the methods of Augustus. Perhaps he had noticed one or two curious things about the way in which Augustus dealt with the marriage of Agrippa. It seems very probable, too, that he was not happy about the marriage laws of Rome, which did not recognize the marriage of slaves and thus placed freed-men in a very ambiguous position. We hear nothing, for instance, of his father's marriage. Horace may have preferred not to attempt marriage on his own account. Women probably regarded him as a funny little man who liked to spend many months in lonely country places, while they preferred the excitements of Rome. Even in his light love-affairs he seems to have been jilted several times, and he is almost pathetically proud of the fact that Cinara once forgot her greed and looked on him kindly. The emperor's own household very soon became an illustration of the *"vanae leges"* of which he wrote. To point out the futility of those laws without morals was not a very likely way to flatter the imperial law-maker;

and in this, too, he surely showed a sturdy and an honorable independence.

"Horace had no divine law of duty to appeal to as we have," says Sir Theodore Martin; and really, at this, any honest observer of the modern world, remembering how that poor heathen, Horace, did appeal, again and again, to that very law, can only throw up his hands in stupefaction.

Many of his feminine characters are very clearly drawn. There is a great difference, for instance, between Pyrrha and Phidyle. The poem about Pyrrha, as we remarked earlier, may be a memory of his student days in Athens. Anyone who has read the delightful paraphrase by a Harvard scholar who identified the slender youth with an undergraduate and transferred the whole scene to his own campus, must see at once how perfectly it fits into what may be called the atmosphere of that student world. Phidyle, I feel sure, is a very real person indeed; and, fortunately, one may take this view without any question of a love-affair. It is one of the most exquisite poems of his life at the Sabine Farm. The gist of it is simply that in the sight of the gods clean hands and an innocent heart are better than sacrifice.

It is possible that this poem enshrines another memory of the farm at Venusia; and that it was brought to light by similar happenings at the Sabine Farm. It is one of the most beautiful of his odes—as graceful in outline as a figure on a Grecian urn. Ruskin in his "Queen of the Air" is mistaken, I think, in supposing that this poem was addressed to a very young girl, though he describes it charmingly. "Horace," he said, "tells the farmer's little girl that the gods will love her, though she has only a handful of salt and meal to give them." This would do very well for the last stanza of the poem; but surely not for the first. "Little girls" would not be using the incense, or offering up the swine in the sacrificial rite. These, and other details in the poem, give it a much more interesting character. It is a picture of a hard-working peasant woman, perhaps not unlike some of the simple country-folk in Hardy's Wessex. Horace calls her Phidyle (thrifty), and thrift is not a juvenile characteristic. She may have been the *vilica*, one of whose tasks was to bring the other slaves together for worship and to preside on occasions when the master of the house was away; or, perhaps, she was the wife of one of the poorer tenant farmers of whom there were five on the Sabine estate. She had actually brought to the sacrifice a good deal more than the salt and meal of which Ruskin speaks, though Horace tells us in the last stanza that the gods require no more of her. She has brought incense, corn of the new harvest, and an *"avida porca"* (a guzzling swine). Quintilian seemed to think that Virgil had saved the poetic quality of one of his lines by using the word *porca* rather than *porco;* and perhaps his remark applies to Horace also. But neither of these words would help the reader who wished to idealize the picture. It is of the earth earthy. It is its nearness to the soil and the crude realities of the Italian farm that make us feel by contrast the extraordinary beauty and tenderness, the almost compassionate tenderness, of the words which close the poem.

It has so often been translated as though Phidyle were a juvenile character, that I may be forgiven, perhaps, for trying to emphasize, in the original meter, some of these other aspects. My translation, of course, is not absolutely literal. I could find no good English equivalent for the adjective *rustica*, which Horace applies to Phidyle. The Latin word suggests the hard-working servants of the farm who were, in fact, "slaves." The combination of this idea with the meaning of Phidyle suggested a phrase which at least fits harmoniously into the picture and may help to correct the false impression created by those translations in which Phidyle becomes just one more of the poet's young women—the Italian counterpart of the dainty country lasses of Herrick. The slaughtered *porca* settles all that; and, if we want a modern comparison, we are more likely to find it among the Breton peasants.

> If suppliant palms, upraised at the sacrifice,
> Placate the gods, my field-weary Phidyle,
>   At each new moon, if hard-won first-fruits
>   Plead, and the darkening blood between them,
>
> Fear, then, no more that wind out of Africa!
> What need hast thou of costlier offerings?
>   Far, far from here, though the axe be waiting,
>   Feeds upon Alba the Pontiff's victim.
>
> Our Lares ask—no gift of thy lowlihead!—
> Crown them with sprays of myrtle and rosemary!
>   Their small bright statues, no less kindly,
>   Cherish your hearth and your clustering vineyard.
>
> O guiltless hands, your touch on the altar-stone
> Moves all the heavens, though nothing of cost you bring,
>   But crackling salt and sacred wheat-cake,
>   Piously flung to the dying embers.

XII

NUNC EST BIBENDUM

THE FINAL WAR BETWEEN OCTAVIAN AND ANTONY BROKE OUT in 32 B.C. To Horace, who could not have foreseen its finality, the outbreak must have seemed only the beginning of one more of those carnivals of blood in which Italy had been a prey to so many rival factions for so many decades. He could not have viewed the war with enthusiasm. Antony being the enemy, Horace was naturally on the side of the new régime, but in his heart and mind he was ingeminating peace.

By a curious overflow of patriotic sentiment, after the First World War of 1914, it became the fashion among some of the writers on Latin poetry to say that "Horace, of course, left his Sabine farm and accompanied Maecenas to the sea-battle of Actium." Tenney Frank went so far as to say that it was "now generally agreed that Horace went to the war and was present at the battle of Actium." The word *"now"* in that sentence did not mean that a single grain of new evidence had been discovered. It meant simply that a world war had *"now"* been fought in modern Europe; that the air was *"now"* full of war sentimentality to which cold facts are merely irrelevant; and that it had *"now"* become a kind of patriotic act, and indeed almost a piece of recruiting propaganda, for the eminent commentators to send Horace to the sea-victory at Actium.

There are some very curious and amusing points about this academic attempt to serenade the Sabine farm with the cheerful strains of

We don't want to lose you, but we think you ought to go.

They do not make even a guess at the capacity in which Horace, the world's worst sailor, was to serve at sea. They are not interested in the land forces on the coast of Epirus, which so bad a sailor would surely have preferred; nor will they allow the unfortunate poet who was "unfit for war," and already prematurely grey and middle-aged, a few months to get his sea-legs. He was to appear for positively one occasion only, at sea, and at the victory of Actium. Proof? With a gravity that is somewhat difficult to share, they point to a single word in the ninth epode, which they suppose he actually wrote on that salt and heaving scene—the word *nauseam*.

Professor Campbell's book *Horace: A New Interpretation* is full of really good things; but he is a supporter of this curious view of the *provenance* of a poem. He thinks that the poet was seasick; and that he not only wrote the poem but actually read it to the assembled officers of the ship, during this fit of seasickness, while the "battle," or rather the flight of the enemy, was proceeding. Emotion recollected in tranquillity! But this is what he says:

So long as no other occasion was suggested commentators have to follow the scholiast in supposing that when the poet calls for a special wine of anti-emetic virtues, he is anticipating the effects of too copious celebration of the good news. It was not until 1878 that the happy suggestion was made by Bücheler that the "nausea" here complained of is nothing less reputable than common seasickness! The poem, in fact, pretends to be writing itself (and almost certainly was so written) on board Maecenas' galley, rather early (I suggest it was read out to enliven the lunch party) on the second of September B.C. 31, the actual day, though this of course could not have been predicted confidently, of the naval battle which was to prove final victory.

There is something wrong with that last sentence and, since Horace actually mentions the flight of the enemy ships, and is also alleged to have read the poem before the battle was over, the whole affair—composition, sea-sickness, reading, and lively lunch party—must have taken place during the battle. There is not a word, of course, in the ninth epode about any galley belonging to Maecenas. Horace mentions the palace of Maecenas in Rome and wonders when they are going to drink Caecuban there to celebrate the news of victory. He pictures a company drinking sweet wine (Chian and Lesbian), and it was a common custom among the Romans to follow this with Caecuban to counteract its effect. Professor Campbell, however, complicates the matter by sending Horace to a sea-battle on a galley, and then suggesting that as Horace himself was very fond of Caecuban wine (the anti-emetic), he brought his seasickness into the poem as an excuse for demanding his favorite tipple at the lunch party, in the officers' mess. I admire the ingenuity of the suggestion; but I cannot help thinking that it shows little acquaintance with the probable effect of seasickness on the writing of a poem, and that it is crediting a party of sailors during a naval action with somewhat more interest in literature than was likely.

The whole of this airy fabric rests upon the one word *nauseam*, which, as Professor Campbell says, commentators were obliged to accept in its obvious meaning until the "happy thought" occurred to Bücheler that it meant seasickness. An attempt to support this theory has been based by the same writers on the first epode. In this earlier poem Horace, apparently thinking that Maecenas is going to the war, tells him that he wishes to share his hardships. It was undoubtedly a misunderstanding of this poem that some years later caused an obscure writer to suggest in an elegy that Maecenas had actually been present at Actium. The plain facts are these. Before Octavian left Italy with his army and fleet in the Spring of 31 B.C. he summoned a council of the chief men of Rome to Brundisium. Maecenas was the most prominent among them. Horace, hearing that he had left Rome for the great sea-port, jumped to the conclusion that Maecenas would be going to the war. He thereupon wrote the first epode, expressing a wish that he might follow his friend, and complaining that he had not been allowed to accompany him. Maecenas attended the council at Brundisium; and, after a consultation with Octavian, returned to govern Rome during Octavian's absence. There was therefore no necessity for Horace to drink Caecuban at sea. The poem, in fact, is an expression of friendship; and, behind it, there is the perfectly true suggestion that neither of them would be of the slightest use on Liburnian galleys. Maecenas would be a fledgling, and Horace would be too ill to play the part of "a mother bird protecting her young." Wickham and Greenough, and a host of other reliable authorities, accept the account of Dio, the historian, and of Seneca, that Maecenas was left in charge of Rome while Octavian was away, watching Agrippa bring his campaign to a successful conclusion.

In the ode *Nunc est bibendum* (I, 37), written a year later, after the suicide of Cleopatra, Horace declares that it would have been wrong to bring out the Caecuban earlier. This surely indicates that the picture of the earlier celebration was a mere imagination—a picture of things as they might be in the first excitement of the news of victory in Rome. But the ode on Cleopatra is a strange poem and by no means so simple as it appears at first sight. We must remember again that poetry is "like shot silk, glancing with many colors"; and that Horace was an extremely subtle master of irony who, all his life, had kept himself at a sufficient distance from the politics of the time to observe them objectively. This poem is not a mere invitation to drink in celebration of a victory. In the unpredictable way of poets Horace, apparently sets out to write a paean in the manner of Alcaeus, whom he actually translates in the opening words (νῦν χρὴ

μεθύσθην . . .). He calls for wine and a sacrificial banquet, at
which the images of the gods were to be placed on couches,
and food set before them. This is followed by a fierce attack
on the Egyptian corruption which surrounded Cleopatra.
The name of Caesar is mentioned exactly once as the titular
victor. Antony, curiously enough, is not mentioned at all. But
the most remarkable thing about the poem is that Cleopatra
really steals all the poetry and receives the tribute. As soon as
her fleet is destroyed, a change comes over her, and over the
poem. Horace describes her flying from Italy like "a gentle
dove pursued by a hawk," or a hare followed by the hunter over
the plains of snow-bound Thessaly. There is a strange mixture
of ideas here; for Horace says that the hunter (Caesar) is
chasing the hare (Cleopatra) in order to put the "accursed
monster in chains":

> *. . . accipiter velut*
> *mollis columbas aut leporem citus*
> *venator in campis nivalis*
> *Haemoniae, daret ut catenis*
> *fatale monstrum. . . .*

"Chains" and "accursed monster" must surely be ironical as
applied to a gentle dove or a fugitive hare. It is possible that if
Horace had seen the image of Cleopatra carried through the
"shouting varletry of Rome" with her pitiful young son walking
in the procession behind her litter, he might have felt some kind
of revulsion against the proceedings. The gods, the real gods,
not those who were laid out on purple cushions at the banquet
described in the opening stanza, could hardly have looked with
favor on the ghastly and cold-blooded murder of her two other
young children; and, though Horace locked a great deal in
silence, he seems to have reversed his usual procedure in this
poem. The irony comes at the beginning, and in the middle.

Possibly there was irony in what he said in the ninth epode about the Romans drinking till they were sick in honor of one more "glorious victory." No matter who won, his deepest feeling about war was that it was always evil and cruel. Like a true Roman, he could not help admiring the last act in which the defeated Cleopatra foiled the hope of Octavian and prevented herself being made a spectacle for the rabble. They could carry her image in triumph through the streets, but they could not take her alive. It is this feeling that makes Horace close his poem with a passage in praise of Cleopatra which may almost be compared with the close of his ode on Regulus:

Bent on a nobler death she did not shrink with womanly fear from the sword, nor seek to win with her swift ships some far off shore, but dared to look upon her fallen palace with a serene countenance, and bravely took the deadly asps and their black venom to her heart, defiantly resolved to die; disdaining the thought of being borne on the cruel Liburnian ships for the proud triumph of her enemies.

ausa et iacentem visere regiam
vultu sereno, fortis et asperas
tractare serpentis, ut atrum
corpore combiberet venenum,

deliberata morte ferocior,
saevis Liburnis scilicet invidens
privata deduci superbo
non humilis mulier triumpho.

To Horace, as to Cicero before him, Antony had been the enemy; and Horace naturally rejoiced over the victory at Actium in 30 B.C. It is extremely misleading to represent his ode on that subject as a recantation of his political views. Octavian was the titular head of the victorious side, and the ode celebrating the victory could hardly ignore the titular victor; but this is a very different thing from the political tergiversation which Swinburne and others appeared to think it. Antony was the enemy at Philippi, when Brutus fought him. Antony was the enemy at Actium, when Octavian fought him. And, as at Philippi, so at Actium, Horace was on the side opposed to Antony. Octavian, on the other hand, whatever his motives may have been, had passed through many phases.

It must be remembered that in the civil conflicts through which Italy had been passing, it was almost impossible for any man to see his way clearly through the constantly changing political combinations. Cicero discovered this to his cost. He decided to support Octavian against Antony, whom he seriously regarded as the enemy, though he was justly anxious and justly doubtful about what Octavian would do next. Almost before the ink was dry on Cicero's letters against Antony, a new combination was formed whereby Antony and Octavian became friends—for the moment—and Octavian agreed to the murder of his own supporter. If one compares the faces of such men as Cicero and Seneca, as the sculptors have recorded them, with those of the emperors who ordered their deaths, the tragedy of the intellectual and spiritual man at the mercy of the "beast"— I use the word of Plutarch—is only too apparent. Historians, essayists, even poets like Browning, carried away by the glamor of power and fascinated by what they are never tired of calling the "eagle beak" of the superficially handsome Augustus, are inclined to overlook the goodness, the truth, the sorrow, the bewildering care written and engraved upon more sensitive and intellectual faces.

The letters of Cicero to Atticus are full of that ghastly fear from which, in the twentieth century, our charters have not yet delivered the world. It has nothing to do with vacillation or cowardice. It is the fear which the bravest may feel, if they are capable of thought, in the presence of unpredictable evil, where no man knows who can be trusted and—in the political world—all distinctions of right and wrong have been obliterated or subordinated to the advantage of a moment. Many a man capable of the greatest courage if he could be sure of his cause may be shaken to the depths of his soul, if he finds that the ethical chart has been thrown overboard; that no political ally can be trusted; and that he cannot accept any agreement with the slightest confidence that it will be kept. The wild beasts that roared in the triumph of Rome when the young son of Cleopatra walked behind the litter in which the image of his dead mother was carried must have stirred strange thoughts in the mind of a poet like Horace.

Seneca has been called "time serving," though he held Nero in check for a generation. Critics even take a curiously cruel pleasure in condemning Seneca for what they call "consenting to the murder of Agrippina," by her son. As if Nero ever asked for the consent of a philosopher before achieving a little thing like that! And as if Agrippina were not herself a murderess of considerable distinction! They admit that Seneca tried to resign all his possessions and they sneer at his failure to do so, forgetting that he was dealing with a capricious beast who once ordered a man to be killed because he did not drink as much as the beast had requested. It amused Nero to load the apostle of plain living and high thinking with extravagant wealth. The philosopher who, by one of the most superb examples of intellectual control that the world has ever seen, had kept the imperial monster in check for years was at last defeated. He retired to the country and then—by the caprice of the monster—was ordered to die. This he did with the spiritual dignity of a Socrates. The words with which he parted from his friends were not unworthy of the comparison. Other ages have recognized this; but his achievement, since it had no big battalions behind it, is not enough, apparently, for the moralists of the atomic bomb period. To the fathers of the Church he was a not unworthy Stoic counterpart of St. Paul. He had certainly fought with beasts, and one cannot help wondering how some of those who judge him so severely would bear themselves if they had the opportunity of holding a Nero in check for a whole generation, with nothing but their own souls to sustain them, and in hourly danger of death.

Horace could not see into the future; but he had read enough in the history of the past and seen enough in his own life-time, to put no trust in princes. With the victory of Actium the period of civil conflict and massacre was brought to an end. It did not change the personal character of Octavian. There is no more cruel and wicked act in history than his cold-blooded murder of the two young boys—Caesarion (aged sixteen), the son of Julius Caesar by Cleopatra, and Antyllus (aged fourteen), the son of Antony by Fulvia.

Apart from any other consideration, what are we to say of the murder of the young son of Julius, the adoptive (and supposedly beloved) father of Octavian himself—Julius, whose death had once agitated Octavian and Antony against the slayers; Julius, to whose memory Cleopatra appealed, not for herself but for the boy, before she committed suicide. The murder is often deprecated by Octavian's admirers, but glossed over as "politic." I suppose that historians say these things because they have not imagination enough to see the frightened faces of those pitiful youngsters as the executioners approached them. But we shall never have a better world until many of our history books are re-written and this unconscious deference to the powers of darkness in high places is expunged. It is a standing danger to the education of the world, and an encouragement to all the evils against which the last World War was fought.

Horace probably did not know of this incidental murder when he wrote his poem on the victory of Actium; but he does pay a chivalrous tribute to the defeated Cleopatra, and he would certainly have been disgusted at the spectacle in the streets of Rome when her surviving child was forced to walk behind the image of his dead mother through the yelling and triumphant mob.

Milton (and Bossuet, in his universal history) painted a beautiful picture of the *pax Romana,* which was to usher in the birth of Christ:

> No war, or battle's sound
> Was heard the world around;
> The idle spear and shield were high up-hung;
> The hookèd chariot stood
> Unstain'd with hostile blood,
> The trumpet spake not to the armèd throng
> And kings sate still with awful eye,
> As if they surely knew their sovran Lord was by.

But Octavian knew nothing of the advent, and, in the reign of his successor their sovran Lord was crucified; while Pilate, the prototype of the modern political relativists, washed his hands of Truth altogether. If, to the Roman poet, the future presented no better prospect than the cessation of internecine bloodshed and the coming of peace, he certainly did not have to change his political coat to embrace that hope. Octavian was now the undisputed ruler of his empire. On the urgency of Maecenas and Agrippa he was apparently attempting to restore much of the Italy that Horace loved. As a highly politic move, the murderer of little children was restoring religion and morality to his bewildered people. Those who are puzzled by his apparent inconsistencies, have only to look at the real explanation, so often minimized by the historians—that two very remarkable men were doing their best, behind the scenes, to control and guide him: Agrippa, a soldier and administrator of great wisdom; and Maecenas, the cultivated scholar, man of affairs, and lover of art and letters, who really presided over all that was best in the Augustan age, and who had called Augustus himself, on one occasion, "Carnifex."

The addresses of Agrippa and Maecenas to Augustus, as recorded by Dio, have the ring of truth. Although they are not the actual words, any more than those attributed to Pericles by the greatest of Greek historians, they present a true picture. Pericles himself lives by a similar record; and the true characters of Maecenas and Agrippa shine through the speeches in Dio. Nobody can read them carefully without feeling something of the true situation, in which two men of wisdom are trying by every means in their power to coax and guide a comparatively immature mind into doing the best for his country. The advice given by Maecenas in passage after passage coincides with the ideas and principles expressed in the writings of Horace. We have already seen this in the case of the poem on the *Ship of State*. Augustus apparently needed to be cajoled and persuaded into adopting their ideas and dropping others. Agrippa and Maecenas talked to him as if they were trying to educate a difficult character into good behavior. It is all the more remarkable because Dio himself makes no suggestion of that kind. We gather it entirely from the tone of the speeches. This immaturity of character accounts for many minor details. When the rest of Rome was calling him Caesar, Cicero exclaimed in something like pity and wonder: "He is such a boy." The man who would choose those three emblems for his signet ring, the Sphinx, the head of Alexander the Great, and his own head, was surely dramatizing himself in a manner which all psychologists will recognize. It accounted for his curiously crude and unsophisticated letter to Maecenas about Horace—"He will leave that parasite table of yours and come to this royal one." It accounts also for the tone, sometimes only half-serious and sometimes very serious indeed, in which Horace himself so freely admonishes the ruler of the Roman world.

The closing of the bronze doors of the temple of Janus, after the battle of Actium, was a central and symbolical event for the thought of Horace, as for that of Virgil. Only once before, since the reign of Numa, had those terrible gates of the war god been closed for the advent of peace. The news that they had again been barred with their "hundred brazen bolts and the eternal strength of iron" (*aeternaque ferri robora*) brought fresh hope to Italy. Horace naturally shared it. Whenever he passed through the Forum after that, his glance would not miss the bronze doors of that little temple to the north. They symbolized something that profoundly affected his feeling towards the régime of Augustus. He still excuses himself from the attempt to write grandiose things about victory. In any case, Virgil and Varius had celebrated the epic history of Rome in the most perfect way, he tells the Emperor. The character and features of her famous heroes were delineated by Virgil "as clearly as in the work of the sculptor's hand, and in a form more enduring than bronze."

If I had the power to do what they have done (he says, in the first epistle of the second book), I should not prefer my pedestrian conversations in verse to the story of heroic deeds, far off lands and rivers, citadels on the mountain-crags, barbarous kingdoms; and, under your auspices, the closing of the gates of Janus, and the ending of all wars throughout the entire world:

> *. . . tuisque*
> *auspiciis totum confecta duella per orbem.*

That bolting and barring of the twin gates of war seemed infinitely more important to Horace than the personality of the Emperor. It happened under the Emperor's auspices; but the policy of the Emperor was very largely that of his chief adviser, Maecenas, who, in some respects, played the part of Richelieu to the Louis the Thirteenth of Augustus. The execution of the policy was the work of his best soldier, Agrippa, who has been described as an outstanding example of a first-rate man, content to play a secondary part for the welfare of his country. This was even more true of Maecenas. He remained a member of the equestrian order, refusing all honors, seeking no recognition for his work; but with one hand laid upon the tiller, and an assumed carelessness, piloting the Ship of State through those very perilous seas. He did it in such a way that Augustus could not only take the credit, but probably could believe he deserved it. The character of Maecenas is one of the most remarkable in history: contemporary honors meant nothing to the "descendant of Etruscan kings"; and he had the great advantage, therefore, of not wanting anything for himself. He was like some of those "commoners" of England who, being on the Plantagenet roll, have no particular use for a new title. Behind the externals of a dilettante, he concealed a statesmanship that has rarely been excelled. His strong face has puzzled some of the historians by its contrast with his traditional reputation as a mere connoisseur of the arts. He is said to have been something of a fop in his attire; but he detested the toga, and preferred the informality and perhaps the unencumbered efficiency of the tunic worn by the work-a-day world, though it was probably of a finer texture and better cut than most. This trivial point is worth noting, because it helps to absolve Horace from the charge of satirizing Maecenas, in a certain early poem, for the way in which he wore his toga. Maecenas played games to keep fit. He took charge of Rome with what Velleius Paterculus calls "sleepless vigilance," while Augustus was watching Agrippa win his victories else-where. It can hardly have been a coincidence that, when Augustus became estranged from his pilot, the luck of his house began to fail. It was certainly not a coincidence that the really endur-ing glory of the Augustan age—its literature, and especially the works of Virgil and Horace—came so swiftly and surely into their own abiding place, under his direct and affectionate care. Nor is it a coincidence that his advice to Augustus, as recorded by Dio, formulates just those salutary principles which, so far as they were allowed to operate, even through the madness and disaster of other reigns, prolonged the life of the Empire for four hundred years.

Horace and Virgil were not "popular" writers in the modern sense. Without the backing of Maecenas, Horace might not have found it so easy to stand up against the literary fashions and professional critics of his day. It is a great mistake to sup-pose that, because he is now seen to have been stating and de-fending ideas that have become part of the intellectual heritage of the world, and are as familiar as proverbs, he was merely on the side of a contemporary convention. It is true that he would not have written differently for the sake of achieving a false novelty, even if the literary world of his time had conventionally been accepting what he believed to be really true. But he was actually in opposition to the contemporary fashions, both in thought and in style. His criticism of Lucilius and some of the older writers, although he gave them their full meed of praise, incurred the wrath of many contemporaries. He was not fighting for his own hand, but for a real advance—a higher perfection of the language of Latin poetry on the one hand, and a return on the other to the old and clear fountains of the great tradition of lyrical poetry in Greece. Even in this return, he was really progressive. He took the true line of progress, which is develop-ment; and, whereas Catullus who, for the most part used very much easier metres, reproduced the Sapphic form with no new note of his own, Horace did actually give it a new strength and weight by a certain prosodic change, adjusting it more perfectly to the Latin tongue, as he had justly claimed. At the same time he maintained all that marvelous precision from which not a syllable could go astray and which is the perfect illustration in verse of the dependence of the highest kind of liberty on the harmonies of law. This was both too original, and too "traditional" in the right sense of that great word to be understood by his own generation. It was the same with his utterances on religion and morals. The attempts to revive them under the Augustan régime, for which Maecenas was really responsible, were resented by the growing license of the generation, to which the *Ars Amatoria* was to make so wide an appeal. The mystical religious sense of Virgil; the almost Socratic irony with which Horace smiled at his own foibles and saved himself from the least appearance of the "unco' guid," while he hammered his ethical maxims home, were certainly not "conventional" or insincere. They give to every man only "as much as he can take"; but they are among the great civilizing influences of Europe; and without Maecenas, they might have perished. Horace could not help saying what he said on ethics. The test case is his utterance on the *vanae leges* of the official attempt to restore religion and morality. Conventionalists were not echoed or quoted by the fiery spirit of Tertullian. In saying that the Augustan laws were futile *sine moribus,* Horace acted as a true *vates,* regardless of the consequences. It was a warning to the Roman people, and it was a warning to Augustus. A mere conventionalist would have glibly praised the new legislation, and probably flattered the people, too. Horace flattered neither, but spoke the truth that was in him. Juvenal, most sardonic of realists, recognized this, when he spoke of certain things as "worthy of the Venusian's lantern"—the light that Horace had held aloft in Rome. The fact that the light was not blown out or the lantern smashed is due in no small measure to Maecenas; and it may be added that Maecenas himself, in turn, was helped and encouraged in his course, and even on "the last dark road," by the lantern in the hand of his friend.

The character revealed in the words attributed to Maecenas by Dio is that of a very real personage. He is represented, in friendly opposition to Agrippa, as telling Augustus that he should aim at personal monarchy. At first sight this might seem to suggest that Maecenas was less fond of liberty, and less aware of the dangers of autocracy, than Agrippa. But careful examination of his words shows that he was very skilfully trying to lead Augustus towards what we should call today a constitutional monarchy, with a responsible cabinet to shape the policy of the government and shield the monarch from criticism. It is quite clear, too, that the really valuable characteristics of the reign were largely due to the spirit and influence of Maecenas. He is at one with Horace and Virgil in his sense of religious and moral values. In fact, as several of the best historians of the period have said, Horace—through Maecenas—was one of the most salutary influences of the government circle. Maecenas had the temporal power and Horace was able to kindle his imagination and strengthen his spirit. The words of Horace on the goddess Fortuna, as an instrument of the divine power and sometimes a chastening one, surely breathed through the appeal of Maecenas to Augustus:

For our own sakes and for that of the city let us obey Fortuna, who gives you the supremacy. Let us be very thankful to her that she has not simply filled us with civil woes, but has put the reorganization of the government in your hands. By paying due reverence to her you may show all mankind that, whereas others wrought disturbance and injury, you are an upright man.

We are drawing near to a very great saying indeed when Maecenas tells Augustus:

Whatever you wish your subjects to think and do, *you* must say and do. You can better educate them in this way than if you should desire to terrify them by the severities of the law. . . .

He warns him against the extravagances of the time, in the very spirit of Horace, and especially against the temptations to deify himself. Here he draws upon Pericles; but he adapts the words and thoughts of the Greek statesman to a very different occasion and develops them to a new purpose, exactly as he did with the parable of the ship from Plato. Maecenas was a student and a scholar, and Dio knew what he was doing when he put words of this kind into his mouth. He makes Agrippa talk in a very different strain:

Never permit gold or silver images of yourself to be made; they are not only costly, but they give rise to plots and last but a brief time. You must build another kind of image in the very hearts of men. These should be both unalloyed and undying. Again, do not ever allow a temple to be raised to yourself. Much money is uselessly spent on these things, which had better be laid out upon necessary improvements. Nor does a temple contribute anything to anyone's glory. Excellence raises many men to the level of the gods, but nobody ever yet was made a god by show of hands. Hence, if you are upright and rule well, the whole earth will be your precinct, all cities your temple, all mankind your statues.

XIII

THE LABOR OF THE FILE

THE NEW LEISURE, THE MOST VALUABLE GIFT THAT THE SABINE farm brought him, was employed by Horace in the most delectable task of the artist. We hear of occasional visits in the winter to Baiae; and, after he had been advised against that fashionable resort, where certain members of the Emperor's household were perhaps already demonstrating the futility of laws *sine moribus,* he went to other and quieter places by the sea, taking a few books with him, and certain manuscripts on which he wished to work. Ovid, a few years later, was less wise.

But the Sabine farm was the real home of Horace, and we may surely picture him, by his water-spring on many a golden morning, or by that ruined temple on the hill, concentrating his whole mind on the attempt to give the last touches of perfection to lines that he had written earlier in the din and smoke of Rome; lines that only needed time and patience, the labor of the file, and Horace, to make them unforgettable. He had brought many of these unfinished poems with him. He liked to hold them back from publication until he felt sure of them; and in that stillness, with only the peaceful sound of the stream below —"thy stream, Digentia"—or the rustling of a light breeze through the stone pine that shadowed his roof, he had his opportunity. Hour after hour would slip by while, forgetful even of food and wine, hardly lifting his eyes, he endured the happy torment of all true artists.

> Yet should there hover in their restless heads
> One thought, one grace, one wonder, at the least,
> Which into words no virtue can digest.[1]

[1] Marlowe.

It is to these "dear delays of art" that he refers in the third satire of the second book. He is not accusing himself of laziness when he makes the bankrupt art dealer, Damasippus, reproach him for producing so little, not asking four times a year for new parchment, but treating his work as Penelope did her web, continually unweaving what he had woven, and angry with himself because, even with the help of wine and sleep, he was unable to finish it. The task, and not the prize, enthralled him while he was engaged upon it; but he could not help being conscious that the work was constantly approaching a perfection which, if he achieved it, would conquer time. He knew, in art, what a later poet felt in a different connection:

> O, the little more and how much it is,
>> And the little less and what worlds away!
> How a sound may quicken content to bliss
>> Or a breath suspend the blood's best play,
> And life be a proof of this!

He had no time to think of it while he was working; but, in those less arduous moments when, much to the amusement of the peasants in the vineyard, he took a little recreational exercise with the mattock or the hoe, and tried to dig stones out of the soil, the thought certainly occurred to him. If he succeeded in his aim, his words, the living cadences of his mind and heart, would speak to men in distant ages. It was only through the completely expressive perfection of form that verse could do that—form, which is not merely external, but is the outward sign of an inner harmony, a symbol and a hieroglyph of another and a deeper perfection. If the form was flawed, the expression was necessarily flawed also, and the idea was not truly conveyed. In such a case it was always possible for someone else to express it better. This was precisely the difference between the enduring and the ephemeral in art and letters. To achieve, or even honestly attempt to achieve, a perfection that would endure, involved an amount of work and an expenditure of nervous energy that—as Stevenson once said—would exhaust an army of stevedores. It is a side of the picture which is often forgotten by those who take Horace too literally when he describes himself as lazy, or "a sleek hog from the Epicurean sty." The firm contours and disciplined style of the Odes were not the product of a slack mind, or a life devoted to pleasure, except in the sense that he loved his work and must have derived a very deep intellectual pleasure from it.

These "dear delays of art" created a real difficulty for the commentators who would write a consecutive account of his life and work, a difficulty which is manifest in many of the books that have been written about him. Sellar's fine essay almost abandons the attempt to be consecutive. We have really to adopt two systems of chronology—one for the origin of individual poems which deal with incidents in his life, and another for the dates of their publication in volume form.

The first book of the *Satires* was published in 35 B.C. Horace went to the Sabine farm in 33 B.C., and all the rest of his work was published after that date. But many of the satires in the second book (published in 30 B.C.) and many of the epodes (29 B.C.) were written earlier. The epode on the Fortunate Islands, as we have seen, was one of his earliest.

At the same time the second book of satires, as a whole, shows a real development. There is a mellowness of tone in many of them which brings them nearer to the spirit of the first volume of odes (23 B.C.), and in form, of course, still nearer to the first volume of epistles (20 B.C.). There is, moreover, a change in the character of the thought, a distinct movement away from the Epicurean philosophy towards that of the Stoics. There is a note of sincerity which can hardly be mistaken in the opening of the sixth satire of the second book, *Hoc erat in votis*. He does not elaborate it, but there is a real religious sense in his feeling that the gods had answered his prayers, even though they might be only the silent prayers of his heart. There is something more here than the Epicurean idea of an indifferent heaven, something considerably nearer to the future thesis of Seneca's *De Providentia*. Horace comments on both philosophies and on many other subjects, in a manner which irresistibly confirms his own statement that he had taken the works of his old favorite, Plato, with him to the Sabine farm. These later satires are full of a genial Socratic irony. He can smile at the extravagances of all the schools. Some of the dialogues—though the verse gives them their own character—catch the very tones of Plato in his lighter moods, to an extent which has escaped the notice of the commentators. In the first satire of the second book, for instance, Horace complains to Trebatius that half the critics think his earlier satires too savage, while the other half think they are too nerveless (*sine nervis*), and declare that anyone could write a thousand such verses a day. He asks for advice in the very accent of that ironic innocence with which Plato endowed some of his characters, and he gets the reply in the very tones with which Socrates maddened the Athenian sophists.

Horace

Tell me what I ought to do, Trebatius.

Trebatius

Keep quiet (*quiescas*).

Horace

What do you mean? Give up writing verses altogether?

Trebatius

Yes.

Horace

Well, may I perish if I don't think that would be best. But, if I do give it up, I really can't sleep.

Trebatius

Anyone who can't sleep should oil himself and swim three times across the Tiber. Then, at nightfall, he should souse himself in wine. Or if your craving to write carries you away, you should be brave enough to sing the deeds of Caesar, the always victorious. Your labors will be quite profitable, if you do that.

Horace

I wish I could, *pater optime*, but I'm not strong enough. It isn't everyone who can paint the ranks bristling with lances, or Gauls falling with shattered spears, or wounded Parthians tumbling off their horses.

Trebatius

Well—you might paint Caesar himself, the always righteous and valiant, as that shrewd Lucilius painted Scipio.

Horace

When the right time comes I shall not disappoint myself. But, unless it is the right moment, the words of Flaccus will not receive an attentive ear from Caesar. If you stroke that horse the wrong way, he kicks back, and defends himself in all directions.

This daring vein of irony in Horace is usually toned down by the commentators to a point where it almost vanishes. Many pages of notes have been written on this passage by critics who take it a word at a time, and there is hardly an intimation that the commentators realize its significance as a whole. We are told the exact meaning of *recalcitrat*; but there is no comment on the remarkable fact that the alleged "varlet" and "court-poet" is here comparing the Emperor with a bad-tempered horse, at about the same time when Virgil was calling him *deus*. One does not wish to stress the comparison too strongly, but it certainly ought not to be completely passed over. Still less ought it to be forgotten when so much stress is laid on the less spontaneous passages of the later work in which Horace could hardly avoid paying a certain conventional tribute to Caesar. Commentators really cannot escape the bluntness of this passage by replacing the word "horse" with the more majestic "steed." Horace is far too subtle to allow that. He actually mentions no animal at all. He merely says that, if you stroke Octavian the wrong way, he kicks out with his heels in all directions, and certainly no poet-laureate has ever said anything quite like that about his sovereign.

Horace published the first three books of his Odes in 23 B.C. About a century later Quintilian spoke of him as the best of the lyrical poets of Rome. Twenty centuries later, one of the best of English critics, Mackail, remarked that "before a volume in which every other line is as familiar as a proverb criticism is almost silenced." We may recall here too that other verdict of the same critic which was quoted earlier—"Horace is at once the widest in his appeal and the most exquisite in his workmanship of all the Latin lyric poets. Many of his penetrating and mastering single phrases have been for many thousands of people through many ages, keys to the whole of life." This judgment has been confirmed by the best poets and critics of almost every nation. Even those concentrated souls whose admiration for one poet forbids them to admire another have usually agreed upon the technical mastery, the metrical variety, the disciplined style, and the mellow wisdom of his pages.

It is no small achievement for a poet to compel praise of that kind so long after his death; and it was compelled by a comparatively small body of work which, despite its range and variety, could be included in a single volume no larger than the meditations of Marcus Aurelius, or the poems of Keats. This is important in estimating the value of the praise; for every syllable in that little volume (a little volume, but great book) has been examined by a host of commentators. More voluminous classics are seldom subjected to so strict an inquisition. Nobody is likely to examine the precise value of every syllable in *The Ring and the Book*. It is true, of course, that the amount of a writer's work must be considered in any critical estimate. The quality of the work must first be determined, and the quantity is the factor next in importance. Wolfe's poem on the burial of Sir John Moore is as good as anything of its kind in Byron; but Wolfe wrote nothing else and he can hardly be compared, therefore, with the author of *Childe Harold* and the *Vision of Judgment*. Horace, however, in this as in many other things, exactly observed the golden mean. He has range and variety enough to rank with the masters who give us "God's plenty," and he is disciplined and restrained enough to give us only the exquisitely chosen flower of his own mind. More than the works of almost any other man, his odes have the selective quality of an anthology, and a very fastidious one, with something of that scrupulous perfection which, as Gautier said, in his most famous poem, can only come from the conquest of a difficult and rebellious medium, whether in verse or marble.

> Strive with Carrara, fight
> With Parian, till there steal
> To light
> Apollo's pure profile.

Horace did, in fact, follow his own advice about the "labor of the file"; and, for all the ease with which the final result seems to be achieved, that compact precision of thought and phrase, that clarity of meaning and lucidity of form bespeak not

only genius, but endless patience. Tennyson said of Virgil that he
would write ten lines at dawn

> . . . and lavish all the golden day
> To make them wealthier in his reader's eyes.

But it was at least equally true of Horace, though he probably
rose a little later. Of this discipline, in the odes especially, there
is no doubt; and in the whole history of criticism there is hardly
a dissenting voice on that score from any competent critic. It is a
little surprising, therefore, to find so good a Latinist as Dr.
Tyrrel, not only denying Horace any merit whatsoever, but
comparing him—of all people in the world—with Tom Moore.
It is apparently the worst thing that Dr. Tyrrel can think of
saying about any poet; and that, of course, is why he says it.
But he could hardly have chosen a more undiscriminating comparison.

Some of the nineteenth-century commentators, possessed
with the popular idea of a Horace crowned with roses and
engaged in perpetual love-affairs, unfortunately talked of him
and translated him in the very spirit of Tom Moore. But this
was about as far from the classic spirit of the real Horace as a
musical comedy chorus from the Nymphs and Graces of the
great ode *Diffugere nives,* which Housman translated so finely.
Sir Theodore Martin, writing of Horace the lover, made sad
havoc of those finely compact and precise lines "How more
than happy are they whom an unbroken bond has joined together, and whose love cannot be torn apart before the day of
their death":

> *Felices ter et amplius*
> *quos inrupta tenet copula nec malis*
> *divulsus querimoniis*
> *suprema citius solvet amor die.*

The Latin of that stanza, in its perfection of form, might, without the slightest incongruity, be wedded to the noble language of a marriage service in Chartres or Notre Dame. But Sir Theodore Martin informed us that the feeling of these lines was "better preserved" in Moore's well-known paraphrase than is possible in any translation. This is Moore's appalling version:

> One hour of a passion so sacred is worth
> Whole ages of heartless and wandering bliss,
> And O, if there be an Elysium on earth
> It is this, it is this!

No words can adequately express the dismay with which anyone capable of appreciating the real values of poetry must contemplate a statement like that of Sir Theodore Martin. Even if we compare Horace with Catullus, it was Horace who was the disciplined artist. The best comparison between these two poets was that made by Merrill in the introduction to his edition of Catullus:

With Catullus died the clearest, if not the richest poet-voice ever lifted in Rome. He lacked the lofty grandeur of Lucretius, the polished stateliness of Virgil, the broad sympathies of Horace. For on the one hand he was no recluse to be filled with heavenly vision, and on the other hand his personality was too intense to allow him to cultivate a tolerant spirit. He delighted in life with a vigorous animal passion . . . and this life he did not study, as did Horace, from the standpoint of a philosopher. Indeed, he did not study it at all, but simply felt it. . . . Such a nature must of necessity ever remain in many essential aspects the nature of a child. And such was the nature of Catullus throughout his brief life—warm in quick affections, hot in swift hatred, pulsing with most active red blood. The great majority of his verses are the direct expression of his own heart at the moment. No poet was ever more unreserved, more perfectly ingenuous. And yet, such was the facility of his genius, his verses show no ruggedness or roughness, but glide along with the utmost ease and swift grace toward their mark. But he was no precisionist in metrics. His hexameters are less perfect and flexible than those of P. Varro or of Lucretius, his elegiacs less harmonious and melting than those of the Augustans, his logaoedics often less melodious than those of Horace.[1]

The form and style alone—the *curiosa felicitas* which Petronius found in him—are enough to shatter the comparison with Moore; but it is worth while dwelling upon this matter a little longer because form and style are far more important considerations in estimating the value of poetry than is commonly supposed by the modern Philistine. They are not merely external qualities. As Matthew Arnold pointed out, the line

> Can'st thou not minister to a mind diseased?

does not say the same thing as the student's paraphrase

> Can you not wait upon the lunatic?

The unfortunate student might affirm that, in substance, he was really saying the same thing as Shakespeare; but the difference in form embraces and embodies a thousand other subtle associations and relationships, and makes all the difference between tears and absurdity, tragedy and farce. When Cornelius de Witte was on the rack, his tormentors are said to have extorted from him only those great lines of the Roman poet, beginning

> *Justum et tenacem propositi virum.*

Even today we can feel how the victim's own tenacity might be imparted to those words, and strike his tormentors like a blow in the face from an unconquerable power.

[1] Elmer T. Merrill, ed., *Catullus* (Ginn and Company).

It is greatly to the honor of Maecenas that he recognized at once the permanent value in the work of Horace. It was through him, of course, that Augustus was convinced of their immortality; and they were received with the same appreciation by a small circle of the poet's friends. But to the professional critics of Rome, and the camp-followers of literature, who too often sway the careless opinion of the merely fashionable world, Horace was only an imitator of Alcaeus and Sappho. The poems were received coldly by the general public and—as Ferrero says—"almost with hostility." It is not creditable to human nature, but it is a melancholy fact that any approach to perfection in art tends to arouse a certain resentment among the artist's less competent rivals. They liked Lucilius better than Horace, because his looser style was more within their grasp. The builder of a mud hut confronted by the Parthenon is disconcerted and murmurs something disparaging about "conventional form." The carver of a totem pole looks at a statue by Praxiteles or Rodin and whispers "insipidly traditional." Without knowing it, people of this kind are really attacking the central principle of beauty itself, that unity in variety, the eternal and universal principle of form, which has a philosophical significance far beyond all questions of technique. But there is a desire to destroy all those fine and difficult things that bar the way to the triumph of mediocrity. Unconscious of their motives, they band together to promote the inferior kind of work that they can do themselves; and, since almost anyone can do it, their theories are often fashionable and popular. They invoke all the conventions of unconventionality to support their claims to original genius. The trick is easy because there are innumerable false and striking novelties to be said on many subjects while there may be only one simple and abiding truth. Professor Tenney Frank in his book on Horace and Catullus has an interesting comment on this matter: it should be remarked, however, that what he says on the subject of original work is not an argument against the true kind of originality. Horace, he says in one place, was condemned for lack of originality because he was too original in the true sense for his own time:

The scholastic insistence upon "original work" has so invaded the field of art that the artist is often prevented from adequate expression by the demand for novelty, and art is too frequently driven to spareness or grotesqueness thereby. One wonders what Shakespeare, Molière or Raphael would have done if compelled to submit to the demands of modern pedantry, always on the hunt for parallels, sources and models. As the Ars Poetica shows, Horace believed in well established and proved standards and forms. They had been tried and presumably had not been found wanting. They provided discipline and prevented waste of time in non-essentials. After all, the greatest poets have found even the sonnet pliable for the deepest utterance. And what was true of form was also true of ideas and fancies. . . . Horace would see no more reason for choosing a less adequate term simply because the best had already been used, than a painter would for employing the wrong color because the right had already been employed by some-one else. The only demand is that his experience, his idea, his con-viction, be thoroughly his at the time; that it permeate him and have full meaning for him.

It should be added, of course, that nobody wants mere repe-tition of what has already been done perfectly. The true origi-nality, in the arts as in the sciences, is a development—along the lines of natural law—from the point where the predecessors ended. In this way, it reveals relationships hitherto unseen and embraces new tracts of experience. Neither Newton nor Shake-speare began from the egg. Progress in art will never be achieved by those who, as Sir Gilbert Murray once said, having grown tired of the good work of the masters, decide that they will deliberately write or paint badly just for a change. Truth is at heart unchanging, and because it endures through all the legitimate changes of external things, they mistake it for what they call "commonplace," though it is exactly in the discovery and revelation of the abiding in the transient that masterpieces are made. It is this, and nothing but this, that makes the *Ode on the Grecian Urn* a masterpiece:

For ever wilt thou love, and she be fair.

In its expression the great artists, the great poets, the great philosophers, may reveal a thousand unsuspected relationships to illuminate and transfigure whole tracts of the universe which had hitherto remained in obscurity. It is this that constitutes the true originality—the revelation and illumination of a reality that had always been there, though hitherto we had not seen it, or had not discovered those relationships which give it a new, a universal value. There is a great deal of confusion at the present day about the nature of true originality. The modern world often prefers the false kind which secures the attention of the moment by a cheap novelty without roots in reality, or by the brilliant reversal of some eternal truth. The academic world has not been blameless in its misuse of the word "commonplace." Some of the editors of Horace not only talk of the "commonplaces" of Stoicism; but, in one case, actually describe him as using the "Shakespearian commonplace":

My way of life
Is fallen into the sere, the yellow leaf.

The lady who found Hamlet too full of quotations was surely a Sainte-Beuve compared with the critic who not only found one of the most exquisite lines in Shakespeare a "commonplace" to his own day, but thought that Horace was a little "commonplace" also for "anticipating" the "quotation" two thousand years ago. There seems to be a further confusion in some of these writers between the familiar, the known, and the "commonplace." One of them refers to the profoundest and most beautiful sentence in the sermon on the mount as "that Christian commonplace"; and he does this in a world which is perishing through ignorance of its value.

Sainte-Beuve remarks in his shorter essay on Virgil, that an empty mind may see nothing but the commonplace where a fuller and deeper intelligence will discover that a great variety of hitherto unobserved relationships has been established between one truth and another. It may have been a commonplace to everyone in Rome that you cannot evolve "plus" from "minus"; but it is a commonplace that is often forgotten by some of the popular exponents of evolution at the present day; and when Horace says of the Father of gods and men (the *Vera Causa*) that "He created nothing greater than himself, nor is there anything like to him, or even second to him," he is quietly unveiling a whole constellation of philosophic truths from which a well-furnished modern mind can draw considerable light on its own problems. It has endless applications. The passage could be used to illustrate the modern philosopher's conception of the Absolute, or the transcendent Deity of the theologian. It could be used, on the one hand, as an answer to the false anthropomorphic conceptions of Deity; and, on the other hand, as a quiet refutation of Swinburne's delirious *Hymn of Man*:

> Glory to Man in the highest! for Man is the master
> of things.

Swinburne at his best is among the first of the lyrical poets of the world; but his wild paean on that occasion has perhaps already been answered and drowned in the blood baths of a tortured and enslaved Europe.

When, in another ode, Horace extends the relationship of

those ideas to the political world around him and tells the Emperor that he rules only because he holds himself in subordination to the gods—

dis te minorem quod geris, imperas—

he is really announcing the central fact which our own second World War was presumably fought to establish, that there is a Power above the State. By this time even that idea may have been outmoded among the last-minute thinkers; but in Horace, it is related to a whole range of other ideas which give it life and place it in an entirely different category from the political catch-words of his time, or ours. It required courage to say it to a Roman emperor.

A recent writer, one of those gay dons who have to keep up with the times, has announced that Horace, of course, did not really mean anything by passages like that quoted above. His reason for saying this is that the present generation—he tells us—is not interested. When the poor pagan Horace really tries to suggest principles of right and wrong, he is not to be taken seriously because the present generation of Christian gentlemen does not take them seriously. The most terrible war in history has just been fought to establish certain principles of international morality. It is surely time that we recovered our belief that they are something more than "commonplace."

One of the greatest passages in the *Odes* is that in which Horace, two thousand years ago, sums up the tragic lesson of two world wars in the twentieth century. "Power without wisdom," he says, "rushes down to destruction by its own weight."

He makes it clear that the wisdom of which he speaks consists in establishing a right relation with certain higher powers, whom he calls the gods. To these everything in the universe is subordinate, though it is possible for the spirit and will of man to cooperate with them, and to draw strength from them. "Power controlled by wisdom," he continues, "is exalted by the gods themselves to greater heights. Force that is intent on every kind of injustice is hated by the gods."

Vis consili expers mole ruit sua:
vim temperatam di quoque provehunt
in majus; idem odere vires
omne nefas animo moventes.

He is not merely saying—as Virgil said—that mind is the real mover of the world. He is making a great generalization, as important to human life and conduct as the law of gravitation was to science. Twenty centuries after he made it, our neo-pagan world is still ready to maintain with a sneer that "God is on the side of the big battalions," or, as a more recent speaker revised it, "God is now on the side of the heavy industries." The man who made that remark would be sneering at God himself, if he really believed in any God at all. In any case, he has already been answered—by "the terrible light of the atomic bomb."

Such men naturally regard the reference to gods as merely conventional; and the terms, of course, are those of the poet's own generation. But the essential meaning is eternally valid; and the conventional critics all overlook the remarkably modern scientific character of the generalization which Horace makes in that passage. He announces what might be called a law of spiritual gravitation, whereby certain things go down to death and dissolution by their own weight; while others move upward because they act in accordance with a law higher than that of the beasts. The man who climbs away from God may think he is going upward to the heights of his ambition; but he is really going downward to his own destruction. It is a truth which by tragic experiment and direct observation has been demonstrated myriads of times in the lives of individuals and in the rise and fall of nations.

No power has ever surpassed the rest of the world in material wealth and armed might to such a degree as the Roman Empire, even when it was moving like an avalanche to its own ruin. Horace felt the approaching peril instinctively; and his feeling was confirmed by his philosophy. To say that he was not always consistently pessimistic, or that he sometimes entertained delusive hopes of the Augustan régime, is merely to say that he was human; or that he was not unaffected by arguments which—in our own day—have persuaded certain eminent historians who have forgotten their Gibbon that Augustus was the greatest ruler the world has ever seen. It is perhaps significant that two of the latest of these historians, Lord Tweedsmuir and Mr. H. A. L. Fisher, were especially interested in the problems of imperial administration. There is no question, of course, about the immediate practical success of Augustus in this field. He owed a great part of it to Agrippa and Maecenas, but the man who specializes in the settlement of political difficulties may easily be led into an admiration for Augustus which is not justified by the picture as a whole. The punctuality of the train-service in Italy under Fascism, and various other administrative improvements, misled many travelers about the goal to which Italy herself was moving, and Augustus was a far more crafty and plausible personage than the modern dictator.

If historians, long after the event, are still at odds about the Emperor's character, there is something almost fantastic about the charges of inconsistency brought against a poet to whom the destiny of the Roman Empire was a sealed book. One thing is quite certain. In all his alternations between hope and pessimism, there is no abandonment of his principles. If Horace was in a hopeful mood, it was because he thought that those principles would be reestablished. If he was in a pessimistic mood, it was because he thought that those principles were being forgotten; and in the political fluctuations of that time, there is no reason whatever to suppose that he was unjustified. There are times when a change of tone is right and necessary. "Up-hill," as Tennyson remarked, "may need the whip. Down-hill may need the chain." It is only the wild modern fanatic who can maintain a steady chant of automatic disagreement on all aspects of every question. To suggest that one of the most independent writers in history was a turn-coat or a "trimmer" because he used his reason is only to find fault with the noblest characteristic of his genius, the very quality which has made Horace one of the most notable exemplars of good sense in the history of literature. This characteristic, this quality, would have lost all its value if it had involved those betrayals of principle that are accepted every day, and admired, in the world of "high politics." The outstanding fact about Horace is that there is not a single instance in which he capitulated or compromised on principle. If he praised Augustus, he took care—in every case—to reaffirm the conditions on which alone the praise was valid.

In the twenty-fourth ode of the third book, for instance, there is another passage which goes to the very heart of the problems of our own world. "Laws," he says, "are futile in a world without morals."

This is the simple, complete, and shattering answer to those who think that the world can be saved by commissioning a "giant" or two to sign lying documents, or to promise that inveterate promise-breakers will not break their promises again at the next opportunity.

> *Quid leges sine moribus*
> *vanae proficiunt?* . . .

There is no merely legal answer to this searching question. Men must regain their moral stature or their civilization will go down in complete ruin. Tertullian echoed the very words of Horace when he spoke to his own time of *vanissimae leges*. The Roman poet had laid his finger on the precise point at which in every age the "social contract" inevitably breaks down unless there is something more than a contract behind it. It is the point at which our own world is now threatening to collapse in a final catastrophe. His generalization is simple, and so terse, that the clever fools who wreck the hope of the world would undoubtedly regard this too as a "commonplace copy-book heading." But it is just this reduction of chaotic facts to an ordered simplicity which gave us the scientific command of nature; and it is just this power to see through all irrelevancies to the core of a matter that makes all the difference between a great leader and an opportunist. As Kipling in his grimmest satire warned his contemporaries, if we choose to ignore or treat lightly the stone tables on which some of those central truths are engraved—

> As surely as water will wet us, as surely as fire will burn,
> The gods of the copybook headings with terror and
>   slaughter return.

In this twenty-fourth ode Horace warns Rome against the material weight that may bring it down to ruin. He begins with a declaration that must have been startling to the victorious and luxury-loving Romans:

> Though thou be richer than all the treasure houses of Arabia and India, thou shalt not save thy soul from fear nor thy head from the noose of death.

He is simply saying in his own terms that the powers of evil may possess wealth. They may possess it, as Milton declared, even in hell; and Milton uses the same oriental illustration:

> High on a throne of royal state that far
> Outshone the wealth of Ormuz or of Ind
> Or where the gorgeous East with richest hand
> Showers on her kings barbaric pearl and gold
> Satan exalted sat. . . .

"Better to live like the wandering Scythians on their frozen plains," declares the Roman poet. "There, at least, a woman will do no harm to her motherless step-children. All the dowry she needs is the integrity of her parents and her own chastity. In loyalty to her own, she would shrink from adultery. With them all sin is evil, and its wages is death":

et peccare nefas aut pretium est mori.

"Let us offer up all our gold and jewels, either in the temples on the Capitol, or by throwing them into the sea, if we truly repent of our wickedness"—

. . . scelerum si bene paenitet.

Moreover, he constantly states the conditions of his own loyalty to the new régime, and tells us what Octavian must do to retain it. "He who would abolish this wicked slaughter and desires to be called Father of Cities must have courage to curb this brutal license."

He is absolutely consistent in his terms; but he is never quite sure about Augustus; and he safeguards himself either with these conditions or, sometimes, by the satiric tone in which he speaks of the Emperor.

Serious as the theme may be in the third ode of the third book, there is a note of subtle irony when he speaks of Augustus reclining among the gods and sipping nectar. Only two lines are devoted to that vivacious picture, but the manner and the style are delicious. He tell us, first, how "Pollux and the wandering Hercules had climbed the steep road to the starry citadel"; and then announces that Augustus himself will one day recline between them, sipping nectar with roseate lips.

quos inter Augustus recumbens
purpureo bibit ore nectar.

The metrical effect of that sumptuously indolent word *"recumbens,"* the color of the next word, the neat sipping effect of the two thin syllables in *"bibit,"* and the full vowel-sound of *"ore,"* closing with a slight smack of the lips on *"nectah"*—(for that surely is how the beatified Augustus was intended to pronounce it)—form one of the most amusing bits of word-painting, visual and onomatopoeic, to be found anywhere. It reminds one of the art with which Aristophanes, in *The Clouds,* and Voltaire, in his Horatian epistle to Phyllis, mingle irony and poetry each to heighten the other.

It is baffling, however, to find that some commentators who refuse to take Horace seriously on much more important matters are determined to take passages of this kind as the real and entirely serious reversal of his political principles. Instead of comparing this passage with Aristophanes, they solemnly compare it with Virgil. They tell us that the phrase *"purpureo ore"* must be applied not merely to the mouth, but to the whole face, and even more solemnly, to the halo of rosy light which surrounds the head of the beatified Augustus. They quote delightful passages from other poets about the rosy face of Venus; but in following that charming idea, they forget the realistic cause of the flush. The most charitable of observers, if he saw a glorified Emperor with a drinking-cup in his hand and a face that might be described as *"purpureo,"* might have justifiable suspicions; and, if the beatific effect was extended to the recumbent monarch's aura, the evidence would at least be circumstantial.

"Purple-stainèd mouth," from the *Ode to a Nightingale,* has been suggested by good Latinists, and it is in accord with the tone of the poem. It should be remarked, however, that in Keats it is used, not of the drinker, but of the cup:

> With beaded bubbles winking at the brim,
> And purple-stainèd mouth.

All that Horace meant to say was that the lips of Augustus looked rosy as he sipped his nectar; but if the phrase is extended to the whole face, Akenside (on lyric poetry) gives a closer parallel:

His cheek displays a second spring
Of roses, taught by wine to bloom.

I suppose it is possible to call this "flattery," but as Horace applies it to Augustus, it sounds a good deal more like raillery. After all, Augustus had written, "Take any liberty with me. It is my wish." Horace knew that the Emperor wished to be mentioned in his poems. If pleasantries of this kind satisfied him, so much the better. He was intended, of course, to share the joke. The poem in which this brief Aristophanic beatification occurs is in some other respects one of the most serious that Horace ever wrote. Toward the end of it, after a passage in which his convictions are expressed with real passion, he pulls himself up and says that this is no strain for the jesting Muse:

non hoc jocosae conveniet lyrae.

But it was the jocose part—the two lines about Augustus—that was really the digression. All the rest is in a very different strain, and the first two stanzas have brought strength and courage to many a lonely idealist:

The just man, tenacious of his purpose, is not shaken in the fortress of his soul by the passions of the mob, demanding what is wrong, nor by the tyrant's menacing frown; nor by the storm wind of the turbulent Adriatic, nor by the thunderbolts of Olympus. Though all the rending heavens should fall upon him, the wreck would find him standing upright still.

But no English can reproduce the iron strength of the interlocking Latin phrases with which, as we noted earlier, Cornelius de Witte, on the rack, defied his tormentors. They are probably the only verses which have ever served so grim a purpose:

Justum et tenacem propositi virum
non civium ardor prava jubentium,
non vultus instantis tyranni
mente quatit solida, neque Auster.

Perhaps it was the thought of Cornelius de Witte that struck the imagination of Browning and inspired one of his finest poems, *Instans Tyrannus*. He took the title from Horace, of course; but he put the dramatic monologue into the mouth, not of the victim, but of the tyrant. Although the approach is so different, no poem in English could so well represent the inner spirit of the Roman poem. The conclusion, when the tyrant has exhausted all his means of crushing the victim into submission, is expressed in the terms of Christendom, but it carries the central thought of Horace to its logical conclusion, establishing all those relations which distinguish it from the statement of a crude commonplace, and make us feel exactly why it has lived upon the lips and in the hearts of so many generations:

Do you see? Just my vengeance complete
    The man sprang to his feet,
Stood erect, caught at God's skirts and prayed.
—So, *I* was afraid.

XIV

REGULUS

ONE OF THE MOST NOTABLE AND BEAUTIFUL EXAMPLES OF THE
way in which Horace would end a poem on an apparently careless note that really deepened the effect of the whole, is the
famous ode *Caelo tonantem*. Landor, not always an appreciative critic of Horace, as the marginal notes in his own copy indi-
cate, was a whole-hearted admirer of this poem. "The finest
odes in the Greek language," he said, "have too many low notes
and somewhat of a wooden sound compared with this." Sellar
finds in it one of the passages in which Horace attains a grandeur
comparable with that of the finest passages in Lucretius. It
begins with a statement which renders to Caesar the things that
are Caesar's; but, as always in Horace, it makes Caesar subordinate to the gods. It is done here, with a touch of irony for the
shallower kind of believers in both the heavenly and the earthly
power; but this is only the poet's way of indicating the deeper
reality. *"We believe that Jupiter reigns because we hear him
thundering in heaven. Augustus will be held a very present
divinity on earth, because he has added the Britons and the
dreaded Parthians to the Empire."* But he swiftly moves on
from this to the story of Regulus, who warned Rome against
the shameful terms which he had been sent by the enemy to pro-
pose, and then, despite the entreaties of his friends, returned
according to his pledged word, to die.

But Horace is not merely telling the story of Regulus.
Through the words that he puts into the mouth of that mighty
representative of the ancient Roman spirit there throbs his own
conviction of the dangers that beset his own time. When Regu-

lus denounces those who had soiled the Roman name, there is a subtle and solemn warning to the contemporary world. We feel it, even though the terms used are those of ancient wars and ancient sorrows. We feel it in that last bitter exclamation of Regulus—"O, mighty Carthage, throned so high upon the shameful wreck of Italy." Regulus turns to go; and there is a momentary pause, a change in the tone of the poem, beginning with the word *fertur*. "It is said"—for we get no further direct word from Regulus—and, at this point, the poem begins to throb with a deep slow pulse, a music measured and precise as a funeral march, but with all the notes of compassion and indomitable fortitude ringing and crying through its majestic and immitigable law:

It is said that he put aside the embraces of his virtuous wife and his little children, as one bereft of his civil rights, and sternly bent his manly gaze upon the ground until he could strengthen the faltering resolve of the Senate by such counsel as no man ever gave before him. Then through his sorrowing friends he went his way, a glorious exile. And yet he knew what the barbarous torturer was preparing for him. In like manner he moved aside the friends who stood in his way and the people who would have hindered his going, as if, the case decided, he were no more than leaving the long drawn out business of his clients and going to the fields of Venafrum, or to Spartan Tarentum.

> *Fertur pudicae coniugis osculum*
> *parvosque natos ut capitis minor*
> *ab se removisse et virilem*
> *torvus humi posuisse voltum,*
>
> *donec labantis consilio patres*
> *firmaret auctor numquam alias dato,*
> *interque maerentes amicos*
> *egregius properaret exsul.*

Regulus

Atqui sciebat quae sibi barbarus
tortor pararet. non aliter tamen
  dimovit obstantes propinquos
    et populum reditus morantem,

quam si clientum longa negotia
diiudicata lite relinqueret,
  tendens Venafranos in agros
    aut Lacedaemonium Tarentum.

The phrase "as if he were going on a journey to Tarentum" gives to the departure of Regulus exactly that air of unconcern which Horace uses in many lighter ways to close his poems; but, in this case, it has a deeper and intensely moving effect.

It may be noted too, that, in one of the stanzas translated above, Horace speaks of the deprivation of civil rights as a thing that might make a man feel like an exile even in his own country. Here, as in a hundred passages elsewhere, it is his own deep feeling for the disinherited and dispossessed, his own experience, or that of his father, that wells up into his mind and gives him the comparison.

The close of this poem is a perfect example of that art of poetry about which, in the mental chaos of our time, there is so much ignorance and confusion. Its metrical precision is one of the factors that lift it completely out of the category of mechanical things into a mysterious accord with the rhythms of universal law. W. K. Clifford, one of the most distinguished of the scientific agnostics of the last century, wrote an extremely interesting essay on this subject. He compares the inspired poet with a musician who, when his cue comes, is caught up by the surrounding orchestra, the orchestra of the universe, and forced to play his part with exactness of tune and time. The metrical "regularity," in which not a syllable can go astray from the controlling pulse of the mind and heart thus attuned, becomes then something very different indeed from the artificial "convention" which those who are ignorant of the world's poetry from Virgil and Dante to Milton and Keats, or Verlaine and Carducci, so commonly assume it to be. Metrical form, verse—the "golden numbers," as Pope would have called them, the quality of song that made Ovid call Horace *"numerosus"*—by its discipline and its restrictions, becomes an infinitely capable instrument of expression. Law and liberty are not contradictory in art any more than in life. It has been said that one of Wordsworth's greatest poems, the *Ode to Duty,* is in form and substance one of the best examples of a Horatian ode in English:

> Me this unchartered freedom tires;
> I feel the weight of chance desires. . . .

The order of the words, the position of the first pronoun at the beginning, and the verb at the end of the line, is of course a recollection of the Latin idiom. But the whole poem with its personification of Duty as the "stern daughter of the voice of God" is very much in the manner and spirit of Horace. It has a very direct bearing upon the subject under discussion, the dependence of liberty upon law, and of the higher flights of expression in art on discipline and perfection of form. The rhythms of the universe which, after all, is a metrical composition, are not a mere "convention." They not only give organic unity and save us from chaos, but they enable us to use our faculties in the most effective way. "Only the feet that move in order, dance. Only the words that move in order, sing."

> Stern Lawgiver! yet thou dost wear
> The Godhead's most benignant grace;
> Nor know we anything so fair
> As is the smile upon thy face:

Flowers laugh before thee on their beds
And fragrance in thy footing treads;
Thou dost preserve the stars from wrong;
And the most ancient heavens, through
    Thee, are fresh and strong.

Wickham, one of the best and most authoritative of all the modern editors of Horace, writing on the close of the Regulus poem, calls attention to the precision of the metrical effects, even to the recurrence of certain sounds in the like endings of two words in the last line:

It belongs partly to Horace himself, partly to poetic art generally. The passion in poetry which gives pleasure is not unbridled passion, but passion felt to be measured and controlled by mind. This is the intellectual side of the pleasure added to poetry by the recurrence of rhyme and meter.

It is not meter that makes the poem, but a meter-making argument, said Emerson. In other words, if the poet has something to say which is true enough and deep enough to find the heart of things, that universal heart will throb through it. It is the battle between blind emotion and the mind that, when the latter eventually takes control, pulses into metrical beauty. The horses of the sun, no longer trying to tear the chariot to pieces, move with the rhythm of a vital function to their desired goal. There is a profound philosophical principle involved in this theory of art, and Horace is quite conscious of it, though he would not have expressed it in the same terms. His own theory, as delivered in *The Art of Poetry*, which is discussed in a later chapter, is in complete accord with it. He acted upon it, and gave perfect examples of it in many of his odes.

THE CLAP OF THUNDER

OUTWARDLY THE LIFE OF HORACE AT THE SABINE FARM WAS uneventful, but it was there that his mind and spirit had their most interesting adventures. The most important of these was in the field of religion, where he began to discover that he believed more and more definitely in a Supreme Power, manifesting itself in the universe, controlling human destinies, and demanding, on pain of disaster, that men should establish a right relationship with it.

One of the most interesting of the poems in this connection is the thirty-fourth ode of the first book, which tells us that "a clap of thunder" out of a clear sky had convinced the poet that the wisdom of the Epicureans was foolishness. The "clap of thunder" is not to be taken literally, of course; but neither is it to be taken "playfully," as one famous critic would have it. Lessing described the poem as "a half-playful record of a poetical mood which it would be sheer pedantry to interpret as a serious recantation." He adds that Augustus was so afraid of thunder that he would hide himself on the approach of a storm. The reader may "playfully" inquire what this information about Augustus has to do with the poem by Horace.

It is sometimes said that Horace was "converted" from Epicureanism to Stoicism, but this is not quite true; for—as we have seen—he had never bound himself to any school of philosophy. He would take from any, or all of them, whatever seemed necessary to his scheme of thought, and he would discard the rest of their doctrine with a gay and impartial smile. It was not necessarily a smile at the tenets of the philosophers. Quite as often it was a smile at himself, or at the limitations of the human reason, including his own. But he was not one of those odd sceptics who mistake their own limitations, or the limitations of mankind, for the boundaries of the universe. The gentleness with which he touches the old Italian religion of the field and fold—as in the prayer to Faunus—was due to his instinctive sense that these personifications were attempts of the human mind to represent the various attributes of a single divine Power, manifested throughout the universe.

Cicero, a generation earlier than Horace, had expressed exactly this view of the matter in his book *De Natura Deorum:*

God, being present everywhere in Nature, can be regarded in the fields as Ceres; or in the sea as Neptune; and elsewhere in a variety of forms, in all of which He may be worshipped.

Lucretius himself, with all his hostility to superstition, continually suggested this line of thought. The splendid address to Venus, in which he celebrates the life-giving and procreative Power that moves through all Nature, is not a mere phantasy. He brings it into focus for the mind of the reader, and for his own mind, by personifying that Power as Venus. The naive question whether he really believed in the goddess Venus as represented in marble by the sculptors thus becomes almost meaningless.

It is almost equally meaningless to ask whether Horace (or Lucretius, for that matter) really believed in the serene heaven of the Epicureans, who—in a sense—were the deists of the ancient world, believing in gods, but holding them to be careless of mankind. The modern world has learned to look on these gods also as they are represented at two removes by the sculptor or painter. But to ask an intelligent Roman if he really believed in those marble figures would be like asking an American if he really believed in the Statue of Liberty. There is as much difference between the Statue of Liberty and the idea of Liberty as there is between the marble Apollo in his temple and the light-giving, music-making, destroying and healing power which even the most Lucretian of the Roman intellectuals could still regard as a reality. Utterly beyond his immediate comprehension, it might still be brought into focus for his mind by the language of art. It would be impossible to give direct expression to all that was meant whenever that power was mentioned, in conversation or in writing; but the single word *Apollo* served as a hieroglyph, or—if the modern world prefers it—a formula, which embraced a great complex of ideas, and yet could be understood by the simplest peasant. Horace was as far from a narrow scepticism as he was from superstition. He was even farther from any mere conventional use of those hieroglyphs, the names of the gods. A dull and conventional man might use them emptily and conventionally; but not an exquisite artist like Horace.

There has been much confusion among some of the commentators on this matter. Dryden—a sound critic on many subjects —was curiously undiscriminating and insensitive in his preface to the *Odes* of Horace. "Let his Dutch commentators say what they will," he remarked bluntly, "his philosophy is Epicurean, and he made use of gods and Providence only to serve a turn in poetry."

This analysis, in the first place, ignores the express declaration of Horace himself that he was bound to no school of philosophy, and his express repudiation of at least one of the central tenets of Epicureanism. In the second place, the contemptuous dismissal of "poetry," as if it were not concerned with truth, is inconsistent with the importance that Dryden attaches to that art. If poetry could really be served by conventional tricks of the kind that Dryden attributed to Horace, it has precisely the value of those tricks, which is nothing. It could be made just as well, and probably better, out of Epicureanism; for there would then be none of those doubts and perplexities.

"God has power to bring down the mighty and exalt the lowly," says Horace:

> *Valet ima summis*
> *mutare et insignem attenuat deus*
> *obscura promens; hinc apicem rapax*
> *Fortuna cum stridore acuto*
> *sustulit, hic posuisse gaudet.*

The latter part of this stanza is an example of Cicero's saying that God can be worshipped under many names. *Fortuna* is here his outward appearance, or that personified means whereby he achieves his purpose. There is certainly no unbridgeable gulf here between the words of Horace and the theme of a great passage in the Magnificat: "He hath put down the mighty from their seat, and hath exalted the humble and meek."

Sir Thomas Browne, in fact, understated it when he said that "The Romans that erected a temple to Fortune acknowledged, though in a blinder way, somewhat of divinity." Pindar called Fortune "the child of God." Perhaps the most beautiful illustration, or illumination, of what Horace is actually saying about God and Fortune is put into the mouth of Virgil in the seventh canto of the *Inferno*. I give John Carlyle's translation of the passage in which Dante asks the question, and is answered by the Roman poet:

"Master," I said to him, "Now tell me also: this Fortune of which thou hintest to me; what is she, that has the good things of the world thus within her clutches?"

And he to me: "O foolish creatures, how great is this ignorance that falls upon you! Now I wish thee to receive my judgment of her.

He whose wisdom is transcendent over all, made the heavens and gave them guides, so that every part shines to every part, equally distributing the light.

In like manner, for worldly splendours, he ordained a general minister and guide, to change betimes the vain possession, from people to people, and from one kindred to another, beyond the hindrance of human wisdom. Hence one people commands, another languishes, obeying her sentence, which is hidden like the serpent in the grass.

Your knowledge cannot understand her; she provides judges, and maintains her kingdom, as the other gods do theirs.

Her permutations have no truce; necessity makes her be swift. . . .

This is she, who is so much reviled, even by those who ought to praise her, when blaming her wrongfully, and with evil words.

But she is in bliss, and hears it not: with the other primal creatures joyful, she wheels her sphere and tastes her blessedness."

It was this sense of a directive Power acting through what is commonly called "Fortune," and taking Horace by surprise, that really constitutes the subject of his ode. He had always had this sense in a certain degree, but apparently something had happened which made him feel it more intensely. This is what he means by the "clap of thunder in a clear sky."

In his next ode, the thirty-fifth of the first book, Horace continues the theme with a more definite personification of Fortuna herself, as a "goddess," by which he means nothing more or less, than a minister or instrument of the Supreme Power. The Romans built many temples to her, of which the chief were at Praeneste and Antium: "O goddess, Queen of Antium, a present power to raise our mortal frame from low estate, or to turn proud triumphs into processions of death . . . Destiny goes before thee with all her iron weapons; but Hope, too, waits upon thee, and Faith, in her white veil. Only the faithless rabble and the perjured harlot turn away from thee."

It is to be observed that ethical considerations are again introduced and bound up with the whole conception of a divine Power, manifesting itself in the universe, and not indifferent to those considerations. It is quite uncritical to suggest, as one or two modern writers have done, that ideas so subtly pervasive were introduced merely to serve an empty convention. Whose convention? Certainly not that of the majority, who were already heading for the very ills against which Horace was warning them. There is nothing in the least conventional about his attacks on the conventional disregard of ethics. *Odi profanum vulgus* might be the motto for all that Horace has to say on this subject. He touched no familiar maxim that he did not revitalize and suffuse with the dry light of the intellect, and sometimes make symbolical of things beyond the scope of intellectual statement.

Horace had always felt that he was in some providential way helped and protected by the gods, as in that episode of his childhood, when he was lost on the hills. A fuller conviction of this apparently developed out of his exploration of Stoicism, of which Warde Fowler remarks that "It woke in the mind an entirely new idea of Deity, far transcending that of Roman *numina* and of Greek polytheism, and yet not incapable of being reconciled with these; so that it might be taken as an outpouring of sudden light upon old conceptions of the Power, glorifying and transfiguring them, rather than, like the Epicurean faith, a bitter and contemptuous negation of man's inherited religious instincts."

One of the most significant of all his poems in this connection is the twelfth ode of the first book, where he expresses, in the terms of his own period, almost exactly what has been said above. This notable poem is commonly described as an "ode in praise of Augustus"; and it is frequently said that, after reviewing the claims of various gods and heroes to be celebrated by the Muse, it culminates in the praises of Caesar. But this comment omits entirely the subject which Horace declares to be the most significant of all; and I do not see how any critic can be justified in simply ignoring that central subject altogether, even to the extent of omitting all reference to the last three lines of the poem—its real culmination.

The two brief clauses toward the end of the ode in which Caesar is mentioned are carefully and deliberately designed to put first things first, and to lead up to those closing lines on an infinitely more important subject—the "Father of gods and men, from whom there is nothing begotten greater than Himself, nor is there anything like unto Him, or next to Him."

Horace makes it quite clear that it is only in establishing a right relationship with that Divine Ruler through justice and righteousness that the rule of Caesar can prosper. Virgil speaks of Augustus as *deus,* merging the man into the god. Horace mentions gods and heroes and men and various forms of earthly power, including that of Caesar; but he subordinates them all to the higher Power which is the central subject of his poem. Not only is everything subordinated to that, but every kind of earthly authority and power and prosperity is shown to be dependent on the "Father who rules the lives of men and gods and governs land and sea and all the heavens." The sceptical modern may, if he please, identify this supreme God with the conventional Jupiter of the classical dictionaries. But this is as misleading in the case of Horace as it would be in the case of Virgil. He does use the figures of his own mythology; but he uses them as a poet; endowing them with meanings beyond those which are commonly attached to them and, in the supreme

instance, infinitely beyond the conventional meaning. He speaks
of the "accustomed praises" of the Father of gods and men who
rules the entire world; and then he adds those four lines which,
for all their simplicity, go down to the depths of the argument
for the existence of God. Consider them again:

From whom there is begotten nothing greater than Himself,
nor is there anything like unto Him or next to Him. Nevertheless
the glory which is nearest to his own belongs to Wisdom.

> *unde nil majus generatur ipso,*
> *nec viget quicquam simile aut secundum;*
> *proximos illi tamen occupavit*
> *Pallas honores.*

These are by no means "accustomed" or conventional praises,
by a poet using his mythological personages merely to fill his
lines. They have a philosophical meaning which might find its
place in an argument of Plato or St. Thomas Aquinas. It is only
by completely ignoring this passage, especially the words, "none
is like or even next to Him," that the modern critic can possibly
maintain that Caesar is the culmination of the poem. The thought
of this passage is continued right up to the last lines, and Caesar is
only mentioned with direct reference to his subordination, along
with that of all other forms of earthly power. "Thou, O Lord,
art more than they" were the words of a nineteenth-century
poet. "Subject to Thee (*te minor*)" was the phrase of the
Roman; and in its terse abruptness, of course, it moves in a
different world. It is less like a prayer and more like a military
salute. It is very much at the mercy of the translators, who are
inclined in that passage to render more to Caesar than the poem
as a whole really allows.

There are many passages in the Old Testament about the
relation of kings to God. Allowing for the difference between

the Hebrew and the Roman mind, they offer an almost exact parallel to this passage in our secular psalter. It is mere habit which has led so many editors to pass over the words, together with all the references to them, which are repeated again and again. It seems to be taken for granted that the work of Horace is a kind of grammatical exercise, and that this excludes a subject so serious. Augustus, however, was a different matter, for he comes into the history books, while God is, of course, just one of those conventional myths. Even if it were as true as it is false, it would still be utterly uncritical to ignore what the poem directly says, and what it also indirectly conveys through its music. We may therefore examine it a little more closely.

The sequence of ideas in this poem is interesting. I think it has a direct bearing on the request of Augustus that Horace should mention him; for it begins by asking the Muse of history what man or hero she would now choose to celebrate on the Latin flute or the Greek lyre. Then he adds almost as an afterthought, "or what god?" In two exquisite stanzas he then makes us hear the musical echoes ringing as of old from crag to crag along the shadowy slopes of Helicon, and from the heights of Pindus; and in the cool groves of Haemus whence in ancient days the woods uprooted themselves and came flocking after Orpheus; for his music—the music he learned from his mother —compelled all things to obey. It stilled the rapid streams and the rushing winds, and it drew the listening oaks to follow him:

> *aut in umbrosis Heliconis oris*
> *aut super Pindo gelidove in Haemo?*
> *Unde vocalem temere insecutae*
> *Orphea silvae.*

No translations can represent the remote glory and cool shadows of those musical hills and glens. But Shakespeare made a song of his own out of those two stanzas:

Orpheus with his lute made trees,
And the mountain tops that freeze,
  Bow themselves when he did sing;
To his music, plants and flowers
Ever sprung as sun and showers
  There had made a lasting spring.

Everything that heard him play,
Even the billows of the sea,
  Hung their heads and then lay by.
In sweet music is such art,
Killing care and grief of heart
  Fall asleep or hearing die.

The idea is older than the legend of Orpheus, and it has taken many forms in poetry; but they all lead up to the same thing. By the analogy of music they suggest an ultimate and harmonious power which can build and unbuild the universe, and control all the operations of Nature. It was not merely because Orpheus looked back at Eurydice that he lost her, but because there was a break in the music. In another legend it is Arion who makes the dolphins obey him through the power of music. In another it is the walls and towers of a city that rise to music, as if by an incantation. Dryden, in his song for St. Cecilia's Day, when he refers to Orpheus, is a little stilted:

Orpheus could lead the savage race;
And trees uprooted left their place,
  Sequacious of the lyre:

but he uses the legend as the nucleus of that greater idea of which we have been speaking:

From harmony, from heavenly harmony
  This universal frame began:
From harmony to harmony,
  Through all the compass of the notes it ran,
  The diapason closing full in man.

Browning, in a profoundly moving way, approaches the same idea in *Abt Vogler:*

Would it might tarry like his, the beautiful building of mine,
This which my keys in a crowd pressed and importuned to raise!

In every case we find ourselves on the borders of the eternal world. In Shakespeare's song we catch a gleam of a perennial Spring where all discords and griefs are resolved. Even in the lighter mood of Tennyson's early lines beginning,

The rain had fallen, the Poet arose,

there is this suggestion of a power in music that can compel all Nature to obey it, and hold all the movements of the material world in a hushed suspense:

And he sat him down in a lonely place,
And chanted a melody loud and sweet,
That made the wild-swan pause in her cloud,
And the lark drop down at his feet.

In all these instances we are really being told that music brings us out of the temporal world into the eternal. It can dissolve all material bonds and show us that beyond the baseless fabric of this earthly vision, there lies an eternal world of the spirit.

It is not by a meaningless accident or a careless and irrelevant use of an unrelated fragment of mythology, that Horace takes the legend of Orpheus as the immediate preface to what is perhaps the most philosophical passage in all his poetry:

Of what shall I sing before the wonted praise of the Father . . . who rules the sea and land and all the heavens with their changing seasons. From Him is begotten nothing mightier than Himself, nor lives there anything like to Him, or second to Him; yet the place nearest to him in honor belongs to Wisdom.

I have translated Pallas by "Wisdom," for it seems quite certain that it was of her attributes as the goddess of wisdom that Horace was thinking when he brought her into that close relationship with the All Ruler. Those editors were surely right who close that stanza with a period after the words *"Pallas honores."* Bentley substituted a comma, and attached to Pallas the words that open the next stanza: *"proeliis audax."* But "boldness in battle" is certainly not the virtue which Horace would place nearest to the divine in that profound conception of a deity controlling all the operations of the universe. It is Wisdom of which he is thinking; and although his idea of Pallas may be as far from the "Wisdom" of the Old Testament as the fourth eclogue of Virgil is from the prophecy of Isaiah, there is, nevertheless, a real relationship between them. From a far distance he seems to have caught an echo of the Book of Wisdom itself.

Moreover, the words, "bold in battle" are necessary to the meaning of the next stanza. There would be no conceivable point in his introduction of the god Liber (whom Horace identifies with Bacchus), at this particular stage of the poem if it were not for these words. Bacchus here, of course, is not that chubby, rose-garlanded toper, half-Silenus and half-cherub, of later times. He is the god described again and identified with Liber in the nineteenth ode of the second book. Horace is carrying on the idea of the absolute supremacy and unapproachable godhead of the All-Father, and referring to the battle in which the impious crew of Titans attempted to storm Heaven, and with their leader Rhoetus were hurled back by the god Bacchus with his lion's claws:

> *Tu, cum parentis regna per arduum*
> *cohors Gigantum scanderet impia,*
> *Rhoetum retorsisti leonis*
> *unguibus horribilique mala.*

In the third ode of the third book again Bacchus is compared with the man who holds unshakably to the cause of right, undeterred by tyranny or the blind forces of Nature. "It is for such virtue, Father Bacchus, that thy tigers drew thee."

If the words, "bold in battle," are taken away from the conqueror of the impious Titans and given to Pallas, the unfortunate Liber is left standing alone in the poem without any explanation at all, like one of the statues in the groves of Blarney. Pallas needs no more than her attribute of wisdom and the place given her next to the divine Power. The meaning of her position there is not altered, even if the other words are attached to her instead of to Bacchus; but the unnecessary addition confuses the firm and beautiful design of the poem. Fortunately some of the best modern editors (including Macleane, Wickham, and Smith) have seen no textual reason for following Bentley. Other eminent Latinists have followed him; and the textual argument has usually omitted any consideration of the poetical and philosophic values. Bentley's emendations of *Paradise Lost* illustrate the dangers of this. A very great scholar, absorbed in textual criticism and all the delightfully kaleidoscopic results that can be achieved by varying the punctuation, may sometimes look directly into an immortal face without seeing it.

XVI

THE ART OF POETRY

THERE IS INTERNAL EVIDENCE TO SHOW THAT HORACE WAS disappointed at the cool reception of his odes by the professional critics. He whistled to keep up his courage. There is a touch of defiance in the consolation which he draws from the appreciation of the few; but it is not altogether with a light heart that he announces his intention to abandon these toys and take to philosophy. This is the note struck in the first collection of his epistles which he published in 20 B.C. If he was to be denied the higher flights of poetry, he might still continue with his conversations in verse. But, in whatever form he wrote, he could not help being himself and, beautifully mature in wisdom as these epistles are, he could not help saying what he thought. So he found himself once again in opposition to the majority. The world was not going the way Maecenas, Horace, and Virgil had hoped it would go. The Emperor's own family were setting the example of breaking those "Augustan laws" which, *sine moribus*, as Horace himself had said, were futile. The most delightful essays ever written on the conduct of life are not likely to find favor in a world which prefers to misconduct itself. He had to wait for posterity to give the final verdict, which has been summed up by Shorey in a single sentence: "in urbanity, gentle good sense, and genial world-wisdom, they are justly deemed the finest flower of Latin literature."

It is probably to this period of disappointment that the epistle on the Art of Poetry belongs, though it may have been published later, with the second book of epistles. "*Nil scribens ipse, docebo,*" he says, directly challenging the familiar taunt that criticism is written by those who can't create.

The poem usually called *De Arte Poetica* was not thus entitled by Horace. It was an epistle addressed to a father and two sons named Piso. It is said that they were descendants of the Piso who had been lampooned by Catullus; and although Macleane says there is no internal evidence of their identity, Horace at least connects them (in line 292) with a family which claimed descent from Numa Pompilius.

They wanted to write plays and poems, and had asked Horace for advice. He gave it to them. One of the most famous passages is that in which he tells the elder son to show his work to a good critic, and then lock it up in his desk for nine years, so that later on he may have the opportunity of destroying it unseen by the world.

In this, Horace was laying down a sound maxim. He obeyed it himself, though his term of years was usually less than nine. But the longer term recommended to the young Piso has more humor behind it than Tennyson allowed in his lines on "the wise adviser." To appreciate it fully, perhaps, we must picture the disconcerted face to which the advice was so gravely and urbanely delivered.

The Pisos, in fact, were bad poets. Horace was too good-natured to tell them so directly; but he points out, in another famous passage, that mediocrity in poetry cannot be tolerated by gods or men. It has been suggested that the *Art of Poetry* might have been a more valuable work if it had been addressed to good poets; but this is to miss the whole point of it. Horace had no wish to write a systematic treatise. Nor would good poets require or welcome a treatise on how to write poetry. It is just because Horace follows the method of the satires that in trying to set the crooked straight he is able to mingle so much quiet humor with his wisdom and make so eminently readable a contribution to critical literature. Its mellowness of tone when he speaks of himself as about to abandon the writing of poetry beautifully conceals his own disappointment. He applies—perhaps he invented—that adage about critics, with a smile as subtle as it is good-humored, to Quintus Horatius Flaccus. He would return to the writing of epistles (*sermones*), which he regarded as verse, not poetry. He was to repeat this wish to retire from the conflict in other epistles and, later on, in the fourth book of odes. But the *Art of Poetry* seems to find its natural place among the earlier epistles, though it may have been published later. It is a part of the literary discussion which runs through all his work, and it may be regarded as the central chapter of it. Critics have occasionally suggested that it was unfinished; but, if Horace had any additions or improvements to make, it would be absurdly contradictory of the principles which it lays down, to publish it prematurely. There is no evidence that it was first published posthumously; and there is every reason to suppose that Horace regarded it as a finished work.

The only sense in which it is incomplete is that it does not cover the whole ground systematically; but, in that sense, his philosophical poems, and indeed all philosophical poems, are incomplete. Nor would further work upon them change their method and character. The aim of a poem, or an epistle of this kind, is entirely different from that of a textbook. Literature, as Professor Campbell observes in his book on Horace, is a different thing from "learned industry." One or two writers have apparently mistaken the light conversational vein in which Horace breaks off the more serious discussion as a sign of incompleteness. But it is merely another example of that favorite device with which he ends so many of his poems, and which has been examined at length earlier. The *Epistle to the Pisos* should be compared, not with Aristotle's poetics, but with Addison's *Essays on Paradise Lost,* on the serious side, and perhaps with

Montaigne in its more humorous passages. It approaches the subject from the point of view of the artist, rather than that of the philosopher; and, like Pope's *Essay on Criticism*, it abounds in phrases that have become proverbial. It has had a pervasive influence on the course of literature throughout Europe. Like the works of Cicero, it is grievously underrated by those who cannot distinguish, as Campbell does so admirably, between literature and "learned industry." But it contains a sound warning to those who think it is enough merely to make that distinction, or those who believe that mastery in any of the arts can be obtained without culture and hard work.

It begins with an application to the arts of a principle for which he contended in every department of life. It is nothing more or less than his old principle of the "golden mean" developed to a point where we discover that all the heresies of art, like the heresies of faith, are merely exaggerations of a single idea which, if it had been kept to its right proportions in relationship to other ideas, would have been true. Taken out of those relationships and exaggerated, it becomes false, and it misleads many people through the fact that originally it possessed a grain of truth (*decipimur specie recti*). "I strive to be brief and become obscure. I aim at smoothness and fail in strength and spirit. The poet who aims at grandeur becomes turgid. Another creeps along the ground and is afraid to battle with the storm. Another, anxious to achieve variety, puts a dolphin in the forest and a wild boar in the middle of the sea. Even the avoidance of a fault may lead to mistakes of this kind."

It is a lesson which has not yet been learned. Poets have sometimes found that by translating the impressions of one sense into those of another, they obtain a beautiful effect. Sydney Dobell, for instance, once compared a streak of color in a sunset sky to a hunter's horn heard in the distance. This was quite rightly admired, and the occasional use of such a device, in many poets of the past, was entirely justifiable. But when it was seized, elaborated out of all proportion, and announced as a new theory of art, so that the poets began to talk of the smell or music or describe the colors of the vowels and declare that they heard the sunset braying like an ass, it became merely a signal of the incompetent poseur. People who did not know how often it had been done in the right way, however, were misled by the little grain of original truth into thinking it an artistic revelation. They went about anxiously explaining, sometimes to those who had long been familiar with the fact, that the idea was to translate the impressions of one sense into terms of another, and they felt aggrieved when their friends refused to become excited about it. Horace, in fact, struck the first note of warning about a process which in modern times has only too often demonstrated its absurdity, but, if he had lived in the nineteenth century he would have made delicious use of certain modern extravagances. What a picture he would have drawn for us of that unfortunate French poet, Gerard de Nerval who, in the Tuileries, saw the gold-fish in the big fountain putting their heads out of the water and trying to entice him to follow them to the bottom. The Queen of Sheba was waiting for him there, they said. What a picture, too, we might have had of that other occasion when the French poet was found at the Palais Royal dragging a live lobster along at the end of a blue ribbon. He argued with impeccable logic that, as it was allowable to take a dog on a leash for a walk, there was no reason why he should not take a lobster, which even his physicians admitted was a quiet and serious animal that knew all the secrets of the deep sea, and never barked. On another occasion he saw a black sun. He was confined several times in a sanitarium and maintained that he had undergone a grave deterioration when he recovered his reason. But his reputation in literary society unfortunately secured his freedom, with the result that he went out and hanged himself.

The *Art of Poetry* sometimes answers questions which have been set by later writers. Matthew Arnold's use of single lines as a touchstone of poetic value, is often illuminating; but there is an equally useful corrective in what Horace says about the "purple patch," a phrase which he originated. The purple patch sewn on to a plainer stuff, with a splendid irrelevance to the context, may be seen far and wide, he reminds us; and he has no need to say more.

> *purpureus, late qui splendeat, unus et alter*
> *adsuitur pannus. . . .*

By implication, too, he deals with one of the perennial faults of casual criticism which, instead of selecting a purple patch for disproportionate praise, often goes to the opposite extreme, and takes an insignificant line out of its context in order to depreciate a masterpiece. In a long poem, though every rift should be "loaded with ore," you cannot have the rift unless you have the rock. There are many occasions when very ordinary things have to be said. They may be only connecting links between one striking action and another. The most magnificent of heroes may sometimes have to walk quietly across a room. Perhaps it was unnecessary for Thomas Hardy, in *The Dynasts*, to say, in blank verse:

> The Emperor will now go up to bed.

But Wordsworth cannot display some of his glorious mountain scenery unless we are prepared for a somewhat arduous climb up a barren path. Possibly he does not spare his readers as much as he might; but it would still be bad criticism to detach a bare connecting passage as an illustration of its author's power.

Horace, in some very famous phrases, warns us against this. "A bad poet," he says, "if he suddenly produces a good line, may surprise his readers and make them laugh. I feel annoyed when Homer, who is so good as a rule, occasionally nods a little. But one must expect moments of drowsiness in a very long work:

> *indignor quandoque bonus dormitat Homerus.*
> *verum operi longo fas est obrepere somnum.*

Passages of this kind provide a lesson for critics as well as for poets; and it was this aspect of the epistle that, through Boileau, had so great an effect upon French literature. The parallel is very close to Pope's *Essay on Criticism,* which indeed must be regarded as one of his many imitations of Horace. In one passage Pope hits off the very characteristics which have just been discussed:

> Horace still charms with graceful negligence,
> And without method talks us into sense,
> Will, like a friend, familiarly convey
> The truest notions in the easiest way.
> He who, supreme in judgment as in wit,
> Might boldly censure, as he boldly writ,
> Yet judged with coolness, though he sung with fire;
> His precepts teach but what his works inspire.

In an earlier passage Pope places Horace on a level with the greatest of the Greek critics:

> Unbiased or by favor or by spite,
> Not dully prepossessed nor blindly right;
> Though learn'd, well-bred, and though well-bred, sincere;
> Modestly bold, and humanly severe,
> Who to a friend his faults can freely show
> And gladly praise the merits of a foe . . .

> Such once were critics; such the happy few
> Athens and Rome in better ages knew.
> The mighty Stagyrite first left the shore
> Spread all his sails and durst the deeps explore;
> He steered securely, and discovered far.
> Led by the light of the Maeonian star.

Pope tells us further that the poets, though fond of "savage liberty," received the law thus discovered, and were convinced that the man who grasped so much of the laws of Nature was best fitted to preside over the realms of Art.

It was the Maeonian star that led Horace also. In Homer, he found that rational exposition of universal truth which is the secret of all great art. One of the most pointed sayings ever uttered on human nature was that of the nineteenth-century poet who remarked that every man—unless he is on his guard—tends to "impute himself." Dryasdust, in his treatment of the creative artists, is particularly apt to do this. A melancholy example is the learned Porphyrion, who suggested that Horace had actually based his *Art of Poetry* on a systematic treatise by Neoptolemus. This, of course, is contradictory of the accepted fact that the epistle is quite unsystematic. Sellar is inclined to take the suggestion seriously; but he does not accept it completely. To those who do, there is very little that can be said, except that real poets do not consult little books on how to write verse, for they usually know more about it than the men who write them. But one may recall the more modern Dryasdust who thought he had fathomed the success of Chaucer in describing the elegant manners of Madame Eglantyne:

> Hir over lippe wyped she so clene,
> That in hir coppe was no ferthing sene
> Of grece, whan she dronken hadde hir draughte.
> Ful semely after hir mete she raughte.

This, he said, Chaucer had got from a book of etiquette!

A great deal of the *Art of Poetry* is concerned with the drama; and, though it is true that Horace takes the Greeks as the best exemplars, he did not have to go to Neoptolemus for that; and his remarks about them are certainly his own. He takes Nature, here as elsewhere, for his final criterion; and his guides are reason and common sense.

"Give your days and nights to the study of Addison," said a wise adviser to those who would write good English; but he was only echoing the older saying of Horace about the Greeks. "The Greeks are your exemplars. Turn their pages night and day."

> *. . . Vos exemplaria Graeca*
> *Nocturna versate manu, versate diurna.*

He sweeps Plautus away as too crude a model; and who shall say he was wrong? But he affirms that the Romans might rival the Greeks in drama if they had a less materialistic form of education, and were only prepared to work, and use "the labor of the file." They should realize that a good poem demands infinite pains, and must be finished, like the work of a sculptor, *ad unguem.*

But always he returns to the eternal fountains. The true source of all good writing, he says, is wisdom. When you really have something to say, words will not be wanting:

He who has learned what he owes to his country and to his friends; the love that he should bear to his parents, his brother, or his guest; he who understands the duties of a senator, a judge, or the leader of an army in war—will certainly know how to give each character his right part. Those who have mastered their art must still draw from life the living word.

Shakespeare was familiar with this epistle. Perhaps he had pored over it at the Stratford grammar-school. The passage on the drama, in which Horace describes the "ages of man" from childhood to senility, is surely the fountain-head of the famous speech of Jaques. Horace, in fact, can be translated here into blank verse which, however far it fails to do the subject justice, suggests the kinship between the two passages. Thus rendered, this is what Horace wrote:

> At first, the child, with feet new-trained to walk,
> Plays with his mates all day; or, at a nothing
> Bursts into rage which, in an instant, turns
> To laughter, and still changes every hour.
> Then comes the beardless boy, set free from school,
> Riding his horse, rejoicing in his hounds,
> Who haunts the Campus Martius; soft as wax
> If evil moulds him, fretful at the curb
> Of wisdom; careless what the morrow brings;
> Prodigal of his coin; a sprightly colt,
> Swift to desire, and swifter to forego
> What yesterday he swore he loved the best.
> Then manhood, all for riches now, and friends,
> A slave to proud ambition, and ashamed
> To think his firm intent could ever change.
> Last comes old age, with all its gathering ills,
> Still seeking more, and yet afraid to use
> Its life-long hoard; sans courage and sans fire;
> Full of delays; content with hope deferred;
> Testy and grumbling, wishing that the world
> Were once again as when he was a boy.
> So, with the flowing tide, much good comes in;
> But, when it ebbs, it carries much away;
> And so to every age belongs its part;
> Youth must not play the dotard; nor the boy
> Ape manhood. Nature's law must rule the stage.

This is as literal a translation as many a prose version of the passage which begins with line 158 in the *Art of Poetry:*

> *Reddere qui voces jam scit puer et pede certo*
> *signat humum, gestit paribus colludere, et iram*
> *colligit ac ponit temere et mutatur in horas.*

It is no more a diminution of the originality of Shakespeare to say that he owed a famous passage to Nature through Horace than to say that he derived the passage about the "peopled kingdom" of the bees from Nature through Virgil.

The immortals are true to Nature, because it is only through such truth that they can lay hold upon the laws which enable them to transcend the visible world and talk with the gods in their own tongue. Order, proportion, harmony, are not always perfect in Nature; but it is through Nature and her laws that we obtain hints of their perfection; and the divine world of which they are attributes. Horace knew, as a fact so elementary that it was not worth mentioning, the discovery of the pseudo-moderns that Art must not be *merely* representational of Nature. But he also knew the far more important truth that Art must not be misrepresentational. It must get its something more by truth, not by falsity. When it begins to distort Nature, it robs the mind of its only clue to the supreme reality and the laws of perfection that are obeyed by Nature up to the limits of her power. It is misrepresentational, for instance, to suggest that you are truer to the "stoniness of stone" by making it vaguely represent human forms of extreme ugliness; for stone *qua* stone does not represent the human form at all, and the artist is therefore contradicting his own theories about representationalism when he makes the stone bulge in those semi-human directions. He is really trying to eat his cake and have it. Stone is not the first consideration when you are pretending to deal with humanity. The significant human form is infinitely more important. The

Greeks did no wrong to their marble. It is misrepresentational again to suggest that Nature is chaotic or evil or mad, as many artists do today. There is disorder and evil in Nature; but they are not its fundamental characteristics, and they are continually being resolved into order and beauty. The leaf falls and rots; but the world itself does not go rotten, as a considerable part of modern literature would try to persuade us.

In some ways the epistle on the *Art of Poetry* is curiously applicable to our own times. It begins with a question which might be addressed to the twentieth century, on some of its own artistic aberrations, though one fears that the answer would not always be what Horace expected:

If a painter joined a human head to the neck of a horse, gave it limbs chosen at random from other creatures, and stuck feathers of every imaginable color all over them; if he gave it the face of a beautiful woman and the ugly black tail of a fish, could you prevent yourselves from laughing, my friends?

The world has moved on since Horace asked that question with such happy certainty of the answer. It would be interesting to know what he would say if he could see solemn men and women in the art exhibitions of the world's leading capitals gaping at a hideous something which might once have been a woman, but now—since art must no longer be representational —had been made to resemble a ton of partially decomposed suet-pudding. Being a scholar, with a sense of the right meaning of words, he would have been amused to hear anything so ponderable and massive described as an abstraction. Being an artist, he would have been puzzled to find it regarded as more valuable aesthetically than the highly organized and significant forms of perfection which had been suggested to Praxiteles by Nature herself. It was just because Nature herself often fell short of that ideal perfection, that the true artist was impelled to complete her incompletions and fulfil her hints and prophecies.

This, in fact, was the only important reason for the existence of the artist at all. It was his chief function to bring mankind into touch with the realms in which the "broken arcs" are rounded, and all those incompletions completed. To surround men with hopes and imaginations of that kind was a work worth doing. To surround them with ugliness and evil was the way of spiritual death.

Horace himself was not unaware of ugliness and evil. Those savage epodes, discussed earlier, would dispose of that idea. But the whole attitude and approach are different. They are the work of a man who believes in truth and beauty, and hates their opposites. He was not what Buchan called "a minor intellectual with a genius for disintegration," an insincere and affected theorist who has lost faith in beauty and truth, and does his best to distort and destroy them wherever they might naturally be found, making it the chief function of the artist to lead mankind back into barbarism and the jungle. If Horace wished to paint an ugly character, he would do so with consistency, and the reader would realize its true place in the scheme of things. It would really be a protest against ugliness, an attack upon ugliness, which would naturally turn the mind to beauty again.

He would have recognized the symptomatic connection of the mental confusion, the moral chaos, the spiritual degradation, so widely manifested in modern art and literature, with the atrocious deeds of the modern world. He would have looked with pity and wonder at the satisfied faces of those who prided themselves on being "in the movement." Instinctively he would have felt under his feet the nature of that movement—the steady, slow, relentless, glacier-like descent of an entire civilization into the abyss. *Fecunda culpae secula* . . . He had felt it before that other decline and fall. The later movement is on a scale so vast that most of its victims are hardly more aware of it than of the earth's motion.

The passage in which Horace once more takes up the legends of Orpheus who tamed the wild beasts with his lute, and Amphion who built a city to music, has been treated too often as if it were merely a piece of mythological ornament. It may have become so to the unfortunate "modern," if he has lost his imagination and is unable for a moment to see with the eyes of the poet. But it was not so with Horace. The passage was an essential part of his plan. Just as in that other splendid and profound piece of symbolism Prometheus brought fire from heaven, so Orpheus—the interpreter and prophet of the gods— brought a more heavenly breath of inspiration to men who were still savages in the forest. It was his music, says Horace, that turned them from bloodshed and foul living. This civilizing function of the arts is always in the mind of Horace; and he underlines the symbolism of the legends to emphasize this function. "For this reason it was said that Orpheus could tame tigers and ravening lions." For this reason, too, it is said that Amphion was able to build the walls of Thebes and move stones by the music of his shell.

A solemn commentator affirms that, in all this, Horace is "unhistorical," and those who are blest with a little poetry and imagination can only wring their hands. There is no reply to such a remark except that Horace did not take those legends as literally true. It is for this very reason that he points out their symbolism, and is able to use their inner meaning, not as ornament, but as an essential part of his plan. It is a perfect illustration of the saying of Aristotle that great poetry is more philosophical than history. History is concerned to establish particular facts, which may after all turn out to be false; while great poetry elucidates the universal laws to which all real facts conform.

Asked—in connection with this—whether a good poem springs from Nature or Art, he replies that all the study in the world would be useless without the natural gift; but that the natural gift requires training and study, discipline and hard work, if it is to achieve its end.

He who would win the race, must have endured and done much as a boy; he must have sweated and shivered; lived chastely and abstained from evil. The skilled musician once learned from a master. But now everyone thinks it is enough to say, "I make marvellous poems. It's as easy as playing skittles." I should be ashamed to be left behind and have to confess that I don't know what I never learned.

He thrusts aside the fallacies that are so common in our own day. "Because the gift is more than the discipline of art, the foolish critic would drive all the sane poets away from Helicon; and crowds of the other sort think that by neglecting their nails and beards and not going to the barber, they can get the reputation of a poet."

The epistle on the *Art of Poetry* is the longest of all the poems of Horace. It abounds in wisdom and humor, and has become a treasure-house of critical maxims. Following the apparently casual method of the satires and *sermones,* it is far more comprehensive than it is usually said to be. It maintains a fine balance between its allegiance to what is permanent in the great tradition, and its encouragement of the true originality along the lines of natural law and rational development. When these are sincerely followed, the new work is found to be organically related to the tradition. Its typically Horatian conclusion is one of the most delicious things in literature. His picture of the crazy poetaster is a comic anticipation of Shakespeare's more solemn hierophant, with eyes in "a fine frenzy rolling." Both of them glance from earth to heaven; but the Roman prototype, like a man bent on catching thrushes, forgets to glance from heaven to earth, and falls into a deep well. He cries for help, but nobody comes to pull him out; for, as Horace says, he may have done it on purpose, like Empedocles, and it would be a pity to deprive him of a famous death. Besides, it is by no means certain how he came to be afflicted with verse-making. Perhaps he had defiled the graves of his ancestors!

In the first epistle of the volume published in 20 B.C. Horace again affirms his desire to abandon the writing of lyrical poetry. He addresses it to Maecenas and compares himself with a retired gladiator who is anxious now only to enjoy his freedom. Personal freedom is the note struck all through the book; and not merely freedom in the political sense but freedom from unnecessary conflict in the world of letters. To quote Macleane again, "malice was never less justified than when it attacked Horace. He has not been in the least spoiled by his good fortune." But mere good nature, if he went on publishing masterpieces of lyrical poetry, was no defense from that peculiar brand of malice which in every age has been devoted to the discouragement and, if possible, the destruction of any outstanding gift of the gods. Horace was of a more resilient temperament than Keats; but he says enough in his epistles to make it certain that he passed through a period of great discouragement, very different in degree, but not different in kind from that which dictated one of the saddest prefaces in literature—the prefatory note to the unfinished fragment of *Hyperion,* announcing that the author had no heart to continue. Horace, of course, was in a very different position, as well as of a very different temperament. While he had his Sabine farm, he could smile at the attacks of his enemies, from a worldly point of view. But, from another point of view, it was not a smiling matter. For some years the lyrical impulse was stifled in him. His epistles are undoubtedly among the finest things of their kind in Latin literature; but, even so, one would give a good many volumes

of epistles for one more collection of lyrical poetry as good as
the first volume of odes.

It is pleasant to note the charming short letter (*Epist.* I, 4)
to a younger poet, probably Tibullus, whom he addresses by
the name of Albius. Early manuscripts, grammarians, and
the life by Suetonius call him Albius Tibullus; but Postgate, in his edition of that poet, thinks that this is a mistake,
and that he cannot be identified with the Albius of Horace in
this epistle. Macleane and others appear to have no doubt of it.
The reasons given by Postgate for doubting the identification
are not at all satisfactory and are based on very literal interpretations of a poem which certainly cannot be taken in a completely
literal sense. When the Latinists differ so entirely, there is
perhaps room for suggestion based on the values of poetry.
There is a gentle vein of irony and raillery running through
it, very like that in the thirty-third ode of the first book,
which was undoubtedly addressed to Tibullus. Postgate's argument is that in the epistle Horace tells Albius that the gods
have given him riches and that Tibullus had complained of
exactly the opposite. It is a common complaint; and Horace was
obviously rallying him on it. It is very difficult indeed to imagine
that Horace would do anything quite so banal as to write to a
rich man merely in order to tell him that he had money in the
bank. But he might very well write to a man who thought himself poor, to remind him that he was better off than he thought.
A second argument of Postgate is that Suetonius in the biography
tells us that Tibullus was not very good looking (*insignis
forma*), whereas Horace in his epistle actually tells him how
handsome he is. As Horace was not only gifted with a sense of
humor, but also trying to cheer the rather melancholy elegiac
poet, we can easily see the twinkle with which he wrote that
very mild piece of flattery. Horace also reminds him that he is
famous; and here Postgate overlooks an obvious argument in

favor of Tibullus rather than a more obscure writer. Here also Horace teases his younger friend a little. He asks him if he is walking about his pleasant woodlands meditating a poem which shall rival those of a somewhat insignificant minor poet, Cassius of Parma. Postgate again misses the raillery and says that Horace is using a comparison which might be addressed to some rich literary amateur, but not to the acknowledged master of elegiac poetry at Rome. I am afraid that Postgate must have encountered the "brindled Andrew" in controversy over this, for he adds that Horace might as well have exhorted Tennyson at the end of his life to try and excel "the minor productions of Mr. Andrew Lang."

There never was such a jumble of fallacious reasoning. Even this last rather unkind and uncalled-for dig at a kindly critic is quite topsy-turvy, for Tibullus was not an old man, but considerably younger than Horace. In the thirty-third ode, moreover, Horace does undoubtedly write to him telling him that he ought to get more enjoyment out of life, and rallying him a little about the excessive melancholy—as Horace apparently thought it—of his love-poetry in elegiacs. It should be added, however, that the Albius of the fourth satire could not possibly be Tibullus as Ullman suggests. It is true that Tibullus was sixteen years of age when that satire was written, but Ullman appears to have overlooked the fact that the incident referred to in the satire is dated a good many years earlier, when the father of Horace, escorting his son to school, asked him if he had noticed the unhappy plight of some other Albius.

It should be noticed that, in spite of the gentle irony running through the epistle, it is really couched in the most kindly and affectionate terms, giving advice in exactly the way that might most effectively help the younger man to throw off his melancholy and enjoy his life more fully. It may further be noticed that, when Horace mentions his own poems in this epistle, he refers only to his satires, as if he had become sensitive about mentioning his lyrical work:

Albius, candid critic of my satires, what shall I picture you doing now at your country place? Writing something to beat the opuscula of Cassius of Parma, or strolling quietly through your salubrious forests, meditating on all that is worthy of the wise and good? You were never a mere soulless body. Why, the gods made you handsome, they gave you plenty of money and the power to enjoy yourself. What more could the fondest nurse ask for her foster-child, if he can think and speak wisely, if popularity, fame and health are so abundantly his, and if he has a decent living and a purse that is never quite empty (*non deficiente crumina*)?

Having said this, Horace brings his letter to an end with that pleasant old trick of surprise—in this case, a somewhat startling comment on the philosophy he had once most affected.

These, Albius, are my maxims; and if at any time you feel inclined for laughter, you will find me here in good case, a sleek hog from the herd of Epicurus.

There is a double irony in this ending; for Horace knew his Epicurus (the master of Lucretius) far too well to adopt in earnest that popular misconception of his philosophy. It is true that Epicurus taught that the gods themselves lived an untroubled life, caring nothing for mankind; but his conception of the physical and material pleasures of human life was not so very different from that of the Stoics so far as physical and material pleasures went. Epicurus himself was troubled all his life with painful diseases. For many years he was unable to walk, and he died of *renal calculus*, one of the most painful of all afflictions. Even those who know better appear to be sometimes unconsciously affected by the modern associations of the word "epicure." He carried the doctrine of plain living a good deal farther than most of the Stoics. It is said that his usual diet was bread and water. In one of his letters, however, like the marooned sailor in *Treasure Island*, he says to a friend: "Send me some cheese of Cythnos, so that I may have a sumptuous meal when I like." In another letter he says that, while Metrodorus had reduced his expenses to fourpence a day, he himself had succeeded in living on considerably less. Individual freedom was one of the first principles of his philosophy. He hated falsehood and deceit. He was kind and generous to his slaves and numbered some of them among his pupils. It is said that he bore the extreme pain of his last illness with great fortitude, and there is a very beautiful fragment of a letter written at the very last to the foremost of his disciples, in which he says, "On this last, yet blessed, day of my life, I write to you. Pains and tortures of body I have to the full, but there is set over against these the joy of my heart at the memory of our happy conversations in the past. Do you, if you would be worthy of your devotion to me and philosophy, take care of the children of Metrodorus."

This is a very different picture from that which is usually implied in the descriptions of Horace as an Epicurean; and, when Horace refers to himself as a hog from the Epicurean sty, the irony of it raises several questions which have not been answered by the commentators.

Like Cicero, and most educated Romans, Horace was eclectic in philosophy. When he adopted one or two of the tenets of Stoicism, he did not reject, and there was no reason why he should reject, the Epicurean principles of kindness, generosity, and love of freedom. Indeed the two philosophies overlapped in many of these principles. The Stoic did not require the self-mortification and suppression of all emotions, which is commonly associated with the modern use of the word Stoic. But he did believe, exactly as Horace believed, that true happiness depends upon the control of anger and fear, and all immoderate passions. The famous opening of the sixth epistle, *nil admirari,* means just this. It certainly does not mean that a man should not admire, in the modern sense of the word, what is truly admirable. It means that he should not be carried away by excessive and irrational emotion, a rather different thing from the bitterness of Tennyson's lines:

> For not to desire, or admire, if a man could learn it,
>   were more
> Than to walk all day, like the Sultan of old, in a
>   garden of spice.

One thing, however, the Stoic did believe in, which is a real addition to the creed of Epicurus. He believed in a Divine Providence; and this belief, though for a time he had apparently lost it, Horace had felt both in his early and in his later life. The epistles themselves, like some of the satires, as we noted earlier, have a great deal of the manner and effect of the lighter discourses of Plato. But it seems quite absurd to suggest, as some of the more recent commentators are inclined to do, that the constant preoccupation of all these writings with the principles of right and wrong was either an insincerity or not a natural and spontaneous product of the poet's heart and mind. It is surely something less than logical to allege, as a reason for this conclusion, that "the younger generation today is not interested."

Some of the most famous lines of Horace really depend for their full meaning on an ethical context which is completely forgotten by many of those who quote them. The famous lines about the rustic "waiting for the river to run by, although it glides on and will continue to glide on, rolling away into the endless ages," are a case in point. Everyone knows those lines. Everyone quotes them, if only the first two words:

> *Rusticus exspectat dum defluat amnis; at ille*
> *labitur et labetur in omne volubilis aevum.*

From the technical point of view the alliteration of the four l's and two v's in the second of those lines, and the way in which *"ille"* at the end of the first line glides into *"labitur"* at the beginning of the second is a masterly piece of onomatopoeia. But ninety-nine out of a hundred of those who quote it forget or ignore the fact that it is not merely a picture of a silly yokel waiting for an absurd breach in nature. They rightly admire its art, but they forget that art includes, or should include, a great deal more than verbal skill. In fact, in this case, the exaggeration is so palpable, or the rustic so half-witted, that the lines themselves, taken out of their context, would be somewhat foolish. Those who quote them usually give them an application of their own. They use them to illustrate the unfortunate plight of someone who is merely expecting something impossible to happen. But Horace used them to illustrate something very much more important than that. The passage in that second epistle of the first book, to Lollius, is one of the most striking in Latin literature:

Thieves rise up at night to cut men's throats. Can you not wake to save yourself? If you will not take exercise when you are sound in health, you will have to do it when you have the dropsy; and so, if you don't call for a book and a light before daybreak, if you don't set your mind on honorable studies and pursuits, you will be kept awake and in torment by envy or passion. Why do you hasten to remove the things that hurt the eye while, if anything is eating into your soul, you put off the time for curing it till next year? Well begun is half done. Dare to be wise; begin! He who keeps putting off the time for right living is like the rustic who expects the river to flow by.

What a world of significance that passage brings into that final line about the river. "It glides on and will continue to glide on, rolling away into the endless ages." The last words of the last line of the passage *in omne volubilis aevum* become not merely brilliant verse, but living poetry, with deep undertones of meaning and a sense of eternity in them.

The passage can hardly be regarded as a "commonplace" by those who have any remembrance of certain other words that have echoed and re-echoed through Christendom for centuries and seldom failed to stir some chord in the intellectual world until, in the twentieth century, having lost its religion, it began to lose its memory also.

Horace ends the first book of his epistles on a note of gentle sadness, indicating that he hardly expected his verse to meet with a very favorable reception from a generation which cared for none of these things. His little epilogue takes the form of an address to his own book. It has been imitated by hundreds of writers in succeeding generations, some of them melancholy, and some of them cheerful. One of the most cheerful is that of Stevenson:

> Go, little book, and wish to all
> Flowers in the garden, meat in the hall,
> A bin of wine, a spice of wit,
> A house with lawns enclosing it,
> A living river by the door,
> A nightingale in the sycamore!

That is pure Horace; but the address of Horace to his book of epistles is in a more ironic vein. He pretends that the book itself is anxious to go out into the world and be published, against its master's will, and that the master, after warning it of all the dreadful things that will most certainly befall the poor misguided creature, finally sends it out very much as a man might push a recalcitrant mule over a cliff. However, he entrusts it with a beautiful little message to the outside world from himself, perhaps the most mellow and exquisitely good-tempered that has ever been addressed, or is ever likely to be addressed,

by a writer who had been unjustly treated, to the outrageous
critics:

> Say, that though born a freedman's son, possessed
> Of slender means, beyond the parent nest
> I soared on ampler wing; thus what in birth
> I lack, let that be added to my worth.
> Say, that in war, and also here at home,
> I stood well with the foremost men of Rome;
> That small in stature, prematurely gray,
> Sunshine was life to me and gladness; say
> Besides, though hasty in my temper, I
> Was just as quick to put my anger by.

In the year 19 B.C. Horace lost two of his friends—Virgil
and Tibullus. There is a mystery about the desire of Virgil to
destroy the *Aeneid* which has never been explained. The suggestion that he wished to have this done merely because there
were some unfinished sections in it, is contrary to reason and to
all that one knows of his character. Critics have again and again
called attention to the extreme beauty given to many passages
by the very fact that certain lines were left unfinished. Incompleteness of the structure as a whole would be an equally inade-
quate reason for the destruction of so grand a work. One does
not destroy the Parthenon because a few columns are missing.
There must have been some more serious reason, and one may
suspect that Virgil had undergone some profound disillusionment. Perhaps he had begun to see that the almost Messianic
hopes which he had entertained of the reign of Augustus were
doomed to defeat. His idealism must have suffered a severe
shock when he was ordered to omit the original tribute to his
friend Gallus in the fourth book of the *Georgics*. Gallus was a
poet and had greatly befriended Virgil in earlier days. He made
mistakes in his official career, and Augustus treated him with a

severity that led to his suicide. Virgil had brooded over his fate and, if one may hazard a conjecture, it seems possible that the story of Orpheus, which he substituted for the tribute to his friend, contains a subtler and more tragic reference to Gallus— the poet torn to pieces and rolled down another and a darker Hebrus because "hell knew not how to pardon." If, in the course of time, it had dawned on Virgil that the political world was not capable of building that abiding City of which he had dreamed; and if, with his strangely prophetic insight, he had caught even a glimpse of the terrible things that were to befall Rome in the not so distant future, we can easily imagine that he might have undergone a strong revulsion against much that he had said in the *Aeneid*.

Horace must have felt his loss deeply, and we may imagine him, at the Sabine farm, perhaps with Maecenas, recalling some of those golden memories of the past, when Virgil read his poems to them. It is a far cry from the Sabine farm to the apocryphal fifth book of Horace, in which Kipling collaborated with a former member of the staff of *Punch*. It has been noted earlier how that finely-edited and finely-critical journal has reproduced certain aspects of the Horatian spirit. The verses of C. L. Graves (from that alleged fifth book) in which Horace and Maecenas, at the Sabine farm, recall an evening with Virgil, are a beautiful example of this:

> Can you forget, Maecenas, how together
>   Virgil and you and I once sped the hours
> Rose-wreathed, anointed, in the summer weather,
>   Under the shelter of my trellised bowers?
>
> Clear was the sky, the moon aloft was sailing,
>   Flooding the valley with a silver gleam;
> Still was the night, save for the never-failing
>   Murmurous music of the rushing stream.

> Dear is to me the voice of running waters,
>> Dearer that night was Virgil's voice of gold,
> Gift of the Muses, Jove's melodious daughters,
>> Fraught with the wisdom of the seers of old.

He pictures Maecenas asking Virgil how, in his serene and sequestered life, he could have probed hearts torn with passion, trampled in the dust. And Virgil replies: "Ah, but I knew them." The human heart is the same in every generation, and there were neighbors of his own at Parthenope in whose lives the tragic story of Dido and Aeneas had been enacted.

> Late was the night ere Virgil ceased from telling
>> How past and present mingled in his view,
> And the worn features, lit by fire indwelling,
>> Changed to the marble mask that others knew.

> Clearer uprose the murmur of the river
>> Hurrying onward past the orchard lawn,
> And the tall poplars with their leaves aquiver
>> Trembled and whispered in the breath of dawn.

It was the desire of Maecenas that Horace should write the verses to be sung at the national celebration of the *ludi saeculares* in 17 B.C. It was this that drew him back to the field of lyrical poetry, not, as too many critics have suggested, to glorify Augustus, but to celebrate something that far transcended the reign and achievements of any one man. Horace had no illusions about a Golden Age; but he, too, had a City. It was not permanent in the heavens like that of Virgil; but the sun in all its courses had seen no greater on earth. He could not deify the Emperor, but he could ask the gods to help his people in what appeared to be the new ways of peace.

XVII

CARMEN SAECULARE

IN THE YEAR 17 B.C. HERALDS WERE SENT OUT FROM ROME TO proclaim a great religious festival, "the like of which no living man had ever seen, or would ever see again." The College of the Fifteen Men (the Quindecemviri), who kept and interpreted the Sibylline books, and exercised a certain pontifical authority over prayers and rituals, declared by an oracle that another *saeculum* was closing (or, as in the Fourth Eclogue, beginning) and that the time had come for another celebration of the ancient *ludi saeculares*.

The celebration of 17 B.C. went far beyond the proclamation of the heralds. It not only surpassed what any living man had seen; it was by far the most magnificent religious festival in the history of pre-Christian Rome—the richest in color, ritual, and poetry, and all that could appeal to the imagination; the most stirring in its national aspirations; the most moving in the deeper and largely unconscious implications of its prayers to the gods from the heights of the Capitol and the Palatine.

On the third day of the celebration, in the culminating act of worship and supplication, the *Carmen Saeculare* was sung by a choir of twenty-seven young men and twenty-seven girls. A certain divine significance was attached to these multiples of three and nine. The hymn for this occasion has justified its author's belief that his works would prove to be more durable than bronze or marble; but, as Professor Rand observed, in his fine book, *The Building of Eternal Rome:*

Many a modern friend of Horace has visited the Museo delle Terme to pay his respects to certain slabs of marble there, on which in beautiful Augustan capitals fragments of the official account of the *ludi saeculares* have been preserved. The words that this traveler seeks first of all read:

Carmen composuit Q. Horatius Flaccus.

It was a great event in the life of Horace, and it has been seriously misrepresented by some of the commentators during the last century. Their habitual phrases often imply unworthy motives on the part of the poet—surrender of principle, political subservience, flattery of Caesar, and all the other pleasant charges which it is so easy for this noble and idealistic world of ours to bring against the solitary artist and man of genius. The very fact that the man is without worldly power or wealth makes it easy to suggest those charges, if he has any intercourse at all with the great ones of the earth, even though all the approaches be on the other side. But there is an insufferable lack of generosity in the charges when they are brought against the Roman poet who, with all his worldly disadvantages, nevertheless stood up to the most formidable embodiment of power the world had ever known, maintaining his own independence and philosophy of life as perhaps no other man in such circumstances had ever done before him. The quiet smile with which he did it has apparently led many readers to forget the steadfast courage and the momentousness of the achievement. His memory does not depend on bronze or marble; but it would be a poor spirit that grudged him that inscription on the fragment in the Museo delle Terme.

The real misjudgment of the *Carmen Saeculare* began unintentionally enough with the English Victorians, some of whom were apparently more interested in the Anacreontic odes and the lines about Pyrrha; while others, like Milman, could not bring themselves to believe that the religion of the ancient Romans could be anything more than an admiration of the sculptor's art. Milman described the *Carmen Saeculare* as a neat example of that admiration, culminating in an apotheosis of Augustus. If this were really true, it would discredit the sincerity of Horace. One would not like to see him taking any part in the deification of the Emperor. It is not true; but it was a characteristically English criticism in that period. It has influenced American commentators to some extent by mere repetition of habitual phrases; but the general tendency of the American critics—although they have no monarchical prejudices —is more just toward the real aims of the poet. The Italian and French critics, for the most part, are happily unaffected by considerations of that kind. Nor would it ever occur to them that there would be anything wrong if, at some dinner with Maecenas, the son of a manumitted slave had anticipated Voltaire and declared, "We are all poets or princes here." The bare imagination of such a scene appeared inexpressibly shocking to Professor Saintsbury. But the guests, and their host, the descendant of Etruscan kings, would have laughed. Augustus himself would probably have drunk the poet's health. Italian and French critics, as a rule, understand that kind of thing. Voltaire, who admired Horace immensely on all other grounds, called him *adroit esclave*, a phrase which like Swinburne's "valet-souled varlet of Venusia" puts the critic out of court because it really attacks the poet's birth rather than his work. Usually, however, it never occurs to the French and Italian critics to suspect Horace of insolence or subservience. They know that if Horace was proud of his friends, the pride was not all on one side. The fragments of the great marble column are there to prove it. Rome boasted of her poet to twenty subsequent centuries in that column. We may certainly regard this as evidence that Horace was in no unduly subservient position at the time. As we have seen earlier, there is good reason to count him among the counsellors of Augustus, either through

235

Maecenas, or through the direct suggestion of his writing. He had, in fact, his own poetical and philosophical kingdom, of which Sainte-Beuve writes in his own inimitable way, supporting a delightful remark of Scaliger:

At the beginning of our own renaissance, Scaliger who praises Horace, criticizes him, and prefers Juvenal to him in satire, suddenly cries out, à propos of the Ode *Quem tu, Melpomene,* and that other *Donec gratus eram tibi,* that he would rather have written those poems than be king of all Aragon.

To those who complain that the poetry of Horace is not elevated enough for them, Sainte-Beuve replies, with a dry irony, *"Que voulez vous? Horace est un homme!"* There is nothing whatever in the *Carmen Saeculare* to justify the suggestion that the poet had abdicated in either of these realms. In order to deal with the *Carmen Saeculare,* it is necessary first to obtain a just picture of the ceremony itself.

It is important, for instance, to remember that it was not an Augustan invention, but a revival of one of those ancient ceremonies in which Horace all through his life had been profoundly interested. Its first observance was in 509 B.C. when Dis and Proserpine were invoked for help during the ravages of the plague. The centennials were not strictly kept, and the next observances took place in 346 B.C. There were two other observances at intervals of a century, in 249 and 149 B.C. The fifth was postponed by the civil wars; and now, with the advent of peace, and the anxiety of the new régime to be regarded as continuing the historic traditions of Rome, it was natural enough that this revival should be suggested to Augustus. Virgil, in his fourth eclogue and in the *Aeneid,* had opened up a vision of the ideal Rome, whose prosperity depended on its right relationship to the divine powers. His vision, perhaps, was for the few. But the *ludi saeculares* might bring it into focus for the whole of Italy. The connection with Virgil and the fourth eclogue is further emphasized by the fact that the College of the Quindecemviri who had charge of the Sibylline books, were asked to prescribe the ritual for the occasion. The *ludi saeculares* were Etruscan in origin, and the elaborate artistry of the celebration in 17 B.C. suggests that a certain descendant of Etruscan kings, Maecenas, had more to do with it than Augustus. It is particularly important to remember (as the reader will observe when we come to the criticisms of the *Carmen Saeculare*) that it was not only a religious festival, but that Augustus himself appeared as a worshipper, offering up prayers and sacrifices to the gods throughout the whole ceremony. It might be the most splendid occasion of his reign; but the character of the festival transcended any particular ruler, dynasty, or system of government. It began with the founding of the Republic, and it was to go on through the centuries to the year A.D. 248. It would be in accord, of course, with the recent Augustan legislation which aimed at the revival of religion; and, from the point of view of Augustus, that might be a merely political convenience; but if—as Gibbon declared—Augustus was a crafty hypocrite, we may remember the adage that hypocrisy is the tribute paid by vice to virtue. The fact that the devil can quote Scripture does not impair the value of the prophets; and there actually was a profound prophetic symbolism, groping after something far greater than it knew, in that vision of the sacred city, an ideal Rome. This—not Augustus with his high heels—is the subject of the *Carmen Saeculare*. It is not the song of a passing day, but—as its title implies—a song of the ages, and a city not built with hands, which eventually merged into the *Civitas Dei*. Cheapened as the phrase has been by common usage in modern times, there has been nothing stranger or more beautiful in the whole history of the human mind than the vision which is summed up in those two words, the Eternal City. It has manifested itself in the most unexpected ways down to the present day. We find it in non-Christian as well as in Christian writers of the nineteenth century. We find Byron invoking it:

> Oh, Rome, my country, city of the soul,
> The orphans of the heart must turn to thee.

He was probably unconscious of all the impulses that were concentrated in that sudden cry of his own pagan spirit, but in the first line he was certainly carrying on the musical significance of the *Carmen Saeculare*.

Kipling who, in some of his work, catches the very tone of Horace, looks back at the same vision from the point where all earthly empires fade and disappear:

> My father's father saw it not,
> And I, belike, shall never come
> To look on that thrice-holy spot,
> The very Rome.

At the back of the modern poet's mind, confused as it may be by modern political considerations, there is still lurking this strange wonder, this thrice-holy thing, this haunting vision of an unearthly city. The *Carmen Saeculare* was equally unable to grasp the vision in its fullness. It was addressed to figures and types, to Apollo and Diana; but in these, as Cicero said, the Roman could and must worship different aspects of the one transcendent Power.

We must imagine Horace coming to Rome for this national religious ceremony, a little grudgingly at first, but feeling a certain excitement, and even astonishment, when he saw the crowds which were thronging into the city. The country folk were coming in from all over Italy with their sacrificial offerings to the gods. Everyone was talking about the tremendous festival which no man living had seen before, or would see again, though their children's children would see it, as their father's fathers had done. The very word *saeculares* gave them a sense of something far greater than the present régime.

Perhaps in the jostling Forum the poet would run into Ofellus and one or two other old acquaintances from Venusia. He might be able to tell them where they could get the best view, and where to obtain their torches, bitumen, and sulphur for the preliminary rites of purification. Perhaps he accompanied them, two hours after midnight, to the opening of the festival at the three altars on the banks of the Tiber where they saw Augustus advance through the torch-light, with the Fifteen Men in attendance, to sacrifice nine lambs and nine kids. After the sacrifice, Augustus offered up a prayer to the Moirae (*sacrificii acceptrices sitis*) in the name and on behalf of all the Roman people. It must be emphasized again that through the whole ceremony Augustus never appeared in any other rôle than that of a suppliant worshipper, offering sacrifices and prayer to the gods. This was followed by a scene on a torch-lit stage, in which a hundred and ten matrons went through another rite in honor of Diana and Juno. Other sacrifices and prayers were offered up on two successive nights to the goddesses of fertility and childbirth, and to Mother Earth. On each occasion Augustus offered up the supplication in the name and on behalf of the Roman people. It is important to repeat this, in view of certain misrepresentations of the *Carmen Saeculare* to which we shall come presently.

The daylight ceremonies were the most important. The first of these took place on the Capitol before the Temple of Apollo, where Augustus and Agrippa, with two of the College of Quindecemviri, sacrificed four white bulls to Jupiter. Augustus then offered up a prayer, as before, in the name and on behalf of all the Roman people. The following day, Augustus and Agrippa each sacrificed a white heifer to Juno; and, after Augustus had once more recited the prayer on behalf of the Roman people, a hundred and ten matrons, chosen from the chief families of Rome, knelt and offered up their own prayer to the gods for the safety of their country.

On the third day, after Augustus had again offered sacrifice and repeated the formal prayers, the culminating event—as recorded on the broken column—was the choral singing of the poem of Horace. The two choirs of twenty-seven boys and twenty-seven girls stood facing the glorious Temple of Apollo on the Palatine. Rome spread below them, "all bright and glittering in the smokeless air." Up the hillside and in among the shining columns of the Temple, a great throng, in festal white, grew hushed and still as the work of a sculptor's hand. The clear voices rang out on the stillness in words as lucid and harmonious as the Temple itself, and more enduring:

"O God of light, and thou that reignest over the forests, radiant glory of heaven, adorable and ever to be adored, hear, in this holy season, this our prayer":

> *Phoebe silvarumque potens Diana,*
> *lucidum coeli decus, o colendi*
> *semper et culti, date quae precamur*
> *tempore sacro,*

"When the Sibylline oracles have bidden chosen maidens and unsullied youths to sing a hymn to the gods who love and ever loved the seven hills":

> *quo Sibyllini monuere versus*
> *virgines lectas puerosque castos*
> *dis quibus septem placuere colles*
> *dicere carmen.*

Then comes that magnificent stanza so greatly admired by Goethe. It was probably sung by the boys alone, invoking the gods' blessing on Rome. It is a stanza which, according to Ferrero, "no young Roman can read without emotion, even twenty centuries later":

"O, kindly Sun, who in thy glorious chariot bringest forth the day, and hidest it away at evening, and art reborn, another and the same forever, O, mayest thou never see in all thy course aught nobler than the city of Rome":

> *Alme Sol, curru nitido diem qui*
> *promis et celas, aliusque et idem*
> *nasceris, possis nihil urbe Roma*
> *visere maius.* ·

This is the real theme of the poem—the vision of Rome as it had been announced by Virgil in the *Aeneid*. But Horace, despite the temptations of the occasion and its more immediate and practical purpose, made comparatively few contemporary allusions.

We now come to some of those curious misrepresentations of the *Carmen Saeculare*, and the poet's acceptance of the invitation to write it. We have seen, in an earlier chapter, how Horace refused, with the utmost independence, another invitation from the autocrat of Rome. His acceptance of the invitation to write this hymn to the gods has too often been treated in a way that lends color to the fanatical nonsense of Swinburne and others about the "valet-souled varlet of Venusia." In his alliterative ecstasy the descendant, not of Etruscan kings, but of Northumbrian earls, must have forgotten his own thesis when he used the word "varlet." He was evidently back in the feudal stronghold of his ancestors, hardly a place to sing the songs of Freedom, even before sunrise. But one can imagine the quiet smile with which the son of the "manumitted slave" would have heard that shrill cry of "varlet" from the republican poet of Victorian England.

It is important, however, that some of the unintentional mis-representations, by more sober critics, should be examined, if we are to obtain a true portrait of Horace. There is a fashion among modern commentators, good in its purpose, but often misleading in effect, of attempting to bring the classics nearer to us by anglicizing them. This fashion has been corrected to a certain extent by the more scientific study of Roman customs, by writers like Cyril Bailey and Warde Fowler. In less skillful hands, there is always the danger that science may go to the opposite extreme and turn the classics into a branch of anthropology, treating the Roman and his religion as if he were a primitive savage, with white rings around his eyes, contemplating the grinning heads on a totem pole. Sometimes the two methods are conjoined in the same picture, and the reader can then thoroughly enjoy himself. Warde Fowler, to whose books the world of scholarship owes a very great debt, does sometimes carry both methods to a point where they can hardly be reconciled. Dealing with the satire in which Horace takes a stroll through the Forum and stands in the crowd to watch the diviners extracting omens and predictions from the entrails of an animal, Warde Fowler has a particularly charming anglicization. He says that Horace "looked in at evening service."

It is a perfect picture (even to the rather casual "looked in") of a peculiarly English type. A practised scholar like Warde Fowler, when he says things of this kind, makes all the right distinctions and mental reservations, of course. He probably finds a certain amusement in confusing the ideas of his sisters and his cousins and his aunts. But, while Warde Fowler remains an Englishman, Horace ceases to be an Italian. His toga is replaced by a morning coat; his ivy-wreath by a top-hat; and, as he looks in at that pleasant college chapel, he hears, not the muttering of the diviner over the blood-red entrails, but an

English congregation singing a gentle vesper-hymn by the Reverend John Keble.

The exponents of both methods have much that is illuminating to tell us; but it could be told without destroying the perspective. The fact that the ideal Rome of Virgil catches a gleam from the distant *Civitas Dei* of Saint Augustine would not justify our treating them as identical. The result is too often like a print from a twice-exposed negative. When that happens, the most scholarly of commentators will sometimes write as if the two pictures were really merged into one. This would not matter, so long as the mental reservations are made. The trouble begins when inferences are based upon the false premises.

It is in this way that many English commentators in recent years have misjudged the whole affair of the *Carmen Saeculare*. They use the terms of their own country, for instance, to announce that in 17 B.C. "Horace became poet laureate." They even speak of his official appointment to that position in the royal household. They are not in the least troubled by the fact that no such office existed in Rome. They do not ask themselves whether the official appointment to the non-existent post was for the duration of the festival or for life, but they imply that the writing of a single hymn to the gods constituted an acceptance for life, not only of a non-existent laureateship, but of the less honorable position of "court poet" to Augustus himself. If they do not mention the butt of sherry, they lead themselves and many a reader, by mere association of ideas, to the false conclusion that Horace had abandoned both his Falernian and his sturdy independence as a poet. Writer after writer does this, each copying another, with that awful air of bland satisfaction which their great-grandparents assumed when they heard that Tennyson had been admitted to what they somewhat blasphemously called the "Presence"; a satisfaction that became even more bland upon the false report that, after the interview, he had been admonished by a Black Rod or a Gold Stick in Waiting to walk out of the room backwards. Some of these commentators are unconscious of what they are really doing; but it is in their bones and blood; and the matter is psychologically complicated because they want to have it both ways. They can't resist the satisfaction of making Horace a "court poet"; and they derive a further satisfaction from the twentieth-century feeling that, having imposed the non-existent position upon him, they can comfortably look down upon the "valet-souled varlet of Venusia" who will now have to walk out of the room backwards. It matters nothing to them that occasionally a shrewd Scot like Lord Tweedsmuir (John Buchan), in his life of Augustus, will observe with a twinkle that, if Horace was a "court poet," he was surely the most independent in history. French and Italian critics, with the exception that has already been discussed, may tell us that the term is completely out of character. The radical democrat, Ferrero, affirms with the utmost emphasis that Horace was neither a flatterer nor a "court poet"; and though Ferrero may be regarded as a questionable historian, it is quite certain that he had no prejudices in favor of "court poets," and that as an Italian, he understood the position of Horace in this respect. He has his own prejudices of another kind, for he speaks with apparent approval of Horace as a cynic. He further confuses his brilliant account of the *Carmen Saeculare*. He says first of all that no such glorious hymn had ever before ascended from human lips, and at the end of his account, several pages later, he says that the hope expressed in it was mere "poetical hypocrisy." This is another example of the way in which a writer will allow the political prejudices of his own party, the associations of his own time, and his own violent partisanship to confuse his picture of another period and entirely different circumstances. There is no way out of these inconsistencies, either in Ferrero, or in the other writers mentioned. The poetry itself is our best guide, and a just and impartial examination of the poetry, if we allow the poetry to speak to us, compels the conclusion that Horace really meant what he said about the majestic history of Rome, and its relation to the Power or powers that rule the universe.

But the English commentators are unmoved. They use the phrase "court poet," either with a kind of conservative satisfaction, or in a way that recalls Edward Lear's "affection mingled with disgust." At one moment they are obviously affected by reminiscences of Tennyson and Queen Victoria. At the next they enjoy a vicarious superiority by murmuring to themselves the splendid lines in which that stormy petrel of English poetry—Swinburne—asserted his own Republicanism:

> I have no spirit of skill with equal fingers
> At sign to sharpen or to slacken strings.
> I keep no time of song with gold-perched singers
> And chirp of linnets on the wrists of kings.

There is no consistency about it. Those four lines of Swinburne were a thrust at Tennyson, of course; but, when Tennyson died, Swinburne wrote one of the most exquisitely beautiful tributes ever paid by one poet to another. The British constitution is like that; and so is much of its literary criticism.

Warde Fowler, who gives one of the best and most vivid pictures of the actual singing of the *Carmen Saeculare*, a picture full of poetry and imagination, is prepared to wreck the whole beauty of it rather than lose the opportunity of making a great artist walk backwards before those "whom the mere Fates ordain." Facts, evidence, logic, history, the plain evidence of the poem itself, he throws them all to the winds when it comes to a sturdy British principle of that kind. He speaks of the rough draught of the poem, and the "instructions" given to Horace by Augustus—instructions not only on what the poet was to say, but how he was to say it and what he was to omit. He actually goes to the incredible length of asserting, without a particle of evidence, that Augustus "instructed" Horace not to mention Jupiter in the fourteenth stanza of the poem, because he (Augustus) wanted the floodlight at that particular moment to be turned upon himself. Other references to the gods, at other moments, apparently did not matter. He tells us further that Horace was only too obedient; and he says this of a poet who had steadfastly and openly told the Emperor, with increasing force and courage as time went on, that the prosperity of his rule depended entirely on his submission to the gods and the law of righteousness.

The festival itself—it is generally agreed—was designed to restore the sense of religion. There is no doubt at all that Augustus regarded this as politically useful; but, if so, it is unreasonable to suppose that he would "instruct" Horace to eliminate the Father of the gods, who—as the poet had said— "created nothing greater than himself, nor is there anything like him or even second to him." The very stanza to which Warde Fowler refers—the fourteenth—puts Augustus in the position of a suppliant to Jupiter and Juno. It mentions the sacrifices—the white steers—that Augustus had offered up to them; and it asks that the prayers of Augustus, their suppliant, should be granted. Augustus is not mentioned by name, and is alluded to so indirectly that even the most intelligent listener to a choral hymn might easily suppose the reference was to Aeneas. And, in fact, it really is Aeneas rather than Augustus who is actually mentioned, for Augustus is merged in that representative figure. "The renowned son of Anchises and Venus" is the founder of Rome, and his life-stream (*sanguis*) continues through all the centuries, in the tradition of the Roman people. Augustus in 17 B.C. is whatever the translator may choose to make of that word *sanguis*—"successor" is as good a rendering as any—but he is indicated only by the statement that the *sanguis* of Anchises and Venus is, here and now, praying and offering up sacrifices to the gods. He is not mentioned elsewhere. The gods, on the other hand, although their names in that particular stanza are not mentioned, are clearly addressed in it as *"you to whom these prayers are offered, you to whom these white steers are sacrificed."* The most unintelligent listener would know who *they* were.

The thanksgiving to the gods for the victory over the Parthians and the return of peace occupies another eight lines. It is directed to the gods, and cannot reasonably be taken as an apotheosis of Augustus, who is not mentioned even by allusion this time; and the poem closes with a direct invocation of Jupiter, whom Warde Fowler tells us the poet was instructed not to mention in an earlier passage. It can hardly have taken the choir more than a minute to pass from the lines in which Jupiter was supposed to be unmentionable, though they are directly addressed to him; and, within that minute, the choir burst into a full chorus, actually calling upon the Father of gods and men by name to confirm all the hopes and aspirations of the Roman people.

The stiff and formal language of the prayers prescribed for Augustus himself by the Quindecemviri is in marked contrast with the poem of Horace, in which—as Ferrero says—"the stanzas rose and fell like flying birds." They certainly escaped the net of the emperor, if he ever hoped to tame them.

It must be concluded, therefore, that Augustus neither sent Horace a rough draft of the poem, as the eminent English critic suggested, nor instructed him to omit what he so clearly included. The tactful Augustus would hardly have instructed any poet with a sense of humor, and a sense of religion, to give him precedence over the Father of the gods on the eve of such an occasion. If he had instructed Horace to do this, the little man would have been so shaken with laughter that his fingers would have refused to hold the pen. Even if a rough draft had been conceivable in such circumstances, the creation of a poem would involve departures from it which are apparently not considered by the critic. A thousand new suggestions and new meanings would be introduced in its cadences. Again, poetry "is like shot silk," "glancing with many colors"; and what could a rought draft, by an emperor, do to a thing like that. Horace, and Horace alone, was responsible. The fragment of the official account on the marble slab in the Roman museum was accurate:

carmen composuit Q. Horatius Flaccus

XVIII

DIFFUGERE NIVES

IT WAS WITH EVIDENT RELUCTANCE, AND UNDER SOME OUTSIDE pressure, that Horace made his fourth book of odes. There had been an estrangement—temporary, but none the less definite— between Maecenas and Augustus. Murena, the brother-in-law of Maecenas, had been accused of a plot against Augustus, and had been put to death. It is possible that Maecenas, urged by his wife Terentia, had made a vain effort to save Murena. The accounts of the estrangement with Augustus are conflicting; but this, by far the most probable cause, has apparently been overlooked. The suggestion that it was due to the misconduct of Augustus with Terentia is possible; but, in the light of her brother's execution, is hardly consistent with the admiration bestowed on the Emperor by some of those historians who suggest it.

The inscription on the broken commemorative column is proof enough of the importance attached to the *Carmen Saeculare*. Augustus naturally wished Horace to continue; and it is said that some of the odes in the fourth book, particularly those celebrating the victories of Tiberius and Drusus, were written at the Emperor's wish. With a certain coolness still existing between Maecenas and Augustus, it is quite likely that, for his friend's sake, Horace would do his best to smooth things over. He collected these poems with others that had probably been written earlier, and published them in 13 B.C. The praise of his city, *magna Roma*; the celebration of her history; the prophetic annunciation of her future; and above all, the blessings of peace, are still his theme. There is no change whatsoever in his principles. The new régime had eventually emerged from an age of civil war into an era which, as far as human eye could see at the time, promised to restore what Horace had always loved and valued most in the life of Italy. This has been universally recognized by historians; and there is no reason for the ungenerous and discreditable suggestions of political apostasy which are sometimes made about Horace than there would be for maligning the beautiful Ara Pacis, which nobody can look at, even today, without some stirring of the mind and heart, and some feeling of its lost idealism. Neither the poet nor the sculptor was a courtier. The "tremendous majesty" of the Pax Romana was in itself a temporary thing. It was brought about, not by the cold craft of Augustus, not by the practical wisdom of Agrippa, not by the humanism of Maecenas, but by forces utterly beyond the range of human planning. Those forces made it, on the eve of the greatest event in human history; and, at last, those forces broke it. There is a real sense, both in Horace and Virgil, of the mysterious workings of a Power beyond their ken, which is to remake the world. The fourth eclogue is the most familiar, but by no means the only outstanding illustration of this. Macleane, one of the soundest in judgment as well as one of the most erudite of all the editors of Horace, goes so far as to compare the fifth ode of this book with the prophecies of the Old Testament:

There could not be a more comprehensive picture of security and rest obtained through the influence of one mind than is represented in this ode, if we except that with which no merely mortal language can compare (Isaiah XI). The *Carmen Saeculare* contains much that is repeated here. Virgil's description in his fourth eclogue may be read in connection with this ode.

It seems to me that Macleane here, while he has seized the essential character of the poem, has been misled by the legend of Augustus into confusing the issue. Isaiah is perhaps a somewhat extravagant comparison, but it is an excellent thing that Macleane made it, for there is no possible relationship between the language and ideas of Isaiah and the mind of Augustus; nor were the ideas and the language in Horace, which so impressed Macleane, really concerned with the little man in the high heels. There is nothing in the poem of Horace which is out of keeping with the exquisite expression of the same ideas by the sculptor's hand in the Ara Pacis; and I would prefer this comparison to the other. It pretends to less, but it is an equally effective repudiation of the suggestion that the fifth ode of the fourth book was merely a "court poem." The formal recognition of Caesar as the head of the State was expressed at that period in terms which are foreign to our own day (though not so foreign as might appear at first sight). But in Horace they were always subordinated to the things that really mattered. The references to Augustus himself, as a man, have been described as "almost perfunctory." The fifth ode contains one passage, almost the only passage in all the writings of Horace, where one can discover what may be called an expression of real regard for Augustus the man; and this is put into the mouth of a personified Italy, and is supposed to convey the feelings of her peasantry towards the ruler with whom they associated the blessings of peace. It is embodied in a very beautiful little picture of the mother, Italy, waiting for her son, who has been too long delayed overseas. "As a mother calls for her son, with vows and prayers and omens, nor can remove her gaze from the curving shore of the sea, so does his country long for Caesar":

> *votis ominibusque et precibus vocat,*
> *curvo nec faciem litore demovet,*
> *sic desideriis icta fidelibus*
> *quaerit patria Caesarem.*

It is a beautiful picture that Horace paints of the reviving Italy. The reason he gives for her devotion to Caesar, however, is nothing more or less than that she associates with Caesar the recovery of those good things and that good life for which Maecenas and the poets themselves had been steadily contending. The fifth ode, in fact, may be taken as an appeal to Augustus on behalf of the country folk of Italy to live up to those ideals. Maecenas, as we have seen, had told Augustus that, by doing so, he would make an image of himself in the hearts of his people more durable, and less alloyed, than images of gold or silver. He could do this by enabling Italy to rebuild her altars and recover the purity of her household laws. Horace is depicting for the emperor exactly what had been happening, not in Rome, but in the countryside, under those conditions among simple people. But, for his own part, so far as Augustus the man is concerned, Horace looks at him quite objectively; and, indeed, with something of the old irony. Consider the passage, for instance, in which Horace describes how the peasants are inclined to deify Augustus, a process which the emperor himself preferred to discourage in Rome:

Now, on his own hill, every man weds his own vines to the long-widowed elms, until he sees the sun go down. Then he goes home to the wine that makes him merry and, at the second course of his feast, he numbers thee among the gods. Thee with many prayers and flowing bowls of wine he worships, and mingles thy *numen* with his own Lares just as Greece used to be mindful of Castor and great Hercules.

The delightful little touch whereby Augustus becomes a god "at the second course" cannot be destroyed even by the commentators who so anxiously explain that this was the point in the feast at which the drinking began and the libations were poured. Horace himself puts the wine first, and it is quite inconceivable that a master of all the shades of expression, a master too of irony, should have introduced so many of these delicate strokes without a slightly Faun-like smile. It occurs toward the end of the poem, just where he is accustomed to surprise one a little. In the last stanza *"deus"* is dropped for *"dux,"* and Horace comes back to earth again, with the usual formal compliments about the heroes. The thing that moved the heart and mind of Horace has been well expressed by Stevenson:

> They pass and smile, the children of the sword—
> > No more the sword they wield,
> > And O, how deep the corn
> > Along the battle field!

It is difficult to see in what way Horace could have placed himself in opposition to that process. If his acquiescence in it requires any further justification, the conduct of Messalla, one of the foremost men of Rome, may be called to mind. Messalla had fought at Philippi against Antony and Octavian. He fought at Actium, against Antony; and, when Octavian thanked him for his help in that battle, Messalla bluntly replied that he had fought on the right side on both occasions. The answer has been praised for its noble independence. "It was all that befitted an honorable man and a patriotic citizen," says Sellar. Horace behaved in exactly the same way, and with more courage, for he had less worldly power. In those early days at Rome, after Philippi, he addressed the friends of Brutus in his poems and aligned himself with them, when it would have been quite easy for him to keep quiet about the whole affair. Messalla had been among those who were proscribed and listed for death. Horace, as we have seen, called him his friend in an early satire. It is true that it was written after the amnesty, but it must still have been very difficult to foresee how the dice would eventually fall. A merely prudent man, an insincere man, or a Vicar of Bray, would have held his tongue.

It is extremely important to notice how constantly Horace avoids making more than the usual formal bows to Augustus and how swiftly he changes the subject. It is said that the first epistle of the second book which he had published in 14 B.C. was addressed to the emperor at his somewhat imperative request. The emperor undoubtedly expected a personal tribute. What he actually got was a letter formally addressed to him, but concerned almost entirely with the condition of poetry in . Rome. It must be remembered that words and phrases which to modern ears may sound flattering were then conventional forms of address in poetry and meant no more than "Majesty" does today. If possible, Horace puts even the formal compliments into the mouth of somebody else. If he was asked to celebrate the exploits of Tiberius and Drusus, he could hardly avoid, and there was really no reason why he should avoid writing something; and, since modern historians have found so much to praise and admire in the Augustan age, it seems unreasonable to find fault with Horace for occasional expressions of hopeful enthusiasm. The fact remains that his heart was not really in the task of writing lyrical poetry any more. He pictures himself as an elderly lover praying that Venus will not make him her captive again; but it is the Muse of lyric poetry that he is really imploring to spare him. There is a note of profound sadness in one stanza of this jesting protest; and, from all but a few poems in this book, the lyrical spontaneity is missing and the disinclination apparent. Possibly he felt, too, that the trend of the time was going against him, and a younger generation was knocking at the door. A passage at the end of the *Epistle to Florus* indicates this; and there is perhaps a reference to Ovid in its last lines. Horace was too much a man of the world to speak censoriously of the new-comer; but, though he was a supreme artist, he believed that wisdom was the fountain-head of poetry, and the kind of work that Ovid was doing was directly opposed to everything for which he (with Maecenas and Virgil) had been contending. He did not pose as a censor; but, with an inimitable lightness of touch, he announced that it was time for him to retire, for youth was better fitted than he to "play the wanton."

This apparently light-hearted jest at the end of a farewell to poetry, is once more a piece of deliberate art, another example of that favorite device with which Horace ends so many of his poems. It has been examined at length earlier. He uses it again and again in the satires; and very often in the odes. It contributes to the conversational effect, and suggests a perfect ease and mastery which would be lost if the poem ended on a too strenuous note. It will be remembered how he breaks off one of his serious odes by reminding himself that this is not the right strain for his carefree Muse. It is a skilful way of avoiding any suggestion of pretentiousness, and it has been imitated by many later poets. It is precisely the method by which a good conversationalist prevents the talk from becoming too solemn at a dinner-party.

A very good instance of this is the satire—already noticed— in which Horace discusses the doctrine of the Stoics that the only true king is the wise man, and concludes by announcing that this is always true except when the wise man has a bad cold. The end of the epistle to Tibullus in which, after some very charming admonitions to the young poet, he describes himself as "a sleek hog from the Epicurean herd," is another instance. We have already seen how he puzzled the commentators by ending his beautiful praises of country life with the remarks of a rich usurer who had had enough of it and wanted to go back to the city. A very obvious instance is the ode in which he bids Asterie not to weep for her absent lover. Horace lavishes his sympathy upon her up to the last three stanzas, when he ends the poem by advising her not to find the handsome young athlete next door too pleasing. *"Quid fles, Asterie?"*

Nobody can understand the poetry of Horace unless it is realized that this is a deliberate artistic device used for a definite purpose, sometimes to throw a horizon around the poem, sometimes to bring us gently back to earth, and sometimes in irony.

One of the most charming instances is the conclusion of Ode 2, Book IV, which may well be examined here. It contains some of the finest passages of literary criticism in his works. It is the best kind of criticism, for its generous praise helps the reader to see and appreciate. It has often been described as if it were a flattering tribute to Augustus. It is worth examining on all these counts.

The ode begins with a magnificent eulogy of Pindar whom, Horace tells us, it would be fatal for him to emulate. If he did anything so rash, he would end, like Icarus, by giving his name to the crystal seas into which he fell (*vitreo daturus nomina ponto*). The next six stanzas are a really superb tribute to the Greek poet. "A great wind of inspiration lifts the wings of the Dircaean swan when he sails through the high dominion of the clouds":

Multa Dircaeum levat aura cycnum.

This passage was imitated by Gray in one of the finest of his own odes:

> Nor the pride nor ample pinion,
>   That the Theban eagle bear,
> Sailing with supreme dominion
>   Through the azure deep of air.

"But I," Horace continues, "like the Matinian bee, laboriously gathering honey from the fragrant thyme round many a wood and along the banks of Tibur, compose only modest poems with much toil."

He makes this his excuse for not singing the praises of Augustus; and he then tells Iulus Antonius (the son of Mark Antony) that he—Antonius—being altogether a grander poet, is the right person to celebrate Augustus when he drags the savage Sygambri behind him up the Sacred Hill, his brows decorated with the leaves that he has so richly deserved. Antonius is the man to emulate Pindar on a subject like that, and on a ruler "than whom the Fates and the gods have given us nothing greater or better, nor will they give us anything better, even though we do go back to that Golden Age."

Only a really great poet like Antonius could do justice to the feasts and public games with which that triumph will be celebrated, while Horace will just stand in the crowd and shout, in the very tones of a modern nonsense rhyme—"*O frabjous day! calloo, callay!*"

> "*O sol
> pulcher, O laudande!*" *canam, recepto
> Caesare felix.*

If Horace is not ironical in all this, nothing is ironical. Of course, he did not make it so obvious as it appears when attention is called to it. But what would the nineteenth century have thought if Tennyson had excused himself from writing Queen Victoria's Jubilee poem on the ground that he was no Dryden; that a relative of the German Emperor—a mediocre poet—could do the subject more justice; while Tennyson himself would prefer to stand in the crowd and shout "O, what a beautiful day." If the commentators insist on taking this ode with entire solemnity, it may still seem a very strange product for a "court poet." It may be true that Horace was requested to write poems; but he certainly showed extreme skill in omitting what he might be expected to say. We should very carefully examine what he actually did say before we come to the conclusion that he had capitulated to Augustus the man, as distinguished from the titular head of a régime which was apparently trying to heal the wounds of Italy.

But it is the delightful ending of the poem which chiefly concerns us here. "Then Antonius, as you walk in the procession, we will all shout '*Io Triumphe!*,' not only once, mark you, but again and again '*Io Triumphe!*,' while the incense rises to the complacent gods." For this pleasure Antonius will have to offer up ten bulls and as many cows, while Horace will get off with the smaller contribution of a single newly weaned calf:

> *me tener solvet vitulus.*

And then comes the delightful bit of "small talk" on which the poem concludes, apparently casual, but finished with the most deliberate and perfect art: "The calf will bear on its brow a white mark like a crescent moon at its third rising. The mark itself will be snow-white, but all the rest of its coat tawny-red."

> *fronte curvatos imitatus ignis*
> *tertium lunae referentis ortum,*
> *qua notam duxit niveus videri,*
> *cetera fulvus.*

Irrelevant as it may seem to note that mark on the brow of the calf as the final word of the poem, it is perhaps the most delightful touch in the whole ode, and it exactly fulfills the purpose described earlier.

Wickham's reference to the recurrence of sound-effects in Horace raises several questions of technique which may be considered here, as they have a bearing upon a very exquisite effect at the end of the most beautiful poem in the fourth book.

I have not seen anywhere any discussion of what appears to

me to be a deliberate use of rhyme in certain poems by Horace.[1] It is particularly noticeable in the first ode of Book I, where rhymes at the end of the line and internal rhymes at the caesura point occur with a frequency that cannot be accidental. They have, in fact, very much the effect of that early poem of Tennyson which he entitled *Elegiacs:*

> False-eyed Hesper, *unkind,* where is my sweet *Rosalind?*

If the reader keeps that rhythm in mind, stressing the central rhyme at the caesura, it becomes apparent that, in spite of the slight difference in the metre, Horace is obtaining a very similar rhyming effect in lines like these:

> *O et praesidium et dulce decus meum,*
> *Sunt quos curriculo pulverem Olympicum*
> *Collegisse juvat metaque fervidis*
> *evitata rotis palmaque nobilis*
> *terrarum dominós evehit ad deós;*
> *hunc, si mobilium turba Quiritium*
> *certat tergeminis tollere honoribus;*
> *illum, si proprió condidit horreó,*
> *quidquid de Libycis verritur areis.*

There are dozens more of these rhymes, in this one poem, falling on what may be called the long or stressed syllables at the caesura, and at the end of the line, or picked up in those positions a line or so later, with a regularity that cannot be accidental. There is something of the kind in the pentameters of Ovid's elegiacs where, again, the syllable at the caesura frequently rhymes with the last syllable of the line in a way that, if it was not deliberate, must have been dictated by some unconscious rhyming instinct. It occurs again in the tenth ode of the fourth book, an experiment with the beautiful fifth Asclepiad metre.

[1] Since this was written I have seen it discussed in the admirable chapter on the technique of Horace in Mr. Wilkinson's recent book.

The poem itself is not so interesting, or so good, as the two earlier experiments Horace had made with it. But it seems to me that he is obviously feeling his way toward rhyme in it. There were a certain number of rhymes in the two earlier poems; but, in the later, four of the eight lines are perfectly rhymed, and there are many rhymed poems in English which have no more than that. It may be compared with Swinburne's beautiful and absolutely successful experiment in the same metre. Indeed, some of the lines in Swinburne's poem would almost fit into the rhyme scheme of the Latin poem, if the English pronunciation be given to the last syllable of words like *rosae*.

What strange | faces of | dreams, || voices that | called, || hands
   that were | raised to | wave,
Lured or | led thee, a | las, || out of the | sun, || down to the |
   sunless | grave.
Ah, thy beautiful hair, so was it once, braided for me, for me.
Now for Death is it bound, only for Death, lover and lord of
   thee.

And now from Horace:

> *et quae nunc umeris involitant deciderint comae,*
> *nunc et qui color est puniceae flore prior rosae*
> *mutatus. . . .*

In this particular instance, the lyric of Swinburne is far more beautiful than that of Horace. It is one of his most perfect, although it is very little known.

In many of the other odes of Horace there is no question of comparison with anyone. In their own kind they are perfect. One curious illustration of those recurrences which were discussed earlier, is the way in which he repeats a word, almost as if he were abandoning himself to that orchestral rhythm of which W. K. Clifford spoke—a rhythm larger than his own, which he allows to speak for him. Familiar instances are such lines as

> *Eheu fugaces, Postume, Postume,*
> *labuntur anni.* . . .

or the repetition of the great name of Ilion in the third ode of the third book, "When Juno to the gods in council, spoke those welcome words, '*Ilion, Ilion,* a strange woman, and one whose judgment was wicked and fraught with doom, have brought to dust the city that was given over to my vengeance.' "

> *gratum elocuta consiliantibus*
> *Iunone divis: "Ilion, Ilion*
> *fatalis incestusque iudex*
>   *et mulier peregrina vertit*
>   *in pulverem.* . . .

The first ode of the fourth book does it twice in a somewhat different way. In the first stanza, when he asks Venus to be merciful—

> *Intermissa, Venus, diu*
>   *rursus bella moves parce, precor, precor.*

and again in the last stanza but one, when he addresses Ligurinus—"but why, O Ligurinus, alas, why does the slow tear steal down my cheek?"

> *sed cur heu, Ligurine, cur*
>   *manat rara meas lacrima per genas?*
> *cur facunda parum decoro*
>   *inter verba cadit lingua silentio?*
>
> *nocturnis ego somniis*
>   *iam captum teneo, iam volucrem sequor*
> *te per gramina Martii*
>   *Campi, te per aquas, dure, volubilis.*

This poem, also, is an example of a very subtle rhyme system. The rhymes fall in certain stressed positions, not always at the expected place, but sometimes picking the sound up at the same position in a subsequent line. In the second of the lines quoted above, for instance, the word *meas* in the center of the line is answered by the word *genas* at the end of the line. The word *decoro* at the end of the third line elides its final letter because of the open vowel at the beginning of the next line, so that the third line ends with *decor*, which is answered by *sequor* three lines later. In the last stanza *nocturnis* in the first line rhymes at the caesura point with *somniis* at the end of the line. *Teneo* again rhymes at the caesura point with *silentio* at the end of an earlier line, and *volubilis*, the last word in the stanza, echoes the two rhymes at the caesura point and the end of the first line in that stanza, *nocturnis* and *somniis*. In addition to this we have the balancing of the "*o*" and "*or*" sounds of which Milton and Tennyson made such deep music, and the repetition of the word *cur* mentioned earlier; and all this within the space of eight lines. This intricate craftsmanship, an art that conceals its art, would itself seem to justify the phrase about "the nine years pondered lay"; though it may have been achieved almost spontaneously, like the fingering of a violin in the hands of a master.

An antiphonal chord to the repetition of "*Ilion, Ilion*" occurs in the fourth ode of Book IV at the end of that magnificent tribute to Rome which Horace puts into the mouth of her most formidable enemy. The race which, after the destruction of Troy, brought its sacred images, its children, and its fathers over the Tuscan seas, he compares with a mountain oak, shorn of its boughs by the axe, but drawing new strength from the steel. "Drown it in the deep," he says, "and it will rise again more beautiful. Wrestle with it, and it will defeat the proudest of those who attack it. I shall send no more proud messages to

Carthage. Perished is all her hope and all the fortune of our house now that Hasdrubal has gone down."

> *Carthagini iam non ego nuntios*
> *mittam superbos: occidit, occidit*
> *spes omnis et fortuna nostri*
> *nominis Hasrubale interempto.*

Occidit, occidit! That repetition has found an echo in a hundred later poets. We hear it in Tennyson's lines on the enemies that had attacked another mighty tree:

> Our enemies have fallen, have fallen: they struck;
> With their own blows they hurt themselves, nor knew
> There dwelt an iron nature in the grain:
> The glittering axe was broken. . . .

Horace uses these repetitions for many purposes. In that relentless little thirteenth ode of the fourth book, to Lyce, he uses it to make Lyce see her own image in the looking-glass, very much as Lord Leicester's spirit stood behind Queen Elizabeth, in Kipling's poem, until she faced the same bitter reflection. "Whither has fled thy beauty, alas, whither the fair color and the graceful movement? What have you left of her, of her, who once breathed love and stole me from myself?"

> *Quo fugit venus, heu, quove color, decens*
> *quo motus? quid habes illius, illius,*
> *quae spirabat amores*
> *quae me surpuerat mihi.*

Illius, illius! There is no more reason to indict Horace for a lack of chivalry in writing this poem, than there is for indicting Villon for his poem on the Fair Armouress. We cannot arbitrarily decide that Lyce was a real person and reject the reality of others who have at least an equal claim to it. She may have been a figure of the poet's imagination, or—if a real person—entirely beyond the reach of any spoken or written word from Horace. Beautiful once, she is the vicious wreck of her former self, now sodden with drink, a crapulous and maudlin creature, who is yet not beyond the range of memory—*illius, illius.* But she cared no more for that than did the skull of Helen, when Marlowe, translating Lucian, wrote:

Was this the face that launch'd a thousand ships?

There is no subject on which these great echoing repetitions are used with more effect than that of death. It occupied the thoughts of Horace more and more when the gift of the Sabine farm had brought him all that he needed in a material way. In the earlier satires, though he was perhaps less happy, he was chiefly concerned with the conduct of life. In the odes, with that deep sadness of a happy man, which was one of his most striking characteristics, he begins more and more to consider its inevitable end. In both cases there was one thing of which he was quite certain. He said it when he was poor, and he said it when he was comparatively prosperous. The heaping up of wealth was dangerous to the soul. "If you have enough," he said, "what does it matter whether you drink from a little brook or a mighty river?" He always felt that the little brook might be better and more pleasant. The river might be full of all kinds of impurities, while his little water-spring in a mountain-glen, was clear as crystal. But in either case, he gave the same warning (in the third ode of the second book):

Whether thou be rich and born of the ancient line of Inachus, or a poor man of low descent dwelling under the open sky, it matters nothing. Thou shalt still be the victim of pitiless Orcus. We are all of us driven to the same end. For all of us alike, sooner or later the

lot will be shaken out of the urn and will place us in the bark of
Charon for everlasting exile.

Omnes eodem cogimur, omnium
versatur urna serius ocius
sors exitura et nos in aeternum
exsilium impositura cumbae.

In this stanza there are two repetitions of a more subtle kind.
The words are not quite the same, but the *omnes* at the beginning of the first line, answered by the *omnium* at the end, and
the juxtaposition of *serius ocius* has an even deeper and more
powerful effect on the rhythmical sense of the whole poem. It
turns a merely obvious fact into something that vitally engages
our emotions. It was no merely conventional set of reflections
that Horace was expressing in these poems. Dion Chrysostomos,
who was converted to Stoicism, said (about A.D. 100) that a
great poet "gives every man as much as that man can take."
Horace was able to make the consideration of death a contribu-
tory factor to his philosophy. It was a thing that made a real
difference to all his estimates of value, and this—after all—
may be a way of setting the temporal in relation to the eternal.
He did not say "let us eat and drink for tomorrow we die." He
did say *"carpe diem."* He did urge men to take the good that
the gods provided, but it was a real good, and it was characterized
by temperance and a love of the things of the mind. If he had
little or no hope in any spiritual life beyond the grave, he still
had fortitude, the old Roman fortitude, which he described in
his portrait of Regulus; and he was able to impart this fortitude
to others. He was a stronger character than Maecenas. This is
perfectly plain from the lines in which he told Maecenas not
to give way to his fears of the last journey. "We shall go together," he said, "you and I, on that last road." *"Ibimus, ibi-*
mus!" It is one of the most beautiful of his repetitions, and it is

not said in self-pity, but to hearten a friend. Moreover, he kept his word.

The fourth book of odes contains two poems, *Quem tu, melpomene* and *Diffugere nives,* which outweigh all the others in that volume. The latter is one of the most beautiful in the whole range of literature, but it is also one of his most profoundly sorrowful. It is impossible in English to do more than faintly suggest the lyrical pulse of the original:

> Fled in defeat are the snows, and the grass grows green on the
> hillside.
> Green grow the leaves on the tree.
> Earth in her orbit returns, and the river that flooded the
> ploughland
> Sinks, and flows on to the sea.

Then comes that wonderful contrast between the return of the unchanging Spring, the immortal loveliness that accompanies her, the apparent permanence of the lights of heaven, which sink but always repair their losses, and the brevity of human life. "For we, when we have gone down whither father Aeneas, and the rich Tullus and Ancus have gone, are no more than dust and a shadow"—

> *pulvis et umbra sumus.*

Very few words have clung to the memory of man like those last four. Their meaning is unfathomable, for they contain something more than the familiar phrase "dust and ashes." There is a moving shadow in them which he may yet encounter in the land of shadows, crying like the spirit of Anchises in Virgil—"Art thou come at last, and hath the love thy father looked for conquered that hard way? Is it given to me to see thy face, O son, and to hear thy voice, and answer it?"

> *datur ora tueri,*
> *nate, tua, et notas audire et reddere voces?*

From that strange land they may never come back to the light of day; for Diana, with all her divine power, does not release Hippolytus from that darkness of the underworld, nor can Theseus break the Lethean bondage of his dear Pirithous. And in the reduplication, the three-fold repetition of the *"o"* sound, at the end of *"caro"* and the two final vowels of *Pirithoo*, the music dies away on a low note of grief such as Dante might have heard on the wind that carried Paolo and Francesca away through the brown air:

> *nec Lethaea valet Theseus abrumpere caro*
> *vincula Pirithoo.*

XIX

ESTO MEMOR

THE SHADOWS BEGAN TO CLOSE IN UPON HORACE IN HIS FIFTY-seventh year. In the last epistle he wrote he had written a characteristic farewell, in which a certain humor—at his own expense —was mixed with a new gentleness and the old underlying sadness. There is nothing quite comparable with it, except the lines of Landor:

> I strove with none, for none was worth my strife.
> Nature I loved, and next to Nature, Art;
> I warm'd both hands before the fire of life;
> It sinks, and I am ready to depart.

There is an Horatian touch in that; but the note of contempt in the first line is absent from the epistle of Horace, who—in fact— had always "striven," if only to convince his fellow-men that greater happiness may be found in a peasant's cottage than in the palace of a king. He, too, has warmed both hands before the fire of life; and it is sinking; but he is content. The younger generation is knocking at the door; and, before going, he questions his contemporaries and himself. "Have you been grateful for each birthday as it came? Do you forgive your friends (*ignoscis amicis*)? Do you grow kinder and better as you grow older?

Lenior et melior fis accedente senecta?

If you don't know how to live rightly, *decede peritis*, make way for the experts, and the young!

Then, with a delicious touch of humor, he sees the younger

generation pointing minatory fingers, and saying, "You have played enough; you have eaten enough; you have drunk enough; it is time for you to go away!"

> *Lusisti satis, edisti satis atque bibisti;*
> *tempus abire tibi est . . .*

The remark is addressed to himself no less than to his friend, Florus. It is one of the great charms of Horace that his didactics so often apply to himself as well as to others. When he does not tell us so directly, it is often quite obviously implied. It was not only for Postumus that the flying years had so sorrowful a cry and so stern an admonition. Already, as he wrote to Florus, "they have robbed me of jests, love-affairs, friendly feasts, and play; and now they are trying to twist my poetry out of me."

They were taking a heavier toll in friendship now. Maecenas, who had become a father and a brother to the always rather lonely poet, died in the year 8 B.C. He left the palace on the Esquiline with all its treasures of art, and all his wealth, to Augustus; but, in his last communication to the emperor, there was another legacy, and an imperishable one. Myriads of wills have been made throughout the centuries and forgotten; but one little sentence in the last testament of Maecenas has already lived for two thousand years, and it will wing its way on through the far future: "remember Horatius Flaccus, as you would remember me"—"*Horati Flacci ut mei esto memor.*"

It was the perfect, though unconscious, answer to those arrogant words of the emperor, written so long ago—"he shall leave that parasite table of yours and come to this royal one."

Esto memor! But the time was brief for temporal favors from an emperor; and it was Horace himself, the son of the manumitted slave, who was to bestow a more lasting remembrance on his friend Maecenas. We can imagine him repeating his friend's own words, half to himself, and half to that remembering mother of all the Muses, who sometimes answers the silent prayer of a poet "with darkness and with dangers compassed round," *"ut mei esto memor!"*

Maecenas loved life so much that by some unreasonably sour critics he is described as clinging to it in a way unbecoming a Roman. In the eighteenth century, Samuel Johnson—perhaps the most Roman character that Britain ever produced—was taunted, behind his back, with a fear of death, mainly because he constantly faced the thought of it with a sober directness. It is sheer hypocrisy to pretend that the majority of human beings do not cling to life, or that fear of death is not almost universal. The medical profession is largely supported by those who desire to avoid it. Nor is there anything shameful about the awe with which any rational soul must approach, not merely that great "leap in the dark," as it appears to the pagan, but the shuddering of that dreadful day, as it must appear to the Christian,

> When friend and home and fire are lost,
> And even children drawn away.

To Maecenas, as to Horace, it was a dark adventure, and if one may judge from the poems of Horace, the consideration of it was never far from his thoughts. To be afraid of it, and yet to face it, is another thing than to be indifferent; and these two lovers of life were neither un-Roman, nor unafraid, for all their philosophy. They were haunted by the profound sadness of the inevitable end. There are plangent undertones in Horace which are like the sound of an iron bell, announcing the universal doom. Piety cannot save mankind from the onset of old age, or offer any long delay to the indomitable shadow of death (*indomitaeque morti*). Each of them must cry, in turn,

> I, too, must go into the dreadful hollow
> Where all our living laughter stops.

Not the fear of death, but the way of facing it is what matters; and one of the noblest ways is that of the pagans who have tried to put themselves into a "right relation with the Power that manifests itself in the universe."

The range of their vision is different; but, between pagan and Christian, Seneca and St. Paul, there is no unbridgeable gulf. Nearly twenty years before the death of Maecenas, Horace had told him, as we have seen, in one of his most moving poems, that he would not be unaccompanied on his last journey: "we shall go together,—*ibimus, ibimus.*"

The death of Horace on the 27th of November followed so soon after the death of Maecenas, and was so sudden, that he has been supposed by some writers to have followed the example of Cato. But this was neither likely nor necessary in the case of Horace; for his time had almost come, and the loss of his best friend must have struck him to the heart. He had no time to make a will; but he is said to have bequeathed his little estate to Augustus. It can hardly have been by his own wish that his ashes were laid by those of Maecenas on the Esquiline. It is possible, therefore, that the order was given by Augustus; and that in this way he fulfilled, as far as was now in his imperial power, the last wish of Maecenas,

Horati Flacci ut mei esto memor.

XX

NON OMNIS MORIAR

THERE IS PERHAPS NO PROPHECY IN THE HISTORY OF LITERA-
ture, which has been so amply fulfilled as those words of Horace
about his own poetry—*non omnis moriar*. His influence is so
all-pervading that it is impossible to estimate it systematically.
He has been translated and imitated by scores of writers in almost every civilized country for many centuries. His indirect
influence is even greater.

Innumerable echoes of his "penetrating and mastering
phrases" resound through writer after writer. We find them in
an amazing diversity of places—in the satires of Juvenal and
Persius; in the rhymed medieval lyrics of love and wine; in the
Fathers of the Church.

In the opening of his *Hymn at Candle-light*, Prudentius,
whom Bentley called "the Virgil and Horace of the Christians,"
showed that—like many of the doctors of the Church ap-
plauded by St. Jerome—he could "spoil the Egyptians, without pollution from the spoil." He begins thus:

"O Creator of the golden light, good Leader . . . Christ,
restore Thy light to Thy faithful."

> *Inventor rutili, dux bone, luminis—*
> *Lucem redde tuis, Christe, fidelibus.*

He thus directly appropriates the phrases used by Horace
in the fifth ode of the fourth book:

> *Lucem redde tuae, dux bone, patriae.*

The fact that Horace was apparently addressing Augustus did
not deter Prudentius from using the same words in the sacred
context: Horace himself was not praying for the mere presence
of the Emperor. He was praying that the return of the man
who represented the sovereign power of his country might
bring to Italy the divine light of peace, and an ideal world.
Those modern critics who would limit the significance of
"*lucem*" to the mere presence of Augustus, as if he were a kind
of imperial "Bong with a luminous nose," are following the
wrong "gleam." The process of "spoiling the Egyptians" is
curiously illustrated by the poetic idealization of the word
"Falernian," which Horace used as a kind of hieroglyph for the
perfect wine. As a direct result of this, the word "Falernian"
actually found its way into liturgical use. In the *Missale Gothi-
cum* (quoted by Rand in his *Founders of the Middle Ages*) the
benedictio populi of the mass on the eve of the Epiphany prays
that dull hearts may be converted, "even as at the wedding of
Cana plain water was converted into *Falernian*."

There was certainly no irreverence in those who used it,
simply a robust power of intellectual assimilation.

Through a long period in the Middle Ages it was the cloister
that saved Horace from oblivion, as it saved so much of the
world's literature. A monk of Fleury bequeathed a manuscript
of Horace to the library of his order, and thus—it was rumored
—delivered his own soul from hell. Occasionally enthusiasts
went too far. Miss Helen Waddell, in her enchanting book *The
Wandering Scholars* tells the story of Vilgardus of Ravenna, a
poor little grammarian who, in the year 1028, "saw Virgil and
Horace and Juvenal in a dream, like unto gods, and was thanked
by them for his good offices to their memory and promised a
share in their immortality. After that he taught openly that the
words of the poets are in all things worthy of belief, even as
Holy Writ, but he expiated that heresy in the fire."

Yet the poems of Horace were set to music and sung in those days, as they have been sung in the public schools of modern England. Music, including the special music of poetry, has a language of its own. It can resolve many contradictions and transcend many of the limitations of the rationalist. A sceptical lover of music once declared that, though he had no religion at other times, there was a certain musical setting of the Nicene Creed which, whenever he heard it, convinced his innermost soul of every syllable. The paganism of Horace ceased to be paganism when the music of the *Carmen Saeculare* was caught up and prolonged, in the strangest and most beautiful ways, through some of the mediaeval Latin hymns. The Sapphic measure of the poem, sung by the two youthful choirs on the Capitol might be thought to have died away forever when Imperial Rome went down, but it rose again from the dimness of the cloister in the sonorous hymn of St. Gregory, invoking a new and deeper light:

> *Ecce jam noctis tenuatur umbra,*
> *lux et aurorae rutilans coruscat*
> *supplices rerum Dominum canora*
> *voce precemur.*
>
> *Ut reos culpae miseratus omnem*
> *pellat angorem, tribuat salutem,*
> *donet et nobis bona sempiternae*
> *munera pacis.*

And that, after all, is not so far from the prayer of the Roman poet, in his hatred of bloodshed and his conviction that the only way to peace was for men to recover a right relationship with the Power that rules the universe. St. Gregory was not primarily a poet, any more than Horace was primarily a moralist. Artistically the two poems are not comparable, for—in the art of verse —Horace was supreme. It was his life, his pagan life. The light

to which he prayed was no more than a shadow of that other
Light; but there is no unbridgeable gulf between the perfection
of which he caught a glimpse and that other perfection which
filled the mind of St. Gregory. The music of the pagan poet
entered into the life-stream of Christendom, and it was the
pulse of his own heart that sent it there.

Some of the Latin hymns composed by Urban VIII, and still
used in the breviary, are modelled on the less familiar metres
of Horace. The vesper hymn for the feast of St. Martina, for
instance, is in the third Asclepiad:

> *Martinae celebri plaudite nomini*
> *cives Romulei, plaudite gloriae,*
> *insignem meritis dicite virginem,*
> *Christi dicite martyrem.*

He connects Rome with Romulus exactly as Horace does in the
fifth ode of the fourth book, of which this is the opening stanza:

> *Divis orte bonis, optime Romulae*
> *custos gentis, abes jam nimium diu;*
> *maturum reditum pollicitus patrum*
> *sancto consilio, redi.*

In fact Urban VIII follows the model in one technical detail
not usual in Horace, and somewhat dangerous for any poet
unless he has the technical mastery of Horace. In the second line
of the stanza last quoted the word *nimium* ends with a long
soft-sounding syllable which is repeated at the end of three
other words in the third line—*maturum, reditum,* and *patrum.*
If the stanza is read with the proper rhythm, the pulse of the
metre falls on each of those soft-sounding syllables, with exactly
the right effect. It suggests the note of a cello heard through the
lighter tones on a violin. Urban VIII, in the opening stanza of
his hymn, does very much the same thing. The first and last

words of the third line, *insignem* and *virginem*, end in a syllable which is picked up at the end of the stanza in *martyrem*. In this case, it is a lighter syllable, but the pulse of the metre falls on it with the same precision, and, by the repetition of like sounds, obtains something of the metrical effect which, in a different way, is obtained by rhyme. Such details, of course, are not thought out by the poet. When his fingers are on the strings he does not count the vibrations. It would be very absurd if he did. It is more important to observe the continuity of the tradition which brought Apollo into the Vatican gallery, and made the Vatican library a treasure house of classical literature.

The old Horace of the beautiful poem *Diffugere nives* comes to life again in the young April of French poetry. We find him in that paradise of roses with Ronsard:

> *La du plaisant Avril la saison immortelle*
> *Sans eschange le suit.*

But we, but we, when once the night has taken us—*pulvis et umbra sumus*. It is the old sad cry, and, though the prince of poets had a better hope, the music of Horace continually breathed through his own.

His influence on that "wisest of Frenchmen," Montaigne, can hardly be overestimated. The songs of the valley of Digentia, echoed and re-echoed through the valley of the Dordogne. The desire of Montaigne for the peaceful life of a lover of books at his country manor is strikingly like that of Horace for his Sabine retreat. The epistles of Horace are the very fountainhead of those essays which have set the pattern for an entire literature, ranging in English alone from Bacon to Emerson and Stevenson. Little felicities from Horace are sprinkled through the pages of Montaigne like flowers in a spring meadow. He will sometimes quote his favorite poet three or four times in as many paragraphs.

As we have seen earlier, it was Horace claiming another kind of immortality—*exegi monumentum aere perennius*—who breathed through the lips of Shakespeare that still prouder prediction:

> Not marble, nor the gilded monuments
> Of princes shall outlive this powerful rhyme.

All those "barbarians of genius"—the Elizabethans—knew Horace and loved him. Ben Jonson translated his *Art of Poetry* and continually preached his doctrine of clarity, and the hard work necessary to obtain it. Obscurity to Jonson, as to Horace, was merely a proof of the artist's incompetence to finish his work and convey his idea. Like Horace and Stevenson, he urges the necessity, for those who would write well, of learning from the masters.

Herrick, a little later, translated scores of lines from the odes, and imitated even more, in his praise of the country life and his admonitions to seize the flying hour: "Gather ye rosebuds while ye may." As Horace himself said, "Hither let them bring wine and oil of crocus and the brief blossom of the lovely rose, while fortune and youth and the dark threads of the three sisters allow":

> *Huc vina et unguenta et nimium breves*
> *flores amoenae ferre iube rosae,*
> *dum res et aetas et sororum*
> *fila trium patiuntur atra.*

Fénelon, in one of his *Dialogues des Morts*, gives us a glimpse of Horace and Virgil conversing in an earthly paradise somewhat more pleasant than the place in which Dante met them. It is clear that they had crossed not only Lethe, the river of oblivion, but also Eunoe, the river of remembrance, which has been strangely neglected by the poets. Their conversation is enchanting:

Virgil

How peaceful and happy we are here in this perpetual Spring on the banks of this pure river, and near this fragrant wood.

Horace

If you don't take care, you'll be making an eclogue. Shades mustn't do that sort of thing. Look, there are Homer, Hesiod, and Theocritus crowned with the bays. They hear others singing their verses, but they don't make them any more.

Virgil

I am rejoiced to hear that after so many centuries men of letters still take delight in yours. You were not deceived when you said with so much confidence that you would not wholly die.

Horace

My writings have resisted time; but one would have to love you as much as I do not to be jealous of your glory. They place you next to Homer.

Virgil

Our Muses ought not to be jealous of one another; they are so different. The marvelous thing about your work is its variety. Your odes are tender, graceful, often forceful, swiftly moving and sublime. Your satires are simple, naive, terse, full of salt. They show profound knowledge of mankind, a very serious philosophy, with a turn of wit which civilizes your readers and educates them with a jest. Your Art of Poetry shows that you had all the knowledge and all the strength of genius necessary to compose the greatest works. . . .

Non Omnis Moriar

Horace

You are a fine one to talk of variety, you who have touched your eclogues with the tenderness of Theocritus and filled your Georgics with all those radiant pictures, giving a spirit to Nature herself; and then, in your Aeneid the beautiful order, magnificence, strength and sublimity of Homer shining out everywhere.

Virgil

But I only followed in Homer's footsteps.

Horace

You did not follow Homer when you wrote the love story of Dido. That fourth book is quite original. Nor can one ever take away from you the praise of having made the descent of Aeneas into the underworld more beautiful than the vision of the spirit world in the Odyssey.

A brief passage follows in which they invite each other to speak more critically; but the good archbishop of Cambrai has not the heart to let them do it. He must therefore bear the blame for the mutual admiration which continues.

Virgil

No man has ever given a happier turn to a phrase or made it convey a beautiful idea so tersely and delicately. Words become new by the way in which you use them, but they are not always equally musical in their flow.

Horace

I am not surprised that you are difficult to please in the music of verse. Nothing is so exquisitely musical as your own. The very cadence of it sometimes brings tears to the eyes.

Horace

Virgil

The ode requires a different kind of harmony, in which you have always succeeded and which is more varied than mine.

Horace

Ah well, I have only carved cherry stones. I have criticized bad writing; I have tried to formulate the laws of good writing; but I have never done anything on the grand scale like your heroic poem.

Virgil

My dear Horace, I think we have been praising one another long enough. It's not quite decent. *Finissons.*

We must come back to the French in the last word; for, as Sainte-Beuve says, it is neither Horace nor Virgil that has been talking, but Fénelon.

Sainte-Beuve remarks that there has never been a period since the Renaissance when Horace was not the personal friend, the most intimately known of all the classics, among a great diversity of readers in almost every civilized country. There have been fluctuations of taste in one country or another when he was not so widely read; but he always had his chosen few; and, when he went out of fashion in one corner of the world, he was usually very much to the fore in several others. He was widely read, for instance, and much translated, during the first half of the eighteenth century in England, although in France his light was a little eclipsed. It was at this time that the Abbé Gedoyn wrote: "What a friendly poet Horace is! And what a pity that he is so little read. I have seen the time when he was the delight of everyone in society who had even a smattering of letters. They knew him by heart and delighted to make apt quotations from him."

It was at this very time of eclipse in France, however, that his light shone out with redoubled brightness in England. Pope based a very large proportion of his own work upon him. Not only in the acknowledged *Imitations of Horace*, but in a very large part of his most important work—the *Essay on Criticism* and the *Essay on Man*—it is the spirit of Horace that shines through the eighteenth-century English and dictates so many of those phrases which have become proverbial.

A little later in the eighteenth century, an incident was told by Dr. Burney and recorded by Boswell, which throws a pleasant and amusing sidelight on Sainte-Beuve's remark that Horace had become a kind of secular breviary:

It used to be imagined at Mr. Thrale's, when Johnson retired to a window or corner of the room, by perceiving his lips in motion, and hearing a murmur without audible articulation, that he was praying; but this was not *always* the case, for I was once, perhaps unperceived by him, writing at a table, so near the place of his retreat, that I heard him repeating some lines in an ode of Horace, over and over again, as if by iteration to exercise the organs of speech and fix the ode (the second of the first book) in his memory:

> *Audiet cives acuisse ferrum,*
> *quo graves Persae melius perirent,*
> *audiet pugnas . . .*

It is interesting to note that he was learning this passage for the discomfiture of the Americans, whose revolution was then in progress.

In the second half of the eighteenth century Horace recovered the ground that he had temporarily lost in France. Sainte-Beuve tells us that thenceforward "Horace became what he never again ceased to be in France—a friend, a counsellor, a household genius." Voltaire, who on this matter allowed himself a few of those flippancies which he could not always control, nevertheless praised Horace "in an epistle which everyone knows by heart":

Jouissons, écrivons, vivons, mon cher Horace.

If Horace had ever really been the "court poet" of Augustus, it would be odd indeed that he should have come so triumphantly into his own in France during the revolutionary period. It is perhaps even more ironical that the son of the manumitted slave should have played the part that he did in the arrest of Condorcet, who had incurred the suspicion of the extremists and was wandering about the countryside, trying to evade the watchful eyes of spies and informers. One day there came into a village inn an unkempt, bearded, ragged and hungry man, asking for food. Probably it was his educated accent that roused the suspicion of the bystanders. He was seized and examined. The only incriminating evidence they could find upon him was a little edition of Horace in Latin. But this was enough; for had not "the common man" come into his own? It must certainly be a nobleman in disguise who was thus secreting a Horace in his rags. He was carried off to Paris to be guillotined, but he died in his cell the night before the date set for his execution. It is said that his Horace was still with him.

It was certainly not because Horace was a reactionary that his poems accompanied men like Condorcet to their death; but, as Sainte-Beuve says again, "in the shipwreck of society he was the faithful companion and consoler of many cultivated men and women who took his poems with them into prison, into exile, or into the armed camp. If there is one classic that, more than any other, helped the revival of letters after the Revolution, it was Horace." The circumstances of the time helped to bring out the truth of the poems which he wrote upon the civil strife in Italy.

In the nineteenth century his influence as an artist extended even further. Tennyson's poem, *Of Old Sat Freedom on the Heights*, in spirit and in form is nothing more or less than an ode of Horace reproduced in perfect modern English. It has the classic phrasing; the golden logic, and that sane love of the central path which characterized Horace:

> Grave mother of majestic works,
>   From her isle-altar gazing down,
> Who, God-like, grasps the triple forks,
>   And, King-like, wears the crown:
>
> Her open eyes desire the truth.
>   The wisdom of a thousand years
> Is in them. May perpetual youth
>   Keep dry their light from tears;
>
> That her fair form may stand and shine,
>   Make bright our days and light our dreams,
> Turning to scorn with lips divine
>   The falsehood of extremes!

Tennyson, on one side of his genius, is the most Horatian of all the English poets. Many of his other early poems almost reproduce the thought and feeling of particular odes and epodes. The sixteenth epode, for instance, supplies the conclusion to the poem in which Tennyson fears that individual freedom may perish:

> Tho' Power should make from land to land
>   The name of Britain trebly great—
>   Tho' every channel of the State
> Should fill and choke with golden sand—
>
> Yet waft me from the harbour-mouth,
>   Wild wind! I seek a warmer sky,
>   And I will see before I die
> The palms and temples of the South.

But perhaps the most Horatian of all modern poems is that in which Tennyson reproduces the more genial and serene atmosphere of the Sabine farm, in an Isle of Wight setting—his epistle to F. D. Maurice inviting him to visit Farringford. The stanza itself is Tennyson's own invention, but it has a great deal of the effect, especially in the fourth line, of the Horation alcaics:

> You'll have no scandal while you dine,
> But honest talk and wholesome wine,
>   And only hear the magpie gossip
> Garrulous under a roof of pine.
>
> .   .   .   .
>
> We might discuss the Northern sin
> Which made a selfish war begin;
>   Dispute the claims, arrange the chances;
> Emperor, Ottoman, which shall win:
>
> Or whether war's avenging rod
> Shall lash all Europe into blood;
>   Till you should turn to dearer matters,
> Dear to the man that is dear to God;
>
> .   .   .   .
>
> Come, Maurice, come: the lawn as yet
> Is hoar with rime, or spongy-wet;
>   But when the wreath of March has blossom'd
> Crocus, anemone, violet,
>
> Or later, pay one visit here,
> For those are few we hold as dear;
>   Nor pay but one, but come for many,
> Many and many a happy year.

None of these instances, however, represents more than one aspect of the genius of Horace, and it would be a mistake to suggest that the terms, or the idiom, into which Jonson or Milton, Pope or Tennyson translated him, represent more than one facet of the original.

The lighter as well as the more serious poets owe him a debt which they have been eager to acknowledge. The Parnassian school in France owed him no less than did Ronsard; and the conversation in verse between Gautier and De Banville is really a continuation of what Horace himself might have said to a contemporary:

> Yes, Beauty still rebels.
> Our dreams like clouds disperse.
> She dwells
> In agate, marble, verse.

Herrick, Prior, and Austin Dobson are no less indebted than Ben Jonson; and, in some ways Cowper, who translated some of the odes, is the most Horatian of them all. His poem *Boadicea* has much of the discipline and terseness of Horace:

> Regions Caesar never knew
> Thy posterity shall sway;
> Where his eagles never flew,
> None invincible as they.

That has very much the feeling of some of the political odes of Horace. Neither of the poets, certainly not the "stricken deer," was an imperialist at heart; but, as we have noted earlier, the music of poetry constantly transcends its apparent subject-matter, and there is no need to attribute the emotion in either case to insincerity.

Some of Stevenson's brief odes and epistles in verse reproduce another aspect of the genius of Horace, both in spirit and in

technique. His lines to his gardener might have been addressed
by the Roman poet to his *vilicus* at the Sabine farm:

> Friend, in my mountain side demesne,
> My plain-beholding, rosy, green
> And linnet-haunted garden-ground,
> Let still the esculents abound.
> Let first the onion flourish there,
> Rose among roots, the maiden-fair,
> Wine-scented and poetic soul
> Of the capacious salad bowl.
>
> . . . .
>
> These tend, I prithee; and for me,
> Thy most long-suffering master, bring
> In April, when the linnets sing
> And the days lengthen more and more,
> At sundown to the garden door.
> And I, being provided thus
> Shall, with superb asparagus,
> A book, a taper, and a cup
> Of country wine, divinely sup.

It is the very style and manner of Horace in one of those
playful moods when he chooses to say small things in a grand
way. In many of his lyrics, too, Stevenson comes nearer than
almost any other poet in English to what I have called elsewhere the interlocking sounds and phrases of the Horatian technique. One stanza of his alcaics, quoted in the preface to this
book, is much the best example of that metre in our tongue;
but, in his English metres, by assonance and internal rhyme, he
very often achieves the Horatian compactness:

> Yet shall your ragged moor receive
> The incomparable pomp of eve.

In that description of a sunset the internal rhyme of the second syllable of "incomparable" with the next word "pomp," gives just that interlocking effect which Horace achieves in a more elaborate and subtle way. The close of his little epistle to Andrew Lang:

> Still like a brook your page has shone,
> And your ink sings of Helicon,

has several characteristics of the Horatian method. The reduplication of the vowel sounds in the third and fourth words of the last line corresponds to a device that Horace constantly employed. Undoubtedly Stevenson was one of those friends of Horace to whom Andrew Lang refers in a beautiful passage of his *Letters to Dead Authors:*

In what manner of Paradise are we to conceive that you, Horace, are dwelling, or what region of immortality can give you such pleasures as this life afforded? The country and the town, nature and men, who knew them so well as you, or who ever so wisely made the best of those two worlds? Truly here you had good things, nor do you ever, in all your poems, look for more delight in the life beyond; you never expect consolation for present sorrow, and when you once have shaken hands with a friend the parting seems to you eternal.

> *Quis desiderio sit pudor aut modus*
> *tam cari capitis?*

So you sing, for the dear head you mourn has sunk forever beneath the wave. . . . Farewell, dear Horace; farewell, thou wise and kindly heathen; of mortals the most human, the friend of my friends and of so many generations of men.

But is it quite true that Horace had no glimmering of any possible future? We do not know how much he may have locked in silence; but we do know that in one stanza of the second ode of

Book III he speaks of Virtue opening heaven wide for those who deserve not to die:

> *virtus recludens immeritis mori*
> *caelum.* . . .

In the word *immeritis*, there is an implied argument, based on an ethical postulate, not unlike that of the Elizabethan poet, Sir John Davies, in his line about the future life—

> If there be none, the gods have done us wrong

It may be compared with Tennyson's lines:

> Thou wilt not leave us in the dust:
> Thou madest man, he knows not why;
> He thinks he was not made to die;
> And thou hast made him: thou art just.

In that closely reasoned stanza, the argument almost takes the form of a syllogism; and it is really saying something very like the inner meaning of the passage in Horace.

The lines of Horace stand perhaps about half-way between those of Tennyson and the verses in which Thomas Hardy declares that "we come to live, and are called to die."

> Life proffers, to deny.

He does not go as far as the hope of Matthew Arnold in the sonnet on Immortality, a somewhat dreadful hope, for it passed over all our poor human failures, and reserved it only for a sublime few who, with all their battles won

> Mount, and that hardly, to eternal life.

It seems to me that the gentle words of Horace *"immeritis mori"* are infinitely more moving. He would certainly not have made that claim for himself. He might, for others. He was not more sceptical than Tacitus and, though he is even more terse, his implied and perhaps unconscious reasoning in *immeritis* is in accord with the noblest passage in the life of Agricola. Horace would not have thought of himself in that light, but he might, and probably did, think in some such way of his father.

If there is a place for the spirits of the good, if, as the wise deem, great souls do not perish with the body, may your rest be quiet; recall us, your household, from weak regret and womanish lamentation to the study of your virtues, over which grief and wailing are wrong. What we loved, what we admired in you endures, and will endure in the souls of men, and in the eternity of the ages, *fama rerum.*

There could be no more beautiful or apt commentary on these lines of Horace:

> *virtus recludens immeritis mori*
> *caelum.* . . .

No English writer is nearer to the spirit of Horace in these things than Thackeray. *Esmond* is full of exquisite little variations on themes suggested by Horace.

It is with a quotation from Horace that Thackeray begins his brilliant imitation of a paper by Richard Steele; and there are scores of allusions to the poems of Horace creeping in and out of his prose like a flowering vine. In *Esmond* particularly he recaptures that pleasant eighteenth-century atmosphere in which Horace may be said to have occupied a seat in Parliament. There is one scene in which he makes a delightful use of Ode 6, Book II:

> *Ille terrarum mihi praeter omnis*
> *angulus ridet, ubi non Hymetto*
> *mella decedunt viridique certat*
> > *baca Venafro.*

Thackeray makes the chaplain, Tom Tusher, quote Horace in
the wrong and pedantic way, and makes Esmond answer him
very gracefully, by capping the quotation in exactly the right
way:

Mr. Tom had divested himself of his surplice, and came forward habited in his cassock and great black periwig. How had Esmond ever been for a moment jealous of this fellow?

"Give me thy hand, Tom Tusher," he said. The chaplain made
him a very low unstately bow. "I am charmed to see Captain Esmond," says he. "My Lord and I have read the *Reddas incolumem
precor*, and applied it, I am sure, to you. You come back with Gadi-
tanian laurels. . . . I wished, I am sure, that I was another Septimius. My Lord Viscount, your Lordship remembers *Septimi, Gades
aditure mecum?*"

"There's an angle of earth that I love better than Gades,
Tusher," says Mr. Esmond. " 'Tis that one where your Reverence
hath a parsonage, and where our youth was brought up."

Perhaps the most perfect illustration of the way in which the
thoughts of Horace can bridge the gulf between paganism and
Christendom is the meditation of Esmond on the theme *Non
omnis moriar*:

As he had sometimes felt, gazing up at midnight into the bound-
less starlit depths overhead, in a rapture of devout wonder at that
endless brightness and beauty,—in some such a way now the depth
of this pure devotion smote upon him and filled his heart with
thanksgiving. . . . Who was he, weak and friendless creature,
that such a love should be poured out upon him. Not in vain—and
not in vain has he lived—hard and thankless should he be to think
so, that has such a treasure given him. What is ambition, compared
to that, but selfish vanity? To be rich, famous? What do these profit
a year hence, when other names sound louder than yours, when
you lie hidden away under the ground, along with idle titles en-
graven on your coffin? But only true love lives after you—follows

your memory with secret blessing—or precedes you, and intercedes for you. *Non omnis moriar*—if dying, I yet live in a tender heart or two; nor am lost and hopeless living, if a sainted, departed soul still loves and prays for me.

The lonely Roman poet never knew the love of which Esmond speaks in that passage, but he had known something comparable to it in the love of his father, the manumitted slave—

> *virtus recludens immeritis mori*
> *caelum.*

In the Roman Empire one of the recognized punishments for slaves was crucifixion. Not many years after the death of Horace an official letter was sent from Rome to a provincial governor concerning a decree very famous in the annals of Christendom: "And it came to pass in those days that there went out a decree from Caesar Augustus that all the world should be taxed." In the strangely interwoven web of history it could hardly have been foreseen that the period when emperors were looked upon as semi-divine was ending and that the place where God and man were really to meet would be in all external circumstances a very lowly one. The poets of the pagan world had at least caught glimpses of a Power that plucked down the mighty from their seat and exalted the lowly.

> *Valet ima summis*
> *mutare et insignem attenuat deus*
> *obscura promens . . .*

It is strange to reflect that the thread of the life we have been considering was so closely interwoven with those which played so memorable a part in the mighty pattern. In earlier days at Rome Horace may have actually seen Herod passing in pomp through the streets when he made his famous visits to that city. In later life Horace actually knew Tiberius who, in turn, became acquainted with a certain Pontius Pilate. The Roman poet may have touched the hand that, a little later touched the hands of the most disastrous judge in the world's history, the hands that, with the most modern of all gestures, waved the truth away and then vainly tried to wash themselves clean of the guilt. At only one remove the Roman poet had touched them, not knowing; and not knowing that on the cross of the slaves, of whom his father had been one, there was soon to die the supreme and perfect exemplar of his own poor, groping pagan words:

> *virtus recludens immeritis mori*
> *caelum.*